TT   Pipe, Ann Kimball.
178
.P56   Mastercrafting
         miniature rooms and
         furniture

Cop. 1   17.95

DATE			
1/87	R0052696768		

JUN   1980

Mastercrafting Miniature Rooms and Furniture

Mastercrafting Miniature Rooms and Furniture

Techniques for the Serious Beginner

Ann Kimball Pipe

VAN NOSTRAND REINHOLD COMPANY
New York Cincinnati Toronto London Melbourne

Printed in the United States of America.
Design by Loudan Enterprises

Published in 1979 by Van Nostrand Reinhold Company
A division of Litton Educational Publishing, Inc.
135 West 50th Street, New York, NY 10020, U.S.A.

Van Nostrand Reinhold Limited
1410 Birchmount Road
Scarborough, Ontario M1P 2E7, Canada

Van Nostrand Reinhold Australia Pty. Ltd.
17 Queen Street
Mitcham, Victoria 3132, Australia

Van Nostrand Reinhold Company Limited
Molly Millars Lane
Wokingham, Berkshire, England

16 15 14 13 12 11 10 9 8 7 6 5 4 3 2 1

Library of Congress Cataloging in Publication Data
Pipe, Ann Kimball.
Mastercrafting miniature rooms and furniture.
Includes index.
1. Miniature craft.   2. Miniature rooms.
3. Miniature furniture.   I. Title.
TT178.P56   747   79-257
ISBN 0-442-26557-3

Contents

Introduction

This book has been written for the craftsman who would like to go beyond the building of a simple dollhouse and the making of toy furniture. He may already have made a few pieces, using balsa or basswood and, having become familiar with the blotting-paperlike qualities of those materials, would now like to move on to hardwoods such as walnut, mahogany, cherry, maple, and rosewood. He is ready to use a jigsaw instead of a hand saw or knife for cutting his materials, and would like his finished pieces to be miniature replicas of full-sized pieces rather than toys.

There are certain catchwords and phrases that will have no special appeal to the craftsman for whom this book was written, words and phrases such as "simple," "time-saving," "short-cuts," and "costing only a few pennies." He knows that a minimum number of tools are required for doing serious craft work of almost any kind, and that such work takes time. He may already own some of the necessary tools, and is willing to buy the one or two essential ones that he may not have. As for time—he will spend a certain number of spare hours on his craft in any case; how many of those hours are allotted to any single miniature piece is not important. If quality, rather than quantity, is the goal of the craftsman, this book was written for him.

There has long been a need for a clear definition of the terms used in the making of miniature houses, rooms, and furnishings. Although there is a general tendency to call all miniature houses "dollhouses," and all small furniture pieces "dollhouse" or "toy" furniture, not all miniature pieces are toys. What of the delicate cabinet, for example, whose intricate carving, curved front, and beveled mirror represent weeks of painstaking work? It cannot accurately be called a toy, which any small child will soon learn if he attempts to remove it from its place of display and treat it as one.

There would be less confusion in the world of miniatures if "dollhouse" were used only to refer to a house for dolls—an imaginative, charming house in an unreal world often inhabited by small people made of such materials as china, cloth, leather, and wood. There is a suggestion of realism in such a house, but realism was not the goal of the craftsman who made it. He meant it to be, and it is, enchanting.

On the other hand, a miniature house or miniature room depends for its success upon the faithfulness with which, at every step, it was reproduced. Proportions are exact, and every possible detail—even to the smoke-blackened chimney and the slight darkening from accumulated wax along the edges of the kitchen floor—are included. Dolls rarely live in the rooms of a miniature house; its inhabitants are small human beings who are very much alive, but can be seen only in the imagination of the viewer. These people sleep in beds and sit on chairs that are exact copies of beds and chairs used by the human giants who so often come to stand and stare into their rooms.

The instructions in this book, therefore, are for making miniature, not dollhouse, rooms, and for furnishing them with miniature, not dollhouse, pieces. It is for the craftsman who understands this distinction and wishes to take the time and very satisfying trouble to make true reproductions that this book has been written.

1.

Planning Ahead

Since the best part of any craft project is doing the actual work, it is too bad that the craftsman must be asked to postpone that best for a little while. Although planning ahead in great detail, even if possible, would deprive him of the fun of using his imagination and creativity as the work

1-1. A house? —

goes along, he should at least know in advance whether he prefers to build a house or individual rooms, what the architectural style will be, the general period of the furniture he will make, and what scale he will use.

Before the actual work begins, it is also important that certain chapters farther along in the book be read, particularly Chapter 5, which covers the use of tools, and those parts of Chapter 6 that discuss adhesives and the use of dowels. Less important, but recommended nevertheless, is the reading, or skimming at least, of the entire book before any work is done. Ideas may be picked up that will give the reader a clearer picture of what he would like to do in the work ahead.

For some craftsmen, making such plans is part of the fun and for others it is not. For all, however, it is a necessary part of the project ahead, so the sooner it is finished, the sooner the miniature room or house can be started.

A HOUSE OR SEPARATE ROOMS?

The reader certainly has a right to a fair discussion of the merits of building separate rooms versus a miniature house. The writer admittedly favors miniature rooms, and in an attempt to balance this bias, has made an informal survey of owners of miniature houses. The question was asked, "Why do you prefer to own a miniature house instead of furnishing individual rooms?"

The answer, "A whole house seems more real," sums up the feeling of all the house owners, although one phrased her reply with somewhat more elegance, "I preferred the fantasy of creating a whole environment."

Tradition and nostalgia also play a large part in the decision to make or buy, and to furnish, a miniature house. Some owners remembered the dollhouses they played with as children and wanted their own children to have the same happy memories.

One dollhouse owner mentioned the matter of available space in her own home. Her house and other collected miniatures were displayed in a large room on the third floor that had been set aside for the purpose. However, since not all craftsmen who are planning miniature houses or rooms are fortunate enough to have a spare room on the third floor, the matter of space should be considered before the work begins. Rooms need only to be viewed from the front and will only require space on a wall shelf; a house needs an area away from the wall so that all four sides are accessible. One arrangement is no more desirable than the other; it is simply a point that should be considered in the light of available space in the craftsman's own home.

To this point, the discussion has been limited to dollhouses and their owners. In each case the small house had been furnished with imagination and great charm, but strict adherence to scale and attempts to be realistic in every detail of the furnishings were noticeably absent. In short, they were very successful dollhouses but were not miniature houses in accordance with the distinction between the two made in the introduction.

Assuming the reader has as his goal the crafting of miniature furniture and a house or rooms as perfect in every detail and as realistic as possible, the writer sees these advantages of individual rooms over a house:

1. *Accessibility.* While it is being worked on, a separate room can be turned in any position. This greatly simplifies the careful matching of wallpaper patterns at room corners, the adding of picture moldings at ceiling level, and the precise drilling of holes for curtain rods, lamp fixtures, and so on. With the room turned upside down, a

1-2. — or a room?

chandelier can be glued to the ceiling and the adhesive allowed to set overnight. Working on a flat, horizontal surface simplifies almost every step in making the room detail-perfect.

2. *Flexibility of Room Shapes.* All the rooms in a great majority of miniature houses are rectangular, because the houses themselves are built in convenient, boxlike shapes. Individual rooms can, however, be planned in interesting shapes that need not conform to the style of any one house. The craftsman has his choice of rooms under a steep hip roof, of cathedral ceilings, of rooms with corners cut off because of outside chimneys, and so on. The possibilities are almost endless.

3. *Flexibility of Numbers of Rooms.* The number of rooms in a miniature house is set when the house is built, and there will be no choice but to complete them all. Looking ahead at all the work to be done very often makes the craftsman neglect some of the small, very important details.

When one separate room has been completed, it is an entity in itself. It can be displayed on a shelf and, in the unlikely event that the craftsman does not wish to continue with the work, the lack of more rooms will not detract from the completed one. To the writer, at least, work that does not have to be done is the most fun to do, and regarding a single miniature room as an end in itself encourages the craftsman to add more and more details until he is very sure nothing more can be done to make it perfect.

4. *Use of Available Space in a Home.* This subject has already been touched on. Where there are bookshelves in a home, there is usually space for a few miniature rooms on the shelves. A shelf or two of an existing cabinet can be emptied to make space for a few more. Not everyone lacks display space, but many do, and building individual rooms can solve the problem.

5. *Visibility.* When a miniature furnished room has taken from months to a year or more to complete, it is best appreciated when easily seen in detail. Nothing is missed when a room is displayed, lighted, at eye level on a shelf; a great deal can be missed in a lower room of a house that the viewer must stoop or kneel on the floor to see.

6. *Use of Outside Channels.* When a miniature room stands alone, channels can be built along the outside of one, two, or three of its walls. Lights can be placed in these channels to shine through doors and windows, thus giving the effect of sunlight or daylight. The channels also allow the craftsman to add to the illusion of reality by giving glimpses of a hallway, an adjoining room, an outside porch through the open door of the main room, or a lawn with trees and shrubbery. Methods for building these channels are described later on.

7. *Variety of Styles and Periods.* With separate rooms, the craftsman has the choice of following one period in history or of making each room of a different period or style. If the latter plan is followed, there is usually an underlying theme to tie the rooms together, such as the famous Thorne miniature rooms, which show typical rooms in historical houses. The craftsman also has the choice of making all the rooms that would normally be seen in one house—the living room, dining room, hall, bedrooms, bath, and so on—or, if he prefers, of making five living rooms and no bedrooms at all. Since each room is an entity in itself, it need only have its own character and not conform to the character and style of any other.

1-3. A clock and a chair in the channel suggest a hallway leading to more rooms.

8. *Building to Scale.* When a complete house is built, every part of it including the walls, roof, porches, and exterior trim must be built to scale. It is not always easy to find materials of the exact thicknesses needed. The walls, ceiling, and floor of a single room, on the other hand, can be of any convenient thickness that can easily be disguised.

Although this book emphasizes the making of separate rooms, most of the principles used in their construction can be applied to houses as well, and of course those chapters devoted to making furniture and accessories apply to rooms and houses alike.

CHOOSING A PERIOD AND STYLE TO FOLLOW

If the craftsman elects to follow one particular period in building and furnishing his rooms, obviously the one that appeals most to his own taste is the one to choose. A word of warning, however: the first thought that enters one's mind is not always the best, and since the craftsman may be working with the same styles of furniture for years to come, the choice should be made very carefully.

It is surprising, when the thought of miniature rooms and furnishings first enters the minds of many, how often the word "Victorian" comes with it. The Victorian period, in all its phases, was a rich and romantic one, characterized by roomy, ornately trimmed houses filled with heavy, elaborate furniture that still has a special charm for nearly everyone. The only drawback in choosing this period is that many others have done the same, and rooms of the Victorian period in miniature are seen everywhere.

A little research into furniture styles, ranging from the very early Gothic to modern, might turn up a period that not only appeals to the craftsman, but also has the advantage of being unusual in the world of miniature furniture.

In addition to styles and periods, there are also the various social strata from which to choose. Those range from the very rich home, obviously staffed with servants who see to it that nothing

1-4. The Victorian period was rich and romantic.

is ever out of place, to the middle-class home, possibly furnished with an assortment of unmatched pieces, which has a comfortable lived-in look, or to a small, very simple home with the barest of furnishings, which tells a story of its own.

Any period, style, or class of rooms and furniture can be most attractive to reproduce. It is only important that the craftsman select one whose appeal to him will outlast the making of the first few pieces.

It is also important, when choosing the style of the first room or two, to consider what skills will be required to do the work. It is one thing to envision a splendid room with a marble fireplace, plaster motifs or carved panels on the walls, and plaster medallions on the ceiling, but another to reproduce those things expertly. If that is not possible with the skills the craftsman already has, or is willing to take the time to learn, then another, simpler style should be chosen. It would be far better to start with a plain, detail-perfect room with papered walls and a painted ceiling than begin with a magnificent salon whose elaborately decorated interior is amateurishly done.

1-5. Simple furniture has its own charm.

SCALE

By far the most popular scale in miniatures today is 1-inch to 1-foot. Nearly all the furniture and accessories sold commercially are to that scale, and even though the craftsman intends to make his own furniture, he may still want to purchase metal and glass accessories. Obviously, some 1-inch-scale accessories can be used even if a larger or smaller scale is being followed, but many cannot, and the problem of finding suitable ones is much simplified if one's scale is the popular 1-inch to 1-foot.

The second most-used scale is 3/4-inch to 1-foot, and some commercial furniture is sold to this scale, but the choice of pieces is limited. A few craftsmen work to the 1/2-inch scale, and there are others who prefer a larger scale, such as 1 1/2 inches or 2 inches to a foot. However, usually only furniture is made to the larger scales; houses to hold such pieces are too large and unwieldy.

The writer prefers the 3/4-inch scale for several reasons (limited space for displaying the rooms is an important one), but the underlying, more nebulous reason can probably be summed up by, *de gustibus non est disputandum*—there is no disputing tastes. One-inch-scale furniture looks good to the writer; three-fourths-inch furniture looks better. However, if the craftsman has no such preconceived preferences, it is recommended that he use the 1-inch scale.

If, instead of building his own, the craftsman intends to buy a commercially built miniature house, he should be aware of one point. A house may have been built on the 1-inch scale, as advertised, but its rooms, after they have been furnished, don't look quite right. The living room may hold a chair, a sofa, a table, and possibly a secretary but no more, and the new owner, disappointed with the effect, does not know what is wrong.

It is surprising how many people will consider only the scale when buying a house or miniature rooms, and will not stop to measure the actual size of the rooms. Depending upon the floor plan, a miniature house built accurately to the 1-inch scale could range anywhere from 36 to 70, or more, inches in length. An average living room might be 15 or 20 inches long. Craftsmen who build their own miniature houses or rooms are very conscious of room sizes, but buyers of commercially made pieces are less likely to measure in inches and translate those inches to feet before investing their money. The results, when the rooms are furnished, can be most disappointing.

Similarly, one should have a ruler handy when buying miniature accessories and furniture. Not all described as "1-inch scale" is actually that. There are some companies whose catalogs show page after page of miniatures, pieces gathered from a variety of manufacturers, and who assure the prospective customer that "everything in this catalog is on the 1-inch scale." An examination of the listed sizes, however, might show that a teacup, translated to full size, would be six inches high, and the pot eighteen inches.

DETAIL

In addition to the importance of adhering to scale, the importance of attention to detail cannot be overemphasized. Details and scale are the two qualities that make all the difference between accurate reproductions and dollhouse furniture.

Many times the comment has been heard, "I could never make such furniture; I don't have the patience." It is the writer's firm, personal conviction that doing fine, detailed work in any field requires not patience, but interest and enthusiasm. The craftsman who says, "I don't have the patience," is probably saying, "I'm not interested enough to try."

It can be taken for granted that the reader has some degree of talent for working with his hands or he would not be interested in making miniatures at all. Given that talent, he can do any amount of detailed work if, for the time being at least, it is the one thing in the world he most wants to do.

The comment is also heard, "Oh, I couldn't do anything as complicated at that!" But in most cases a complicated piece of miniature furniture is nothing more than a combination of simple pieces, fastened together. The skill required for gluing together five or six pieces of wood to make a simple bed is the same skill needed for combining perhaps 25 or 30 pieces to make an elaborate one.

To illustrate the foregoing mixture of fact and opinion, the writer feels it would be both fun and informative to carry the making of a fairly elaborate Victorian chair throughout the book, starting with the drawing of its pattern and ending with the larger finished piece shown here. The chair, hereinafter referred to as The Chair, will appear in various stages of completion in the sections on sawing, lathe turning, wood finishing, carving, gluing, using dowels, and so on.

(Note: The metric system, the measuring system of the future in the United States, may be the present system of measuring for some craftsmen. Since the pages of this book are filled with so many figures in inches, and since adding the metric equivalents to each figure on each page would be confusing, those equivalents are given in a table at the end of the book. In the same table are given the figures in inches for converting full-size measurements to the 1-inch and 3/4-inch scales.)

1-6. *Two similar chairs show the size difference between the 3/4-inch and 1-inch scales.*

2.

Building a Room

This and the following chapter give detailed methods for building and lighting miniature rooms such as those shown in the color pages of this book. It should be pointed out, however, that these methods are by no means the only ones by which a successful room can be built. If the craftsman has the necessary tools, and some experience in carpentry work, he may wish to plan and build his own room in an entirely different way.

Since not all makers or collectors of miniature furniture have a basement workshop in which to cut large pieces of wood, the plans for miniature rooms can be drawn and someone else found who will do the actual work. There are many experienced craftsmen who make dollhouses for sale, and it is not difficult to find one who will make rooms on order, and who will charge a reasonable price for his work. The cost will, of course, depend upon how much work is to be done. The owner of a custom-built room can save considerable money if he later adds such details as doors, wood moldings, wallpaper, and so on. He can also make such things as fireplaces, inside brick chimneys, and tile and stone floors and give them to the builder to be incorporated into the room as it is being constructed.

It is not necessary to be an architect, or even experienced, to draw plans for a miniature room. All that need be shown are the shape and dimensions of the room wanted, its ceiling height, the placement of doors and windows, and any other special features such as a closet or built-in window seat.

PLANNING THE ROOM

In essence, a miniature room is a box with the front wall omitted so that its contents can be seen. That missing front wall can be the craftsman's best friend, since on or against it may be a door, a window or two, a staircase, or a fireplace, features that can be assumed to be part of the room but do not show.

The simplest full-size room, however, always has a door or doorway, and nearly always a window. While it is acceptable for the craftsman to fudge a little by placing one of the two elements on the missing front wall, to place both features there, and to show the viewer only three solid walls, would seem to be cheating. The minimum requirements for a seriously built miniature room, therefore, are three walls, a ceiling and floor, and a window or door. From there, as many more features may be added as the craftsman wishes to take the time to make, and within limits, the more the better. He can be sure that whatever details he adds will be noticed and appreciated by viewers, and will enhance not only the room itself, but its furniture and accessories as well.

Assuming the added details conform to the chosen period and style of the room, they can include random-width flooring, with or without pegs, picture moldings at ceiling level or dropped an inch or two, casement windows, double-hung windows, window seats, chair rails, quarter rounds over the baseboards, and so on. None of those details is essential to the success of the room, but any or all will add to its success if included.

The only details that should not be omitted in a room are those which are a necessary part of something else that has been included. An electric ceiling light, for example, calls for either a pull cord on the light itself or a switch on the wall, just as an electric appliance, such as a fan, a lamp, or a toaster, needs a wire running from it to a wall plug. A radiator does not sit unattached on the floor, but has a quarter-circle of pipe going from it into the floor, and a coal stove needs a length of pipe connecting it to the wall. Window shades need pulls, windows need locks and handles, and so on.

Again, however, the convenient front wall that isn't there can be used to good advantage. If the door is located on the missing wall, the light switch can be there also. If the house is steam heated, the radiator might be against this front wall. Similarly, details that are obviously needed somewhere in the room, such as a wall outlet for an electric appliance, might be above a baseboard behind a chair or bookcase where it doesn't show. In other words, details necessary to a room of a certain style and period should be in view, or there should be a logical reason why they aren't.

ROOM SIZES

As mentioned previously, commercially made miniature rooms, especially if part of a dollhouse, are often built too small to hold the same amount of furniture that an average full-size room of the same style would hold. Conversely, however, when the craftsman himself designs a room, he sometimes is tempted to make it larger than it should be. The additional cost and labor involved are negligible, and he reasons that the extra space will give him a chance to add more pieces to his collection later on.

It is usually a mistake, however, to allow the size of a room to be influenced by anything but the style of the furniture that will go into it. An inexpensive, mass-produced oak dining set, for example, of the style seen in catalogs of the early twentieth century or before, was usually used in a fairly small room, often as small as 10 by 12 feet. To put such furniture in a 20- or 25-foot room would detract from its effectiveness, just as a heavily carved, rich mahogany or rosewood set would look wrong in the smaller room.

OTHER CONSIDERATIONS

In addition to size, the style of the room being planned should conform to the style of the furniture that will go into it. Papered or painted walls, and sometimes painted woodwork, would be suitable for the oak set in the small room, while the larger, more elegant set would look well in a large, paneled room, or one with plaster medallions and motifs on the ceiling and walls.

A third consideration when planning the new room is wall space. The missing front wall, which was earlier called the craftsman's friend, now becomes an enemy, since it robs him of more than one-fourth of the total wall space that would be available in a full-size room of comparative size. The space that is left increases proportionally in value and should be studied carefully as the room plans are being drawn. Adequate wall space should be left for major furniture pieces, such as a piano or sofa, and window sills should be high enough to leave room for whatever might be placed under them, such as a radiator, table, or plant stand.

Before the plans are completed, it should be decided which will be the inside, and which the outside walls of a room. (An inside wall separates two rooms; an outside wall stands between a room and the outdoors.)

In most houses, a fireplace is located on an outside wall, while a doorway or hallway to another room belongs on an inside wall. If a closet is located on an outside wall, it must protrude into the room, but if on an inside wall, it is only necessary to show the door; the closet itself can be assumed to be protruding into an adjoining room.

ADDING CHANNELS

Channels along the outside of a room add a great deal to its effectiveness, and they should be used wherever possible. As mentioned in the previous chapter, they not only allow the viewer to catch glimpses of an adjoining room, hall, or outside scene, but they also can be used to hold the lights that shine through windows and doors, giving the effect of sunlight in the main room.

A channel is needed only outside a wall that has a window or open door in it. The normal corner room of a house would have at least one window on each outside wall, and a door on an inside wall leading to another room or hallway. Since too much wall space would be lost if there were openings on three walls, it can be assumed that the door or one window is on the convenient, missing front wall. Only two openings and two channels would therefore need to be planned in a corner room.

A room with only one outside wall would have windows on that one side only and would therefore require only one channel. However, an inside door on a second wall, and glimpses of another room behind it, would make the room more attractive and would help to balance the lighting.

It would seem logical to make a channel only as long as necessary, perhaps just long enough to have room for a light and a glimpse of the area that would be seen through a door or window. In practice, however, it is easier to run any channel the whole length of a wall. Not only will this simplify the work of building the room box, but also it will give the craftsman extra space in which to find the most effective location for the light.

PLANNING THE LIGHTING

In the following chapter, detailed instructions are given for installing lights, but before room plans are drawn, decisions should be made as to what method will be used to light the rooms.

It is possible to depend upon daylight or an outside light source, such as a floodlight or lamp, to light a miniature room, but such a method usually proves to be unsatisfactory. The light may be too harsh or too dim, may cast interfering shadows, may leave corners unlighted, or may simply produce an unrealistic effect.

A popular method of lighting is to place electrified lighting fixtures such as chandeliers, lamps, and wall lights, in view inside the room. Because full-size rooms are lighted in this way, many craftsmen (probably a majority of them) use the same method for lighting their dollhouses and miniature rooms. The writer, however, feels that visible lights detract from the effectiveness of a room unless they are so reduced in intensity that they are then no longer an effective light source. Perhaps this is because the viewer is not built on the 1-inch scale, or perhaps it is that lights minimize important details by shining too brightly in the eyes, or perhaps it is blind prejudice on the part of the writer. Whatever the cause, if such lights are used, it is recommended that they be dimmed as explained in the next

chapter. Miniature rooms may also be lighted indirectly from hidden sources, such as lights in coves or in concealed holes in the ceiling or in other fixtures.

A third lighting method is to place the lights in the channels. Bulbs located outside the room can be considerably larger than those located inside the room. With careful planning, ample and effective illumination can be provided by allowing light to shine through windows and open doors.

Any of the above lighting methods can be used alone or in combination with others, but in the writer's opinion, the best method will always include some lighting in the channels.

If channels are to be used, they should be included in the drawn plans of the room, but other lighting systems need not be indicated on the drawing. It is only important that the craftsman know what they will be so that holes for the wiring, or larger openings for light bulbs and so on, can be made in the walls and ceiling before the room is assembled.

The width of a channel is optional. If it is to hold only lighting equipment, and perhaps a scenic view to be glimpsed through a window, two to three inches is wide enough. If the channel is to represent a hallway, small pantry, or porch, it should be wider, perhaps three to four inches. If part of an adjoining room is to be shown, the wider the channel can be made, the better.

WOOD FOR THE ROOM BOX

Since the wood used for the room box will not show inside the room (the inside walls will be papered, painted, or paneled), any kind of wood or wood substitute can be used. Plywood in desired thicknesses is the easiest to use, but pressedboard or solid wood boards are also satisfactory. (When shopping for solid wood boards, remember that they are not as thick and wide as lumberyard designations would indicate. A so-called 1- by 12-inch board may be only 3/4- or 7/8-inch thick by 11 1/2-inches wide, and so on. Where it is important to be accurate, all boards should be measured before they are purchased.)

The thickness of the wood selected for various parts of the room box need be in scale only if it will show inside the room. If the viewer is to glimpse a hallway or other room through an open door, the wall in which the door is located should be (or at least appear to be) of in-scale thickness. Similarly, the outside wall of a house, as seen through a window, should appear to be thick enough to represent an outside wall.

Inside full-size walls, or partitions, vary from about 4 to 8 inches, and outside walls from 10 to 13 inches, or more. On the 1-inch scale, therefore, a 6-inch-thick partition would require wood 1/2-inch thick, and a 13-inch-thick brick wall would require wood over 1 inch thick. A miniature room of such thick wood would be heavy and awkward to handle, and a whole house would be proportionally more so. Door and window openings, however, can be built with correctly scaled thicknesses, as shown farther along, without resorting to the use of thick, heavy wood pieces for the entire wall or partition.

The choice of wood thickness is up to the craftsman. For most room box parts, 3/8-inch plywood is recommended; it is amply strong without being too heavy. The room whose construction is shown in this chapter is built of this material with two exceptions: Lighter, 1/4-inch plywood is used for the box back, which has no openings in it, and the top and bottom pieces are of 1/2-inch plywood, which is thick enough to take screw holes in its edges. Screws are used to mount the removable panels.

In addition to the above, material is needed for the front, decorative frame. The writer uses 1/4- by 3/4-inch double-bead wood molding, a standard wood trim that can be purchased in 6-, 8-, or 12-foot lengths at lumberyards and in some hardware stores. Also, if the open side is to be covered with glass, a piece of windowpane glass, as explained later, will be required. Glass fronts on the rooms will protect the contents from dust and, even more important, from the exploring, and often damaging, fingers of visitors.

OTHER MATERIALS

Ready-made parts for miniature rooms and houses are now available in shops, or can be ordered from catalogs. More and more such pieces are appearing on the market; most are done in excellent detail, and most are to the 1-inch scale. Windows and doors in a variety of styles, wainscoting, panels, newel posts, and balusters are among the pieces to be found, and they are well worth using if the craftsman does not wish to take the time, or is not equipped, to make his own.

In addition, there are many choices of miniature wood trim to be found, much of which

cannot easily be shaped at home without special equipment. Such moldings as quarter-round, chair rail, dentil, cove, and double bead, for example, can be bought in convenient strips and cut to length as needed.

Unfortunately, most of these pieces are made of basswood, a light-colored, fairly porous wood that is difficult to finish with stain, particularly if it must be made to match a darker, hardwood piece. However, with several coats of stain, a creditable job can be done, and the convenience of the shapes makes the pieces well worth using.

Small bricks can be bought, complete with the mortar for laying them. However, it is the writer's taste not to use them, but to create a more subtle effect by simulating bricks with clay or other materials, using methods described later on. If the craftsman disagrees, he should by all means use whatever looks best to him.

Small room parts made of pot metal can be found in most shops that specialize in miniatures.

2-1. Commercial plywood, trim, and flooring simplify building a room box.

Available are doorknobs, light switch plates, wall brackets, radiators, handles and latches for windows, and so on. Most of these pieces are quite inexpensive and rather crudely made, with ridges of metal left along the edges from the molds. Fortunately, however, pot metal is very soft. The shape of any chosen piece can be improved, and its surface made smooth, with the use of a small file or knife. It can then be painted as desired. There will be more on this subject later on.

Of a better quality are pieces made of brass. Hinges, doorknobs, drawer pulls, curtain rods, chandeliers, candelabra, and other brass accessories will do a great deal to make a miniature room more convincing.

Wallpaper is, of course, an important part of a room's decoration and, like so many other miniature house and room parts, is being offered on the market in a continually widening selection of colors and patterns. The only advice to be offered on this subject is that the pattern should conform to scale. It is a good idea for the craftsman to lean over backwards on this point to maintain wallpaper scale. A paper pattern in a full-size room might be very attractive with brightly colored, oversized flowers, but the same pattern reproduced on the 1-inch scale would probably seem too large for the miniature room and might give the impression that the craftsman just couldn't find the right paper for his scale.

Although wallpaper made especially for miniature rooms is easy to find and use, other sources for wall coverings are wrapping and shelf papers, cloth, full-size wallpapers, and painted "plaster." The latter effect can be achieved by using a fairly thick latex paint or, for rougher plaster, a coat of gesso paint under a topcoat of any other paint desired.

TOOLS AND SUPPLIES

A saw will be needed, and the best saw for cutting room edges straight is either a bench saw or a band saw that is large enough for the job. Second choice is one of two hand-held power tools—a circular saw or a sabre saw. Last choice is a carpenter's hand saw.

If a removable glass for the front of each room

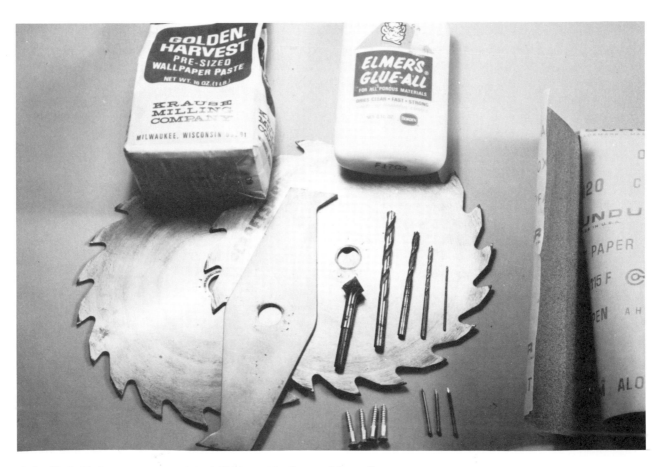

2-2. Dado blades, rose countersink, drill bits, and other useful supplies.

is to be used, a dado blade (for a bench saw) or a power router will be needed to make the required dados. (Dados are grooves in the wood into which the glass edges slide.)

A power drill or hand brace will be needed for drilling holes, in addition to a selection of twist drills in sizes from 1/16-inch to 1/4-inch, and a rose countersink for preparing holes for screws. Screwdrivers of several sizes and a pair of pliers will also be needed, as well as a supply of 1 1/8-inch finishing nails, 1-inch No. 6 flathead wood screws, white glue, and sandpaper.

DRAWING PLANS TO SCALE
Using a Ruler and Graph Paper

With the mechanical help of graph paper and the correct ruler for the craftsman's scale, drawing the plans for a room and, later on, for the furniture, is not at all difficult.

Various rulers have different scales, and which to use depends upon the scale being used. If the 1-inch to 1-foot scale is being used, the ruler should have 12 divisions to an inch. For the 3/4-inch scale, 16 divisions to an inch are needed. The latter ruler is standard and can be purchased almost anywhere, but a ruler with 12 divisions to an inch is less common. If one cannot be found in an office-supply store, a store specializing in engineering supplies will have it. A pica ruler, used by printers, can also be used, since there are 6 picas (and 12 half-picas) to an inch. A pica ruler should be available in most office-supply stores or wherever printing supplies are sold.

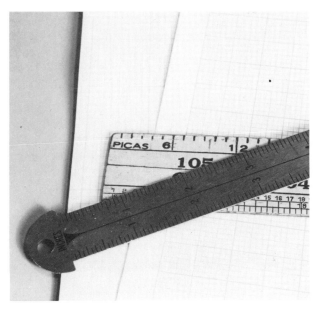

2–3. Graph paper and 1/16-inch and 1/6-inch rulers.

Graph paper with 8 squares to an inch can be found in nearly all stationery and office supply stores, but 12-squares-to-an-inch paper is more difficult to find. Again, an engineering supply company is the most likely source. If it cannot be found at all, any graph paper, with its parallel lines and exact right angles, will still be helpful for pattern-making. In this case, however, the ruler alone must be counted on to give the correct measurements for the 1-inch scale.

Using a Calculator

When converting full-size measurements to those for a miniature copy, an inexpensive calculator will greatly speed up the work, although using such an instrument is not at all necessary. All full-size measurements, converted to inches, are simply divided by 12 for the 1-inch scale, and by 16 if the 3/4-inch scale is being used.

Calculators do not show fractions, but it is easy to convert fractions to decimal equivalents. Anyone who remembers his grade school arithmetic knows that 1/2 = .50, 1/3 = .333 and so on. Therefore, if a cabinet is 6 1/2 feet high and a miniature copy is to be made to the 3/4-inch scale, 6 1/2 feet is converted to inches by multiplying 6 1/2 by 12, or 6.5 x 12 = 78. That gives the height of the full-size cabinet in inches. Those inches are then divided by 16 to give the height of the miniature copy to be made to the 3/4-inch scale. Dividing 78 by 16 equals 4.875, or 4 7/8, the height in inches of the miniature copy.

The following table gives the decimal equivalents for the common fractions the craftsman is likely to use.

For the 1-Inch Scale		For the 3/4-Inch Scale	
Fractions of an inch	Decimal equiv.	Fractions of an inch	Decimal equiv.
1/2	.5	1/2	.5
1/3	.333	1/4	.25
1/6	.1666	1/8	.125
1/9	.1111	1/16	.0625
1/12	.0833	1/32	.0312
1/24	.04166	1/64	.0156
1/48	.0208		

Without a calculator, the same steps given above are followed. The only difference is that the answers must be found by using paper and pencil, a time-tested but more time-consuming method.

DRAWING THE ROOM PLAN

The first step in drawing a room plan is to glue together the edges of as many sheets of graph paper as are necessary to make a single piece a few inches larger all around than the floor of the miniature room itself. The graph paper should, of course, have the correct number of squares to an inch for the craftsman's scale, as discussed earlier.

If the room is being planned for an already existing set of miniature furniture, the pieces should be arranged on the paper and a tentative outline of the room ruled lightly in pencil. If no furniture exists, pieces of paper to represent items of furniture can be cut out and arranged in the room before the outline is drawn.

A third method of planning a room is to give consideration only to its purpose—is it to be a dining room, living room, or whatever? The room can then be designed to fit the style or period desired, and the right furniture can be made for it later.

2-4. Plan for a simple dining room and hall. If someone else were to build the room, instructions should be given at A, B, C, and D regarding the locations and sizes of windows, doorways, removable panels, and glass channel respectively.

When the outside dimensions of the room have been determined, these lines are darkened. The windows and doors are located next and marked, and their sizes, including the heights of the window sills, written beside them. (A front door should be wider than a door between two rooms, and a closet door should usually be a little narrower.) Similarly, windows should be of different heights and widths, depending upon their locations and the period of the room or the house.

The height of the ceiling should be marked on the plan, and if the room is to be made by someone other than the craftsman himself, notes should be included specifying the type of flooring, the placement of picture moldings, and so on. If the maker of the room is an experienced carpenter, the forgoing plans should be all he will need.

Figures 2–4 and 2–5 show a typical floor plan and the room that will be made from it. One side wall will have windows in it, and the opposing side wall will contain a doorway, so they are backed by channels for lighting. Since the door at the end of the hall will be glued shut, the whole rear wall will have no openings in it and therefore does not need a channel.

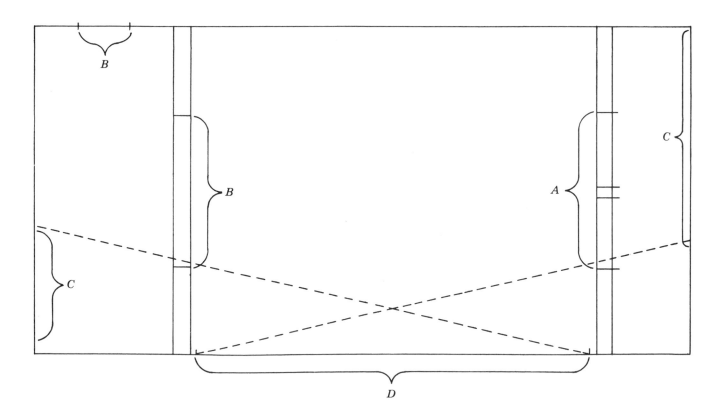

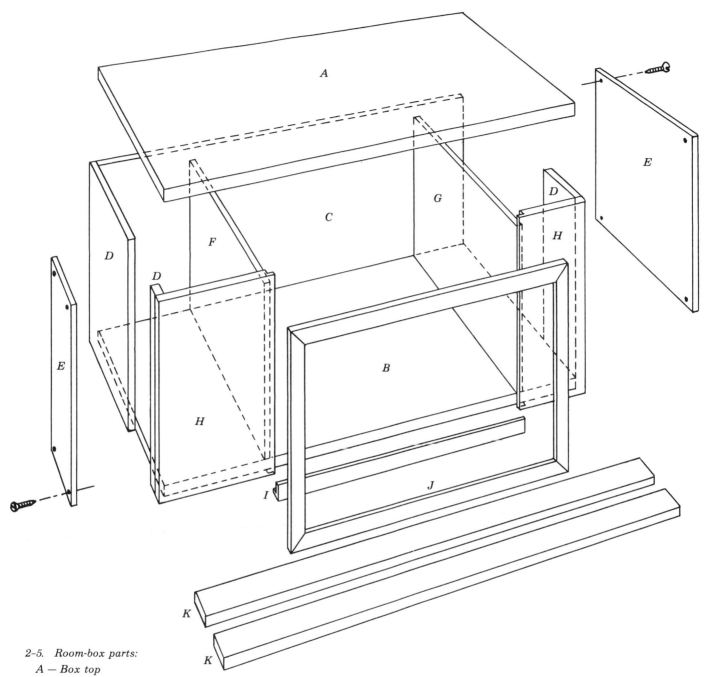

2-5. *Room-box parts:*

A — *Box top*

B — *Box bottom*

C — *Back wall*

D — *Vertical sides*

E — *Removable panels*

F — *Partition*

G — *Outside wall*

H — *Vertical fronts*

I — *Spacer*

J — *Front frame*

K — *Slats to elevate bottom*

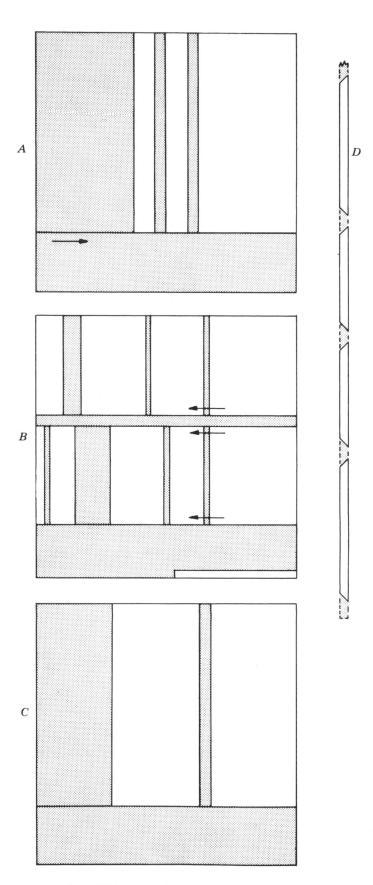

2-6. White areas show how patterns can be used for planning lumber cuts. A, B, and C are 2-foot squares of 1/4-, 3/8-and 1/2-inch plywood. D is a length of double-bead molding.

If the craftsman will make the room himself, and if he is not an experienced carpenter, it will be a great help to him to make paper patterns of the various parts. The pattern pieces will serve two purposes: (1) They can be laid close together on a large, flat surface, and the total area can be measured to determine how much wood should be purchased, and (2) they can then be fastened to the wood with rubber cement and used as guides for sawing. Although using patterns is the safest way to make sure the various parts of the room will fit together, the craftsman experienced in using a power saw can draw his cutting lines directly on the wood.

CUTTING THE OPENINGS

Each door and window opening (or other opening, such as for a fireplace) should be marked on a wall piece in the exact size and place it is to be when finished. A second line is next drawn outside the first one, allowing space for framing trim on three sides of the doors and windows, and for window sills. (Full-size trim is usually 3/4-inch thick; a window sill, 1 1/2 inches thick.) The opening of a miniature fireplace may need to be widened to allow for a brick lining, and other openings may similarly need enlarging to allow for finishing materials.

These enlarged openings are next sawed out and their edges sanded smooth. A band saw makes the smoothest cut, and can be used for both the door and window openings. Since a door is open at the bottom, there is no problem in starting the cut, but a window can be cut by starting at a floor edge, sawing up to the window and completing the cut inside the window area. This will leave a single unwanted cut in the wall between the window bottom and the floor, but this can be concealed by gluing a thin piece of scrap over the cut on the back side, and filling the front side with crack filler.

If a band saw is not available, a power sabre saw or jigsaw can be used instead.

An opening may also be needed in a ceiling for a skylight, or for the wires of a lighted chandelier. Holes for the wires can be drilled with a 1/16-inch twist drill, while a drill of a larger size will be needed if the rod of the chandelier is to go through the ceiling as well. Hidden interior lights (Chapter 3) require 1/4-inch holes.

2-7. *Window openings have been cut out with a band saw.*

All holes should be drilled from the inside so that any possible splintering at the edges will be on the outside where it will not show.

FINAL SAWING DETAILS

If a removable glass front for the room is to be used, a channel to slide the glass into must be provided. The channel is made after all the other pieces have been sawed to shape.

To make the channel, cut rabbets at the inside vertical edges of the two front pieces (*H*) and the top edge of the spacer (*I*) as shown in figure 2–5.

A rabbet is a groove cut at the edge of the wood, so there is only one groove side instead of two (figure 2–8).

Either a 1/4-inch dado head (a special blade used on a bench saw) or a 1/4-inch router bit can be used to cut the rabbets. Each rabbet should be 1/4-inch deep by a generous 1/8-inch wide. This will make a channel into which a 1/8-inch piece of window glass will slide. Measurements for the glass should be taken after the room box is assembled.

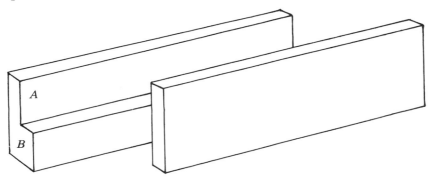

2-8. *A rabbet cut.* A *is the depth of the cut,* B *is its width.*

2-9. *Box parts ready for temporary assembly.*

2-10. *Temporarily assembled room box. White patches are crack filler necessitated by poor quality of plywood.*

24

TEMPORARILY ASSEMBLING
THE ROOM BOX

After the openings for the doors and windows have been cut out, and before any other preassembly work is done, the room box should be temporarily put together with nails and screws. Adhesives should not be used until the final assembly later on. To prevent the wood from splintering, 1/16-inch holes should be drilled for the nails. For the screw heads, 5/32-inch countersunk holes should be drilled in one wood piece, and opposite them in the second piece, 3/32-inch holes should be drilled for the threaded sections of the screws.

When putting the box together temporarily, the screws can be tightened, but nails should be driven in only about half way so they can be removed easily.

With the room assembled temporarily, the fit of all parts should be checked and corrections made where necessary. Next, pencil lines are drawn on the ceiling, back wall, and floor to show where the side walls are located, and the door openings should be marked on the floor.

Lines of visibility should then be drawn, as illustrated in figure 2–11, to define areas the viewer will be able to see through the wall openings into the channels. These lines will be used as guides for laying flooring, papering walls, and doing other finish work.

The room box can now be taken apart and preassembly details completed.

PREASSEMBLY DETAILS

All wall, fireplace, and other required openings must be cut out before the room box is put together. Many other details, such as laying the flooring, completing the doors and windows, adding a staircase or fireplace, paneling the walls, and so on, are more easily done while the parts are still separated. It is also more convenient, although not necessary, to install wall lights, to paint and paper walls, add curtains, and the like while each wall can still be laid flat.

The only details that are better left until the room walls are assembled are such things as baseboards and picture moldings, whose ends will be mitered to meet exactly at a corner.

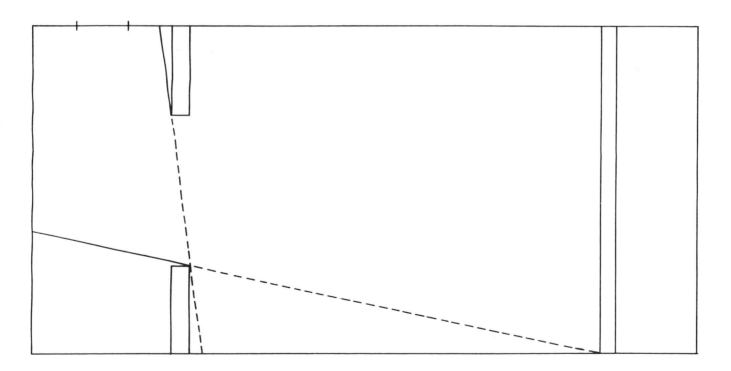

2–11. Visibility lines, partition lines, and others should be drawn on the floor before disassembly.

Wood Flooring

Wood is by far the most-used material for room floors of any period, and although floorboards may vary in widths and colors, and may be held in place with either nails or wood pegs, basic floor styles have changed very little for hundreds of years.

Today's floorboards, cut by machine, are of even widths, but many years ago boards were laid on the floor in random widths, a style that is still used occasionally, but no longer from necessity. All floorboards are of random lengths, so no two side-by-side boards start and end at the same place. The kind of boards used for the

2-12. Squaring off the end of a floor section.

2-13. A hard wax makes an excellent floor finish.

miniature room, and the style of laying them, depends upon the style and period being represented.

Floorboards can be cut individually from 1/16-inch plywood and glued side by side, but unless the craftsman has a band saw or similar tool that will cut perfectly smooth, straight edges, it would be advisable for him to buy ready-made flooring, which is available in either regular or random widths. Such flooring is made of thin sheets of wood, usually 3 1/2 inches wide, which is scored to resemble individually laid floorboards. The craftsman needs only to cut the sheets to length and glue them in place.

Scored flooring can also be made by hand. The scoring is done with the use of a steel ruler and any not-too-sharp tool, such as the back of a knife blade. The scoring should be done with the grain of the wood, and the craftsman's scale should, of course, be strictly adhered to. Nearly all hardwood floorboards are 2 1/2 inches wide, although the boards used in plank floors were usually made of pine and ran as wide as 8 to 10 inches.

Whether miniature flooring is made by hand or purchased, cross lines should be scored here and there to indicate the ends of the boards, just as these butt lines show in all full-size wood flooring.

Any thin sheets of wood can be used to make miniature flooring, although very soft wood, such as balsa or basswood, takes a poor finish. Of the woods that are plentiful in the shops, good-quality 1/16-inch plywood is the writer's first choice, although if thin sheets of hardwood were available at a reasonable price, they would certainly make the best flooring.

If pegged boards are desired, pairs of peg marks can be made by tapping the end of a 1/16-inch brass tube into the wood at each end of a board. Nail marks can be added with a pencil, which can also be used to darken and emphasize the scored board lines, if desired.

To finish the wood, a stain should first be used, followed by a finishing coat of varnish, a plastic-type spray, or wax.

To lay the wood floor, the lines drawn on the floor when the box was temporarily assembled should be followed. (The floor ends should not be run under the walls, as this will prevent the room pieces from fitting together properly.) If there is a doorway through which the flooring must be laid, all the area beyond, within the lines of visibility mentioned earlier, must also be covered.

Floorboards usually run with the length of a room. Starting at the front of the room, each board section should be sawed and glued in place before the next one is sawed. This will ensure the correct fitting of the pieces. If the boards are to run from back to front, the gluing of the floor sections should start at one side wall.

Any desired adhesive may be used, although white glue or contact cement are the two most commonly used for the purpose; each has its good and bad points. White glue must be spread and used quickly before it dries. If commercial flooring is being used, each floor section must be clamped until the adhesive has dried thoroughly or it may buckle in places. Contact cement allows plenty of time for the work and will not buckle the flooring, but the laying must be done very carefully, since there can be no repositioning of the flooring once it has been laid in place.

If preferred, the wood floor can be laid after the room box has been assembled. It will then not be necessary to measure and mark wall lines on the floors, but the craftsman will have to work in more awkward positions as he fits and glues the floor sections.

Constructing Doors and Windows

Doors, windows, built-in cabinets, and any other wood features that will not be glued to two walls can be added next.

Doors can be constructed in a number of styles. If a door is to be left open, its thickness should be to scale, but the thickness and back side of a closed door (such as the one constructed here) is not important. Of course all visible parts of the door must be to scale.

Any desired wood can be used for making doors, but since plywood comes in very thin sheets, it is a useful material for the purpose.

Before constructing a door, the doorway fram-

2-14. The door can be marked as shown to guide the adding of trim.

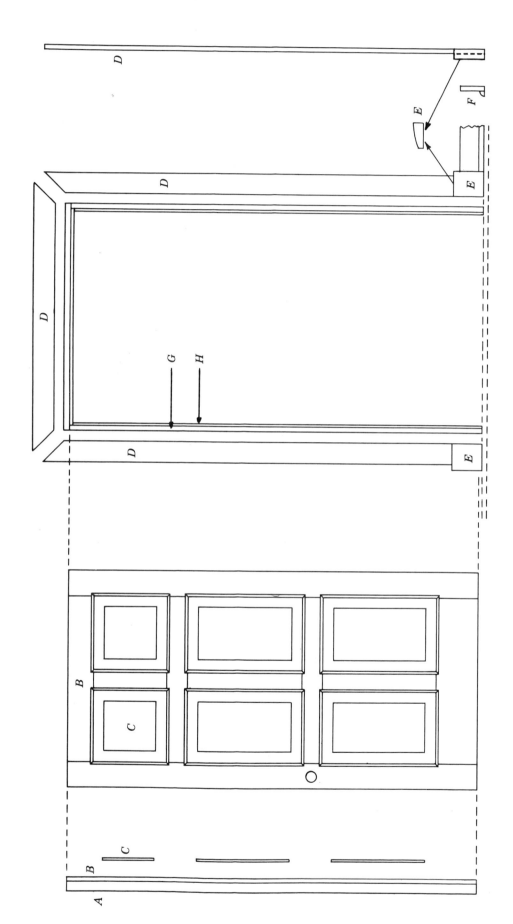

2-15. *Door and doorway construction details:*

A — Door backing piece
B — Various door-face trim pieces
C — Six inset panels
D — Facing trim for door opening
E — Two trim bases
F — Baseboard with show molding
G — Three framing pieces for opening
H — Three door-stop pieces

ing trim and door stop pieces should be installed. The opening in the wall can next be measured, and the door built to fit it. Painting or staining of the door and frame should be done before any hardware is added.

Windows also vary in their styles, sizes, and locations, and the details of construction will vary accordingly. Windows shown in figures 2-16 and 2-17 are the ordinary, double-hung type that are most frequently used in homes with 13-inch walls.

Since the outside wall of the room is made of 3/8-inch plywood, it must be thickened around a window edge so that the viewer, looking through the window from inside the room, will see the edge of what appears to be a 13-inch outside wall. This can be done by lining the window with a frame (figure 2-16) of a width to conform to the craftsman's scale.

With the frame glued in place, the window opening can now be measured to determine the sizes of the upper and lower sashes. When measuring, it should be remembered that when the window is open, the lower sash will rest in front of the upper one, and when the window is closed, the upper and lower sashes overlap each other in the middle where the lock is located. The two sashes should therefore be made long enough to allow for this overlapping.

Window panes may be made either of glass or clear plastic. The writer prefers glass, even though glass is more difficult to cut, and in-scale glass is hard to find. (Glass slides, such as those used in medical laboratories, make excellent miniature windows.) Fortunately, however, glass that is a little too thick will appear to be in scale once it has been installed in the windows.

In-scale plastic (1/32-inch thick) is easy to find and can hardly be distinguished from glass. Moreover, once curtains have been hung on a window, the question of glass versus plastic becomes purely academic. If the craftsman is unbiased on the subject, which the writer is not, he should use whatever material he prefers.

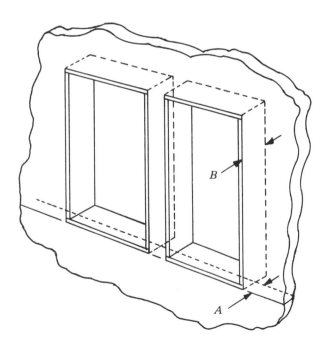

2-16. *Making a room wall appear thick through the windows.* A *shows the actual room wall thickness,* B *shows the width of the frame added inside the window openings.*

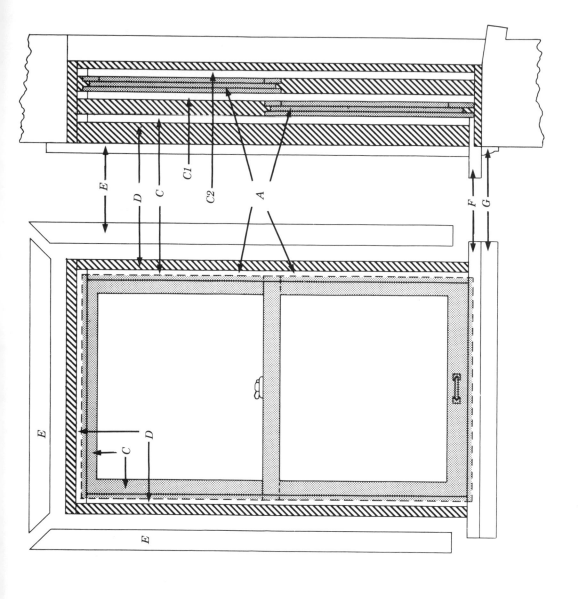

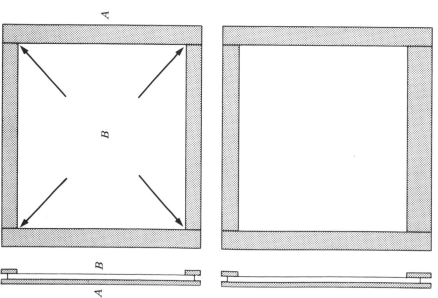

2-17. *Details of the window sash and opening construction:*

A — *Upper and lower window sashes*
B — *Upper and lower window panes*
C — *Three inner stop pieces*
C1 — *Three center stop pieces*
C2 — *Three outer stop pieces*
D — *Framing pieces used to thicken the wall*
E — *Window-opening facing trim*
F — *Windowsill*
G — *Skirt*

If glass is used, it must be cut to size with a glass cutter. Clear plastic can be scribed with an awl, then cut with a fine-tooth blade on either a jigsaw or band saw. The glass should be cut to fit snugly between the frames, but not tightly.

The sashes can be made of narrow wood strips glued around the edges of the glass, or of a frame cut in one piece. (Instructions for cutting a frame in one piece are included in Chapter 5, in the section on using a jigsaw.) Since the outer side of the glass will not show, only the inner side need be framed. Before gluing the sash to the glass, the woodwork should be stained or painted. The frames can then be glued in place using any preferred adhesive. (The writer uses epoxy putty when gluing glass, because the likelihood of squeezeout is greatly reduced. This is explained more fully in Chapter 6, in the section on adhesives.)

When the above work is finished, the hardware can be glued in place as a final step.

Double-hung sashes are held in place by three sets of stops (wood strips), which are glued to the framed window opening. The top sash is held between the outer and center stops, and the lower sash is held between the inner and center ones. The inner stop, which shows from inside the room, is usually made of a strip molding; the other stops are plain wood strips.

If the stops are glued to the window frames only, the sashes can be raised and lowered; gluing the stops to both the frames and the sashes prevents the sashes from being moved. If windows that can be opened are not important to the craftsman, the work is easier if they are glued to the stops permanently.

The inner stops are glued to the sides and the top of the window frame only; the window sill serves as the fourth stop, at the bottom.

Built-in cabinets and bookshelves are constructed just as any piece of furniture would be, except their outsides and backs need not be sanded and stained. They are slipped and glued into openings in the walls that have been sawed out to receive them. Their front edges are then covered with wood trim.

2-18. *Preparing plastic for sawing by scribing with a sharp point.*

2-19. *Lower window with hardware to be attached.*

2-20. *Window wall ready for papering.*

2-21. *Marking floor lines on the wall.*

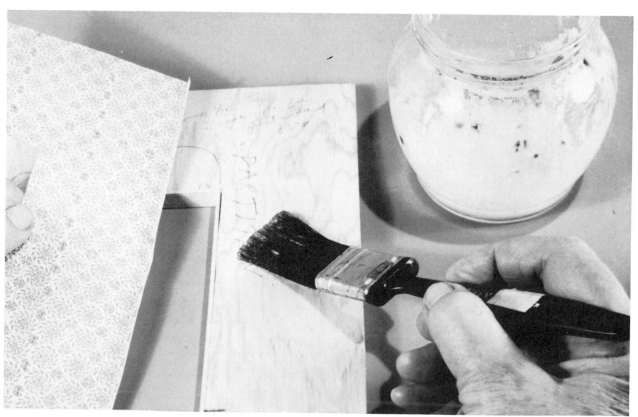

2-22. *Applying a section of wallpaper.*

Papering, Painting, and Paneling

Most of the necessary interior decorating can be done before the room is assembled. With the exception of a pattern that cannot be pieced at a room corner, wallpaper can be applied while the walls are still separated, as can all interior paint and paneling.

Unlike full-size wallpaper, whose edges must be cut to fit existing window and door frames, miniature room paper can be applied right to the edges of doors, windows, and floors; wood trim, which will be added afterwards, will cover any irregularities in the paper edges.

Wallpaper paste (available in some hobby shops and all wallpaper retail shops) should be used for applying the paper, since it allows the pieces to be moved about until they are correctly positioned. In addition, accidental smears can be wiped off without leaving a stain.

Before papering, it will be helpful if additional guidelines are drawn on the walls, where they meet the floor, and around the windows and doors. To do this, the room can be temporarily assembled, or the back wall and each side wall can be held in place, one at a time, and the necessary lines drawn. Using these lines (and those drawn earlier) as guides, the wallpaper can then be fitted and cut.

Wallpaper paste can be applied either to the paper or to the wall. The writer prefers the latter method because some papers have a tendency to stretch when wet with paste. Each paper section should be applied as closely as possible to its correct position, so very little pulling or pushing will be needed to position it exactly. If bubbles appear, they can be flattened with a clean board, or with a wad of paper towel or facial tissue. The prepared wall should be allowed to dry

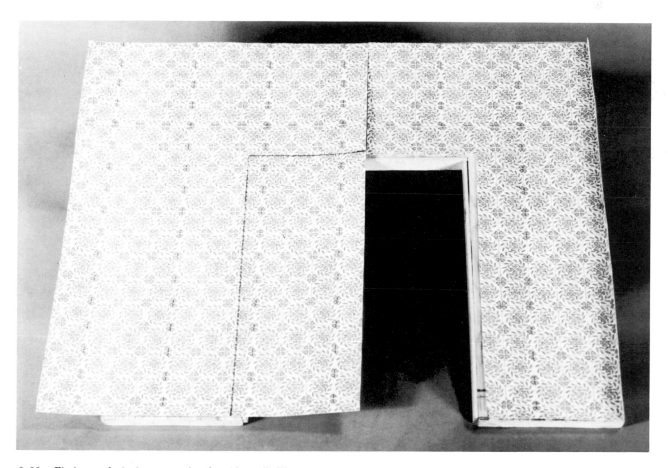

2-23. Fitting and piecing paper for the side wall. The excess at the left will wrap around the front edge of the wall to the other, out-of-sight side.

thoroughly before any accidental smears are removed from the front surface. The cleaning can then be done with a damp (not wet) cloth.

There are two ways to turn a corner with wallpaper. The first is to use a single piece of paper large enough to cover both walls. The first wall can be papered before the room is assembled, and the excess paper can be applied to the second wall after the room has been assembled. The back wall and side wall (figure 2-24) of the hallway were papered in this way.

The second method of turning a corner is to leave a very narrow extension of about 1/8 inch or so at the edge when papering one wall (figure 2-25). The extension is then pasted to the second wall after the room has been assembled.

Because matching patterns at a cut edge is difficult (and they should always be matched as perfectly as possible), wallpaper should be pieced no more than is necessary. The easiest pattern to

match is one with vertical lines, and the most difficult is one with an open, widely scattered design.

If walls are to be painted, the wood surfaces should first be sanded smooth. Any oil-base or latex interior paint can be used, although the latter is the easier to handle. A plaster wall finish can be simulated by applying a latex paint thickly and not too smoothly.

Walls can also be paneled, or partially paneled, if desired. The simplest method is to cover the area to be paneled with sheets of very thin wood (not over 1/32 inch) or, even better, wood veneer, which can be bought in sheets or convenient rolls. Edging strips can then be used to outline the panels in any size or shape desired. The panels in the dining room, shown in the color section, were done in this way, in combination with a fairly wide and a very narrow edging strip.

2-24. First method of papering around a corner. The excess paper will be applied to the hall side wall during the box assembly.

2-25. *Second method of papering around a corner. The slight excess turned up at left has been pattern-matched to the back wallpaper.*

2-26. *Matching paper of the side wall to that of the back wall. The paper will be creased at the place marked, then trimmed along the pattern line adjacent to the crease.*

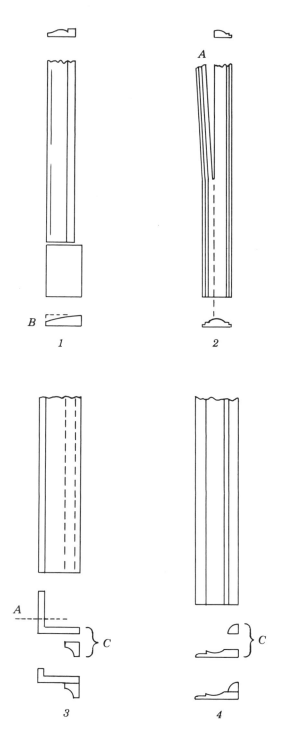

2-27. Altering commercial pieces to make a special trim. A is the saw cut; B is shaped with a file; C shows two pieces glued together.

1 — Facing trim for doorways and windows

2 — Window skirt or wall molding at ceiling

3 — Plate rail

4 — Baseboard with shoe molding

Installing Door, Window, and Other Facing Trim

Commercial moldings, baseboards, window edgings, and the like have many uses other than those for which they were intended. If very narrow stripping is needed, double bead can be sliced in half lengthwise. Baseboards can be narrowed with a jigsaw, and all pieces can be made thinner, if necessary, with the use of sandpaper and a file. Fortunately, making such changes is fairly simple, since the wood used in most manufactured trim is quite soft.

All woodwork pieces should be stained or painted before they are glued into place. They should then be given a coat or two of varnish, Krylon, or something similar; this is especially important if the trim is made of basswood, which is quite absorbent.

When fitting wood facing trim to windows, doors, cabinets, and so on, a miter box should be kept close at hand and used for each cut. Ends of trim that meet at right angles should be cut at 45-degree angles.

White glue is a useful adhesive for adding trim. Since it would be difficult to follow the usual method of applying glue to both surfaces (the papered walls could too easily become stained), the adhesive should be applied to the trim only, which is then positioned very carefully and pressed into place until dry.

ROOM ASSEMBLY

After all possible preassembly details are completed, the room can be assembled permanently. Using nails and glue, the back wall is first attached to the floor. The two side walls are added next, and any wallpaper extending from one wall can now be pasted to the adjoining one.

Baseboards, picture moldings, and other wood trim that extend around the corners can now be glued in place. All such pieces should be carefully mitered at the corners and, again, they should be stained or painted before they are attached to the room.

2-28. *Installing a section of baseboard with a shoe molding.*

2-29. *Installing a plate rail. The contrasting paper above the plate rail was applied after the walls were assembled.*

2-30. *The room is now ready for the assembly of the box.*

FINAL BOX ASSEMBLY

The room box can now be completed. Using the preassembly nail holes as guides, the various vertical pieces are attached next, and the ceiling last. Glue and nails are used for attaching all pieces except the removable panels on the sides, which must be attached with screws. (If any other part of the room, such as the ceiling, is to be removable, it should also be attached with screws.)

To make sure that the top of the spacer (part I in figure 2-5) will be flush with the floor, it is a good idea to press a small piece of board flat against the room's floor and to allow its edge to extend out a little beyond the floor's edge. The spacer can then be pressed against the board and nailed into place (figure 2-33).

The frame pieces at the box front (parts J, figure 2-5) are next glued into place. With the room now completed, its exterior can be painted as desired, and 1/8-inch glass cut and fitted into the channel between the room box and frame.

2-31. *Nailing a vertical piece to the bottom.*

38

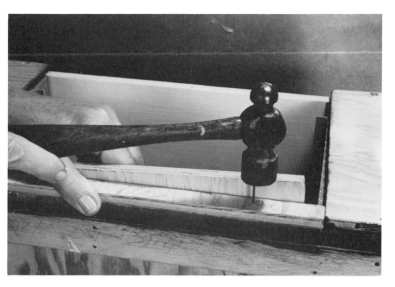

2-32. *The room box is complete except for the frame.*

2-33. *Attaching the box part that supports the bottom of the frame.*

2-34. *With the front frame attached, the room box is ready for wiring and furnishing.*

2-35. *Making a tile floor. Modeling compound is rolled evenly.*

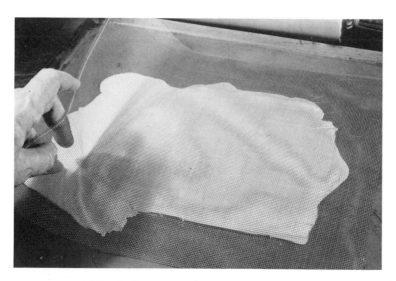

2-36. *Rolling screening into the flattened compound.*

2-37. *A short baking sets the material.*

OTHER DETAILS FOR OTHER ROOMS
Making a Tile Floor

A study of old photographs shows that ceramic tile floors in kitchens and bathrooms, and in such public places as banks, drugstores, and barber shops, go back at least a hundred years. Although large tiles, three to four inches square, were used many years ago just as they are today, it is the small square or hexagonal tiles, not more than 1 1/2 inches across, that seem to be more representative of the period just before and after the turn of the century. The following method of making such a floor was worked out with the use of Polyform, although other clay-type materials might do just as well.

With an ordinary rolling pin, a thin sheet of the modeling compound is rolled out on a non-stick baking sheet. It is extremely important that the rolled sheet be of a uniform thickness (about 1/8 to 3/32 inches) throughout. Since the rolling pin will tend to make the compound a little thinner at the edges, the sheet should be rolled about 1 1/2 inches larger than needed all around. The work is simplified if, after the material has been rolled flat, it is picked up in the hands and gently stretched to almost the size desired. It is then laid back on the baking sheet and rolled until the surface is perfectly smooth. If any small dents appear, they should be filled with Polyform and rolled until they no longer show.

A piece of screening is next used to press the tile shapes into the Polyform. A soft screen, made of nylon or fiberglass, is easiest to handle, although wire screen can be used if necessary. The size of the squares is optional, although those 1/16 to 1/8 inch across make the most realistic floors.

The screening is rolled into the Polyform sheet until it is well embedded, but not buried. Care must be taken that the depth to which the screen is pressed is uniform throughout the whole sheet; if this is not accomplished on the first try, the surface must be smoothed and the screen pressed in again.

The baking sheet of Polyform is next put into a cold oven, the temperature turned to 250 degrees, and the floor baked for about 20 minutes. This slow baking allows the material to retain its light color and to remain flexible, which simplifies the work of gluing it flat later on.

As soon as the baking is finished, the screening is pulled away from the hot material, and the

(Text continues after color pages.)

40

A Victorian bedroom. The ornately carved dresser and wardrobe are of rosewood; the bed and chest are of walnut.

A comfortable living room in a large, middle-class home of the early 1920s.

A kitchen of the 1920s with a linoleum rug on a wood floor.

A college boy's bedroom. The not-too-neat occupant has left a cap and hanger on the dresser posts, and he often forgets to close drawers.

A rather formal dining room with a wide hall at the left and a butler's pantry at the right rear.

An attic sewing room. The window shade and no curtains, the very simple ceiling fixture, and the mixture of furniture styles suggest a catch-all family room.

The office of a lumber dealer at the turn of the century. Copied from a photograph.

An attic playroom. Another catch-all room, with semi-discarded furniture serving as a background for a floor full of toys.

An upstairs hall. With a collapsible gate standing between him and the dinner guests, the family pet has lost interest in his ball and bone.

A bathroom about 1910. The toilet lid and tank are of oak. The footed tub and the exposed pipes under the wash basin are typical of the period.

Toys for a miniature playroom. The dollhouse is 2 1/8 inches high.

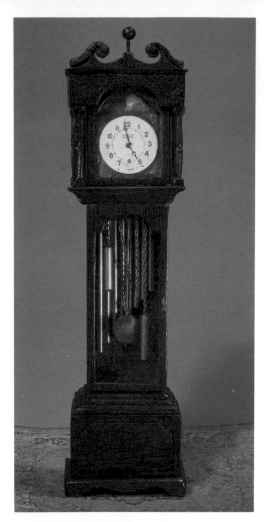

A rosewood grand piano. The legs were carved with an electric drill.

A mahogany grandfather clock. The dial is mounted on thin brass sheet on which are painted phases of the moon.

A maple rocker and a world globe. The globe is a painted one-inch wood bead.

An icebox and kitchen cabinet. The built-in bread box and flour bin were typical of the early 1920s.

Office furniture made of plywood, an easy wood to work with but difficult to finish.

A rosewood Victorian sofa and chair. The wood of the sofa back is bent in one piece.

A copy of an old fireplace seen in a restaurant. The work consisted of gluing together 105 fairly simple pieces, a project that required more time than skill.

"tile" floor is allowed to cool. The edges are then cut to the desired size with scissors or a sharp knife, with care being taken to cut only into the pressed-in lines, and never through a raised tile.

2-38. *The screening is pulled away from the hot material.*

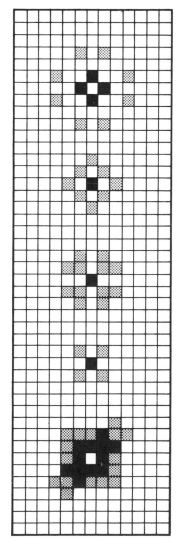

2-39. *Typical tile patterns of the early twentieth century.*

If desired, evenly spaced patterns can be painted on the tiles with the use of a fine brush and water color, a ballpoint pen, a lead pencil, or colored pencils. The scraps cut from the margin can be used for practice to find the right pattern and color combination. It is best to use no more than two soft colors, and preferably two tones of only one color, such as medium and light blue, brown and tan, or two shades of gray. Typical patterns popular at the turn of the century are shown in figure 2-39.

If a pencil or other smearable material has been used to color the tiles, the floor should be given a light protective spraying of Krylon or similar fixative as a final step.

If hexagonal tiles are desired, a piece of nylon netting can be used instead of screen. However, since it is impossible to roll the material into the Polyform without stretching it a little in places, the tiles cannot be painted after baking. Any slight irregularity caused by the stretching does not show in the white tiles, but would if a symmetrical pattern were painted on the floor.

If there is to be a hallway or another room adjoining the miniature kitchen or bathroom, the surface of the new tile floor will be slightly above the wood surface of the adjoining area. In such a case, the edge of the tile floor should be concealed with a narrow wood or simulated marble sill, just as full-size tile floor edges are concealed.

The flooring is glued in place with the same adhesive used for wood flooring—either white glue or contact cement.

2-40. *The completed bathroom floor.*

Staircases

Treads, Risers, and Stringers

There are certain features of a miniature house or room that appeal to nearly everyone, and which most craftsmen will sooner or later want to make. A staircase, or at least a glimpse of the top or bottom steps, is one of those features. (A fireplace is another, and is discussed in the following section.)

Basically, a staircase is composed of three parts (figure 2-41): (*A*) The stringers, (*B*) the risers, and (*C*) the treads. In large homes with spacious front halls, a staircase may be free-standing, but in nearly all others the stringer that supports one end of the treads is fastened to a wall. This arrangement means not only a saving of space in the hall, but also to the craftsman it means a saving of labor, since only one newel post, one hand railing, and one set of balusters to support the railing need be made.

No special skill is needed to cut the parts for a staircase. The dimensions of the treads (which should overhang the risers in front and on one or both ends) and of the risers can be ruled in pencil directly on the wood. Even easier, if wood strips of the desired width can be found, they need only be cut to the correct lengths. The outline of the stringers can be drawn on graph paper, the pattern fastened to the wood with rubber cement, and the two pieces sawed out.

The only real problem to be solved when building a staircase is to find the correct height for the risers so they will all have the same dimensions (or almost) and come out even with the floor above. Mathematically, the solution is simple enough. The total height of the space to be filled with steps (the distance from one floor, through the ceiling, to the floor above) is divided by the height of each step. The result is the number of steps needed.

The heights of the steps in a number of homes were measured by the writer, and all were 7 to 8 inches. In one instance there was some satisfaction in finding steps in a lovely old home that were not all of the same height. The riser of one top step was a full inch lower than the others, and another, a fraction of an inch lower. Apparently, then, even skilled builders of full-sized houses weren't always able to make their steps come out even!

The craftsman should take heart from the above and not feel that each of his risers must be exactly the same height. If his figures show that his staircase will be a fraction of an inch too high for the available space, he can make the top riser a little lower than the others, and if the difference is too large to be absorbed by one riser, he can divide it and make the two top risers a little lower than the others. When determining dimensions of stairs, the craftsman is encouraged to cheat a little if necessary, with only one word of caution: he must not be caught at it. If his figures show that one step will have to be only half as high as the rest to come out even, he should change the measurement of his step height slightly and rework his figures.

For example, if the distance from a floor through the floor above is 10 feet, the possible heights of the steps could be 8, 7 3/4, 7 1/2, 7 1/4, or 7 inches. To find the number of steps that would fit into 10 feet, the feet should first be converted into inches by multiplying by 12. The results, 120, would next be divided by each of the step heights. The results:

Step Heights in Inches	Number of Steps That Would Fit
7	17.14
7 1/4	16.55
7 1/2	16
7 3/4	15.48
8	15

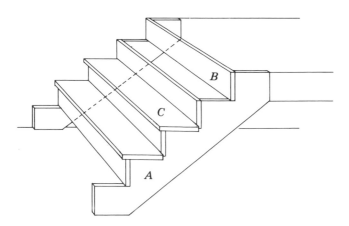

2-41. Staircase parts: A, stringer; B, riser; C, tread.

Obviously, then, the height of the steps should be either 7 1/2 or 8 inches, with 16 or 15 steps respectively. If none of the figures should come out even, the step height should be chosen that results in the highest possible odd step. A figure of 15.97, for example, would call for 16 steps, with the top step being only .03 lower than the others, a difference so slight it would not be noticed.

If a staircase in a miniature room ascends to an invisible floor above, the only preparation that need be made for it in the room is an opening in the ceiling. Of course, if only the bottom few steps are to show behind a wall, the wall itself is the only preparation needed.

A descending staircase, on the other hand, calls for a slight change in room plans. Such a staircase would lead downward from an attic hall, a second floor hall, or from a first-floor hall or kitchen to the basement. The full set of descending steps would not be seen; the top three or four steps would be all that would show from the room or hall being reproduced.

Since, in a normal room box, there is no space below the floor in which to show a few descending steps, space must be created by making the sides of the box two to three inches taller, and attaching the floor above those extra inches. The space below the floor can then be used to show the top few steps of a descending staircase (figure 2–42). It is only necessary to cut an opening in the floor, slip the shortened staircase in place, and glue it.

When sawing staircase parts, the thickness of the wood for the stringers is unimportant. It will not show and can therefore be as substantial as the craftsman wishes. However, the thicknesses of the treads and risers will show and must therefore be in scale.

Figure 2–43 shows the exposed ends of the risers. Some steps are left this way, but in most homes, a thin covering piece, as illustrated, conceals the ends of the risers. The craftsman should look at a few full-size staircases to see how they are finished. The wood used as a covering board should be thin, and its edges should be sanded smooth and rounded off.

After the treads are sawed to shape, the front edge of each and the ends away from the wall should also be rounded by sanding. All cut pieces should then be sanded smooth.

2-42. A descending staircase to the basement is suggested by using a channel to show the landing and a few top steps.

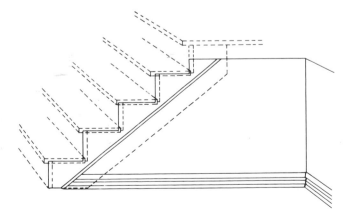

2-43. A thin wood piece, shown by a dotted line, conceals the ends of the risers.

Railings, Posts, and Balusters

Shapes for the hand railing of a staircase are shown in figure 2–44. If the 1-inch scale is being used, the simplest solution is to use a ready-made miniature railing, which can be purchased in strips of convenient lengths and cut as needed.

If the craftsman is using another scale or wishes to make his own railings, he can use a file to flatten one side of a length of dowel. It can then be glued to a flat strip whose top edges have been rounded by sanding.

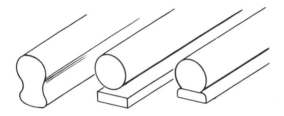

2-44. Hand railings. Left: a manufactured railing. Center and right: a railing made from a flattened dowel and a wood strip glued together.

Balusters can also be purchased ready-made, and if the 1-inch scale is being followed, they should be used. Turning two or three almost identical posts on a lathe is relatively easy, but when a whole series must be shaped alike, there are certain to be discrepancies that the eye will too readily pick out. Ready-made posts can even be used for the 3/4-inch scale if they are shortened as shown in figure 2–45.

In a miniature room, either the top or lower newel post will show, but probably not both. The craftsman can therefore go all out to make the one post as detailed and elaborate as he pleases. A design for it can be found either in books on interiors, or in homes of the approximate period he is following. Most newel posts are round, and must therefore be turned on a lathe. Square posts can be sawed, and those that combine both square and round sections can either be turned from a square stick, with the squared areas left untouched, or separate square and round sections can be fastened together with dowels and an adhesive. In any case, since baluster and railing

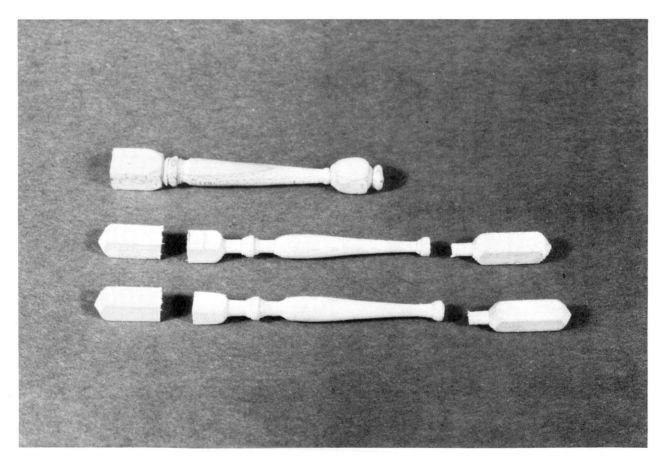

2-45. Manufactured balusters can be shortened to suit the purpose or scale.

styles are quite standard, the newel post can set the tone of the whole staircase and should be made with care and in as much detail as possible. (Making and using dowels is explained in Chapter 6.)

2-46. Balusters have been fastened to the railing with dowels and glue, and will be made parallel as they are glued to the floor of the upstairs hall.

Assembling the Staircase

The staircase parts should be stained before they are glued together. If they are glued first, there is almost sure to be some squeezeout here and there, which the stain will not penetrate. The result will be an unattractive, spotty finish.

When gluing the staircase pieces together, the bottom and top risers should be fastened first to the stringers to hold the stringers apart. The rest of the risers are then glued in place; the treads are glued last. If preferred, heavier blocks of wood of the same length as the risers can first be glued between the stringers at the top and bottom of the staircase (below the step level, where they won't be seen) to hold the stringers apart. The risers and treads are then glued on.

The balusters and railing can be fastened together with dowels and an adhesive, or with an adhesive alone. The latter method is faster, but the former will make the job easier, since the dowels will help hold the balusters erect and parallel until the adhesive dries.

Depending upon the circumstances, the dowels may be used either to hold the balusters to the railing or to the stair treads. Under normal circumstances, however, it is recommended that the balusters be fastened to the treads with dowels and glue, and the railing added afterwards with glue alone.

Doors

A study of the doors in any but the most modern homes (where panelled doors are seldom used) will show panels arranged in a wide variety of patterns. Some are vertical, some horizontal, and some a combination of the two.

The pattern of the door panels, however, is less important than the thickness of the wood used. As with all other parts of a miniature room, the doors must be in scale. If a door can be opened so that both sides will be seen, three thicknesses of wood must be used (the door itself, and the panels on each side). Since doors between rooms in full-size houses vary in thickness from a little more than an inch to about 2 inches, the three layers of wood in a miniature door should total not more than 1/12 to 1/6 inch on the 1-inch scale. The strips of wood that form the panels on the door's surface are usually thicker than the door itself, so the thickest possible miniature door on the 1-inch scale could be made of two 1/16-inch layers and one 1/32-inch layer. A door this thick, however, would be found only in a large, old house. Smaller houses and those of a later date would have even thinner interior doors.

Panel edges on full-size doors are nearly always beveled, but when working with such thin wood, it does seem that the craftsman should be forgiven if he simply sands and rounds off the inner edges of the wood panels. If he wishes to bevel them, the table of the saw should be tilted to a 45-degree angle, as explained in the sawing section in Chapter 5. Beveled cuts are then made on all edges of the inner panels, and on the inside edges only of the strips that will form the border. Again, a study of almost any paneled house door will show how the panels are formed and which edges should be beveled.

Nearly all interior doors have thin panels glued between the edging strips as shown in three of the four doors illustrated in figure 2–47. However, these panel pieces should be of thinner wood than that used for the edging strips. If such thin wood cannot be found, it would be better to omit the panels altogether. In miniature doors, the omission will not be as conspicuous as would be panels that are too thick for the scale used.

After an initial staining of the wood pieces, the door is glued together with white glue, fastened with clamps, and left to dry. The wood should then be finished with a filler and additional stain as described in Chapter 6.

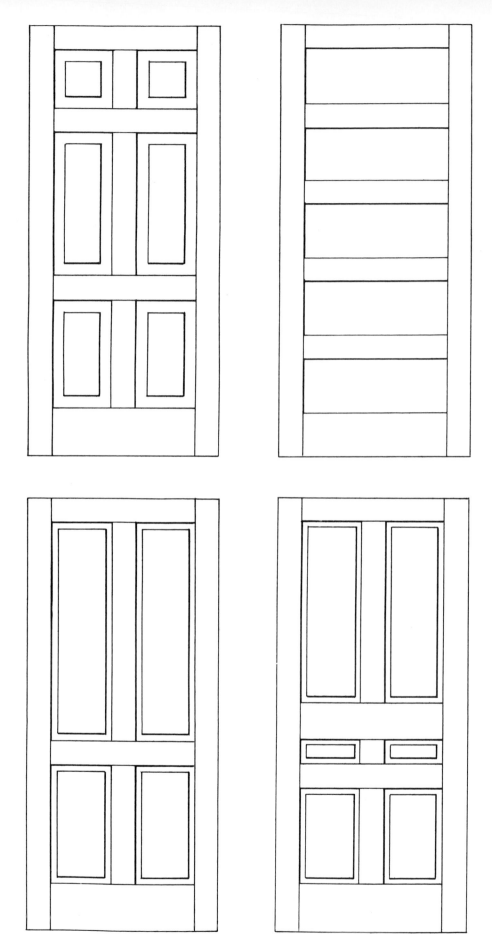

2-47. *Door panels can be arranged in a wide variety of patterns.*

If the door opening in the wall has not already been edged and faced with wood molding, it should be now. The door can then be attached with the use of manufactured hinges. Although most miniature hinges have tiny holes for tacks (and tacks to fit them are available), the door will be held more firmly if the hinges are attached with an adhesive, either a contact-type cement or epoxy putty. For the sake of appearance and for extra strength, the tacks can also be used, but they should not be counted on to support a movable door alone.

Fireplaces

General Construction

To most people, a fireplace has long been a symbol of home, security, comfort, and warmth. A miniature fireplace, like its full-sized counterpart, can do a great deal to make a whole room seem more intimate, and the furniture around it more inviting.

A great many manufactured fireplaces are so well made, and so detailed, they can very well be used in even the most carefully made miniature rooms. That some of them are made of materials, such as plaster and metal, which the craftsman may not be equipped to handle at home, makes them even more desirable when rooms of certain styles and periods are being furnished.

Whether a fireplace is manufactured or hand-made, its manner of installation is most important. The fireplace should not be set flat against the wall, leaving such a shallow fuel-burning area that the miniature room would soon be filled with smoke, and probably miniature flames, if the fireplace were used.

The inside of the fireplace must be large enough to hold a support of some kind for the fuel, and deep enough to reach the chimney opening at the back. A hole must therefore be cut in the wall to accommodate the back of the fireplace. Similarly, a rectangular hole should be cut in the floor so the hearth's surface will either be level with that of the floor, or standing just slightly above it. An open-front box, made of any thin wood and lined with firebrick, stone, or similar material, is glued behind the fireplace opening to form the fuel-burning area.

If the craftsman wishes to make his own fireplace, he will have not only the satisfaction of having created it, he will also be able to design it especially to fit the style and available wall space of the room, and, perhaps best of all, he will not see an identical fireplace anywhere else.

Making a fireplace is no more difficult than making a piece of furniture, and often it is simpler, in that nearly all fireplace designs require only straight cuts on the saw and afford generous gluing surfaces. There is one basic requirement, however. Except for those of very early times, fireplaces contain a great many parts, most of them decorative, and none of them should be omitted. The well-made fireplace will therefore take time to make, but it will be time well spent.

To start, the craftsman should study pictures of room interiors. Some fireplaces that attract the eye at first glance may turn out to be so elaborate and so difficult to make that they will require more time than he wishes to give. Others may contain features, such as carved gargoyles and cherubs, that he does not have enough expertise to make. The fireplace he does select should, of course, be in keeping with the room for which it is planned, and also should have component parts he can visualize and for which he can draw patterns.

Fieldstone Fireplaces

Fieldstone fireplaces have a special appeal to many builders of dollhouses and, if in keeping with the period and style, can be attractive in even the most meticulously built miniature rooms. Part of their appeal is that they are so easy to make. Too many of those the writer has seen, however, have not been carefully built to scale; the stones were too large and, in many cases, spaced too far apart. Pretty, bright-colored, water-rounded stones that have been brought back from a vacation at the beach are not suitable materials for a stone fireplace. Fieldstone is just what the name implies—stone that is found in fields—and the type of stone it is depends upon where it is found. Fieldstone colors are usually soft and tend toward the brown-tan-yellow group. There are exceptions, of course, such as white limestone, a stone once popular for fireplaces in areas where it was native.

Stones used for miniature fireplaces should be as flat as possible. Also, since fieldstone was used as a structural building material for fireplaces as well as a decoration, the stones should be set close, and the shapes fitted together as much as possible.

A fireplace shape, without the mantel and about 1/4 to 3/8 inch smaller all around than the finished fireplace is to be, should first be made of any soft, scrap wood. It is then covered with whatever material the craftsman wishes to use as a base for the stones. Mortar made especially for miniature work can be used, as can caulking material or Polyform. The stones are pressed into the soft material, which is then allowed to dry, set, or harden by baking, depending upon the compound used.

The mantel is next made and glued across the top. A fieldstone fireplace mantel was made either of a single, heavy slab of hand-hewn wood, or of stone—one or two large, flat pieces, or smaller stones set in the same material that was used to face the fireplace. Firebrick, discussed later, can be used to line the fire area.

Brick and Wood Fireplaces

Most so-called brick fireplaces are a combination of brick and wood. In its simplest form, such a fireplace consists of a wood pillar or column on either side supporting a wood mantel. The area between, surrounding the opening for the fire, is faced with brick. From that basic design can be evolved a fireplace as elaborate as the craftsman wishes to take the time to make.

The pattern in figure 2–49 was used to make the fireplace shown in the living room in the color section of this book. Although the fireplace appears to be elaborate, and does have quite a few parts, it is actually rather simple in that there is no carving, and all the pieces, with the exception of the columns, can be cut with a jigsaw. The columns were turned on a lathe, then flattened in back with a file. If the columns were changed from rounded to square in section, a jigsaw would be the only electric-powered tool needed.

Although the fireplace was made of mahogany, any other hardwood would have done as well. The edging strips are not included in the pattern drawing, but are of 1/8-inch purchased double bead, stained to match the mahogany. They outline the whole back piece, the brick sections, and the mirror.

When facing a fireplace or chimney with brick, the craftsman has several materials from which to choose. The easiest of these is a purchased cardboard sheet of colored brick, which can be cut to shape and glued into place. The brick pattern is pressed into the material of some of these

sheets, giving a three-dimensional effect. Such "brickwork" can usually be found in hobby shops and in those specializing in model trains.

Individual miniature bricks, which must be laid separately, can also be purchased in hobby shops. A fine mortar for laying them can usually be bought at the same source.

Fine sandpaper, cut in brick shapes and glued in place, gives a most convincing effect. (Old scissors should be used; sandpaper is hard on scissor blades.)

Instructions follow for making the brickwork shown in the kitchen and living rooms in the color pages. The writer prefers this method because its effect is more subtle than that of the others.

To start, a sheet of Polyform, about 1/8-inch thick, is rolled out on a flat surface. Although an average brick is 8 by 4 by 2 inches, when using this method, the thickness will not show, and only the length and width need be to scale.

2-48. A mahogany fireplace made from an accompanying pattern.

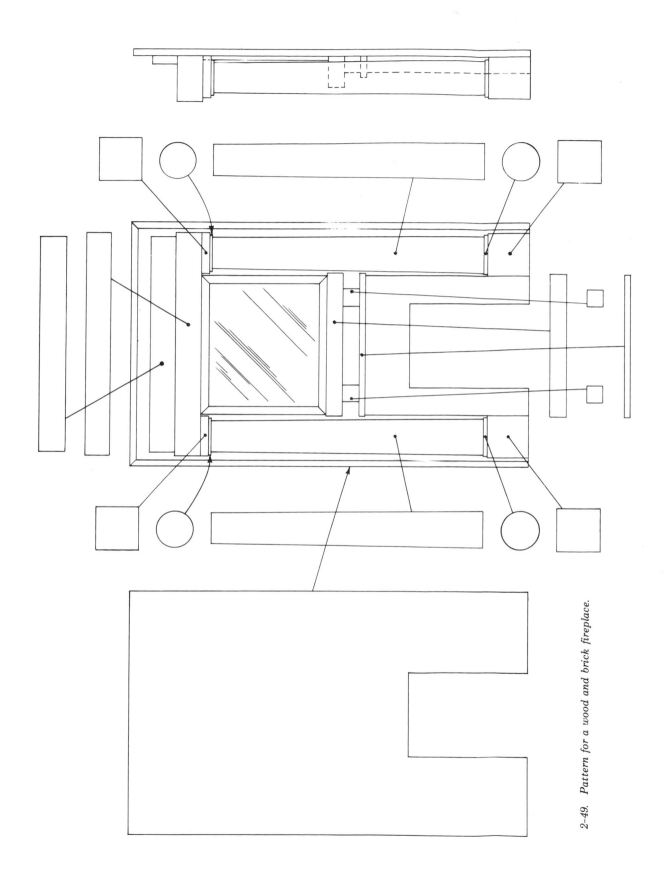

2-49. *Pattern for a wood and brick fireplace.*

A backing piece for the brick area is cut from heavy cardboard or, preferably, from wood. The backing for the fireplace shown was made of 1/32-inch plywood, and for the kitchen chimney of 3/8-inch balsa. A piece of the rolled-out Polyform sheet is then laid on the backing piece and cut to fit. For the kitchen chimney, the Polyform was carried around the edges of the thick wood piece and feathered into the back to hold it in place.

Indentations to define the brick shapes are then pressed into the unbaked clay. For the horizontal lines, a thin-edged metal or plastic ruler can be used. For the vertical lines, a piece of thin cardboard should be cut to the width of a brick, which, on the 1-inch scale, would be 1/3 inch. The vertical lines should be spaced about 2/3 inch apart, or 8 inches, full-size.

The brick piece is then baked at about 300 degrees and watched until the color darkens just slightly. The color of the baked Polyform will be the color of the "mortar" between the bricks in the finished piece, and should therefore be neither dead white, nor overly dark. At the same time, it is a good idea to put a few extra pieces of the rolled-out Polyform in the oven for later testing of colors.

The baked brick can be painted with acrylic colors. Mixing a true brick color is most important. The right shade will not be found in any single jar or tube of red paint, but in a mixture of such colors as red, brown, yellow, or black. If an error must be made in the mixing of the color, it should be on the side of too dull, rather than too bright.

Using a fine brush, scattered bricks are then painted, some more thickly than others so that the shades will vary. When these have dried thoroughly, the remaining paint is thinned with water, and a small cloth is dipped into it, squeezed quite dry, and wiped down over the bricks. The cloth is dabbed here and there to darken some areas. The lines between the bricks will not be touched by the paint if the cloth is kept dry enough.

This method of coloring gives a natural, subtle effect but is not, of course, the only way it can be done. Each brick can be painted individually in any way the craftsman wishes. He should be careful, however, not to paint all the bricks exactly the same shade. Even all-red, full-size bricks pick up the light differently and change colors accordingly.

Firebrick for lining the interiors of all fireplaces is made in the same way as described

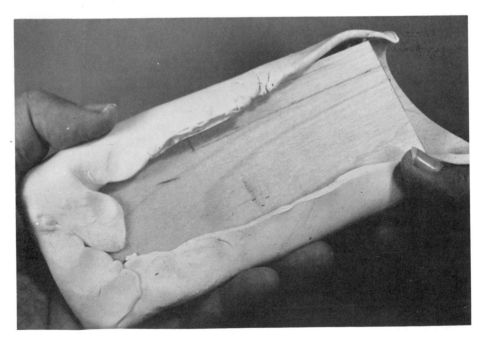

2-50. *Making brickwork. The wood backing is covered with modeling compound.*

2-51. Brick shapes are pressed into the material.   *2-52. Scattered bricks are painted individually.*

2-53. Color is wiped on the rest of the bricks with a damp cloth.

above. The only difference is that firebrick is usually a little larger than the facing brick, and is usually a gray or tan color. When finished, the inside of the fireplace can be irregularly darkened with ashes, charcoal, or a similar substance to heighten the realism.

Brick hearths usually match the facing brick, although they are sometimes of a different color. The hearth is made as described above, and lowered into a hole cut for it in the floor, as mentioned earlier.

Marble Fireplaces

A most effective way to make a "marble" fireplace is to purchase one of the attractive white plaster fireplaces that can be found in almost any shop or catalog specializing in miniatures. It is then given a coat of white enamel. When the paint has dried thoroughly, the surface is spotted irregularly with a brush that has been dipped into a can of wood oil stain of any desired color. The stain should be unmixed in the can so that the brush brings up some of the solid pigment at the bottom.

2-54. *A plaster fireplace is painted white.*

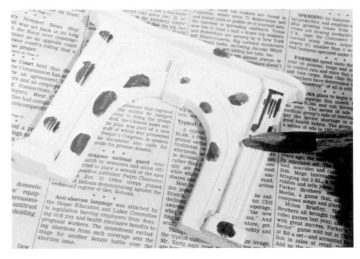

2-55. *Oil stain is spotted unevenly on the surface.*

2-56. *Color is broken into a fine pattern when dabbed lightly with a cloth.*

2-57. *The completed "marble" fireplace.*

A brush or small piece of cloth is then used to dab the stain, scattering and breaking it up into smaller and smaller areas until the surface pattern resembles marble. If the stain has run into small crevices that cannot be reached with a cloth, a dry brush can be used to smooth it out.

Two colors can be used together, or a single color such as gray, slate blue, or tan can be used alone. Paint can also be used in place of the stain, but stain spreads more evenly and makes a more realistic marble.

When the surface of the fireplace looks right, (if it does not, and if stain has been used, it can be wiped off and done over) it should be given a thin coat of Krylon, enough to protect the stain finish, but not enough to give the surface a gloss.

Miscellaneous Attached Furnishings

Before the room box is glued together, the craftsman has one last chance to add, conveniently, whatever small attachments will go into it. If some of them are overlooked and must be added later, no great harm has been done. However, those put in place now will save him the extra time, and the wear and tear, of doing the same work under cramped and sometimes exasperating circumstances.

At this point, it is not likely that the craftsman has made draperies, curtains, or window shades; neither is it likely that he is in the mood to make them now, before the room is even completed. If he does know, however, how the windows will be trimmed, he can save himself future work by drilling the necessary holes for curtain and drapery rods, while the walls are still laid flat.

If light fixtures are to be electrically lighted, and if they are to be glued in place at this time, the necessary wires, as described in the next chapter, should be attached to the fixtures and pulled through the holes in the ceiling or wall to the channel behind them.

3.

Electrical Wiring

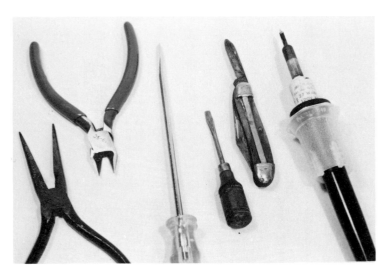

3-1. *Useful tools for miniature room wiring include longnose pliers, wire cutters, medium and small screwdrivers, knife, and soldering iron.*

3-2. *Plastic tape and assorted sizes of wire nuts are among supplies needed.*

INSTALLING THE LIGHTING

If the subject of electricity is new to the craftsman, this chapter will be useful to him only if it is read slowly and digested line by line. None of it is difficult, but, unlike some other subjects that may be learned thoroughly, half-heartedly, or not at all, electrical wiring is either understood or it isn't. There is no halfway point between a bulb that will light up, and one that won't.

To the uninitiated, there is a certain mystique about working with electricity that is due in part to the unfamiliar vocabulary. Such words as volts, watts, and amperes too often seem to have been coined to confuse the beginner. However, where simple wiring (such as that needed for lighting a miniature house or rooms) is concerned, knowing the meaning of the words is not necessary. It is enough to know what to do, and to leave the whys to the experienced electrician.

TOOLS AND MATERIALS

There are only a few tools needed for wiring the miniature house or rooms, and some of these will be useful for other miniature work as well. A small electric soldering iron is essential, as are small and medium screwdrivers, a pair of longnose pliers (for bending and/or pulling wires), a small pair of wire cutters, and a pocket knife (for stripping insulation from wires).

Materials needed include a roll of rosin-core solder (the flux is inside the core). If solid solder is bought instead, a can of rosin flux will also be needed. An assortment of wire nuts of various sizes should also be on hand; their use is the safest and easiest way to join large-enough wire ends without soldering. To cover all the bare metal parts of the wiring, a roll of vinyl tape will be needed and, even better in some cases, a package of epoxy putty, a material discussed in Chapter 6 under "Adhesives." A tube of Duco Cement will also be useful for strengthening and insulating low-voltage wire connections.

SAFE WIRING METHODS
High-Voltage Wires

In the United States and Canada all ordinary wire outlets carry 120 volts. (There are 240-volt special outlets for stoves, air-conditioners, and so on, but they are never used for miniature lights.)

A 120-volt current can be dangerous to anyone who touches a bare wire or metal part carrying it, and a poorly made, loose connection can even start a fire. Therefore, before an electrically lighted room is plugged into a wall outlet, it is very important that all wires carrying 120-volt current are properly joined and insulated.

The wires that carry 120-volt current are those used for lighting 120-volt bulbs, and those leading *to* a transformer from the wall outlet. All such wires must be spliced when necessary by one of three methods (figure 3–4). (A transformer changes voltage from high to low. This will be discussed in more detail farther along.)

To make a splice, insulation is first stripped from a wire end or from a middle section, as needed. About 3/4 inch of bare wire must be exposed. For a wire end, the insulation is cut all around with a sharp knife blade, then pulled off the end. For a center section, two such circular cuts are made, about 3/4 inch apart, and the insulation between them sliced lengthwise and unwrapped from the wire. Lamp cord is made of a number of fine wire strands that are easily cut, so care should be taken to avoid this when removing the insulation. It will not matter if two or three strands are cut through, but if more are broken, the wire's usefulness may be impaired. After the wire is bare, the wire strands should be twisted tightly together.

When wires are twisted to a "point," they should be twisted clockwise. For an end-to-end splice, which makes a neater connection, each wire end is wound around the other, with the two wires being wound in opposite directions. When a center splice is made, only one wire end is twisted around the other. In all cases, the wire should be twisted very tightly, with pliers if necessary.

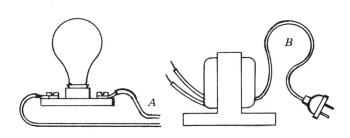

3-3. Wires to a 120-volt bulb (A) *and to a transformer* (B) *require careful handling.*

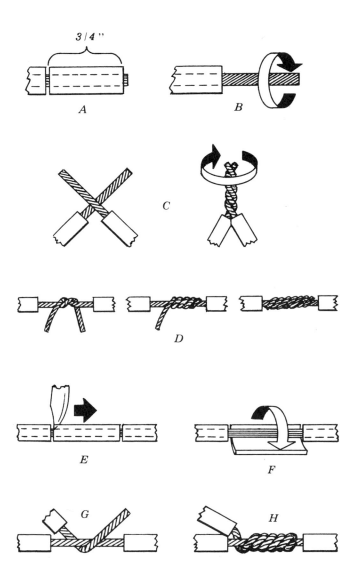

3-4. Three ways to splice two lamp-cord wires: 1. Two ends (A and B) *are stripped and twisted to a point* (C). *2. Two ends are stripped and spliced end-to-end. 3. One wire can be spliced to the center of another* (E through H).

If two, three, or even more wires are twisted to a point, the easiest way to complete the splice is to cap them with a wire nut. The nut should be large enough to cover the bare wire ends completely, but small enough to hold tightly when twisted on (again, clockwise). To finish the joint, several layers of tightly stretched vinyl tape are wrapped around the wire nut base and the adjoining areas of the wires.

Wires twisted to form a point can be soldered instead of being capped with a wire nut. However, all other splices *must* be soldered, and they must first be cleaned with a rosin flux so the solder can bind them. If rosin-core solder is used, the wires are cleaned automatically as the soldering is being done. However, if solid solder is used, it is necessary first to paint paste rosin on the splice. The splice is then heated with the electric soldering iron until the rosin melts away. The splice can then be soldered.

To solder, the heated iron is first held against the underside of the splice until the wires are thoroughly heated. The end of the soldering wire is then held against the top of the splice until the solder melts and runs over the bare wires. (At no time should the hot iron touch the solder itself.) As soon as the splice is covered with solder, the iron and soldering wire are removed and the joint is allowed to cool and harden, which happens very quickly.

The soldered splice is then wrapped with at least two layers of tightly stretched vinyl tape, which more than covers all the bare wire. Care should be taken that the tape end is securely stuck so that it can't become unwound.

Plugs and Switches

A plug with an attached cord is used to plug a miniature lighting system into a wall outlet. The receptacle end of a purchased extension cord can be cut off, and the plug and attached wire used for wiring a miniature room. An alternative is to purchase a separate plug, which is easily attached to a length of lamp cord.

There are two kinds of plugs available. A standard plug has two terminal screws and an insulating disc. The plug is attached to the cord by first stripping about 3/4 inch of insulation from the ends of both cord wires. The wire ends are then twisted tightly. With the insulating disc removed, the wires are inserted into the plug (figure 3-6) and bent around the plug prongs.

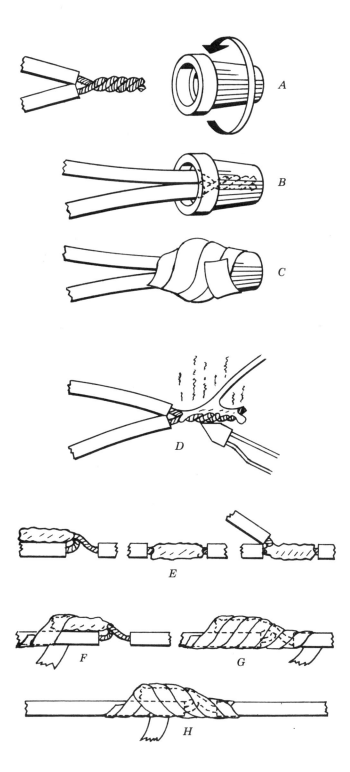

3-5. *Two wires twisted to a point may be secured with a wire nut (A to C), and any splice may be soldered (D to E) then wrapped with tape (F to H).*

Each wire is then curled clockwise under a terminal screw head. Both screws are tightened securely, and the installation is checked to be sure no stray wire strands are out of place. The insulating disc is replaced and the job is done.

Another type of plug requires no tools. The lamp cord, with the insulation intact, is inserted under a hinged cap, which is then forced closed. Internal prongs pierce the insulation to make the necessary contacts (figure 3–6).

If a switch is installed in the cord, it will not be necessary to turn the lights on and off by plugging and unplugging the cord. The easiest to use is an in-line switch, which can be positioned anywhere along the lamp cord. Instructions for an in-line installation are printed on the switch's package. This switch can also be attached to the end of a cord (figure 3–7). It is very important that the longer wire end be curled back inside the switch and the unused hole plugged, so there will be no danger that the wire end will be accidentally touched.

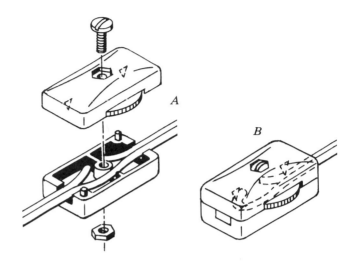

3-7. *An in-line switch can be installed anywhere in a lamp cord* (A) *or at end of cord* (B).

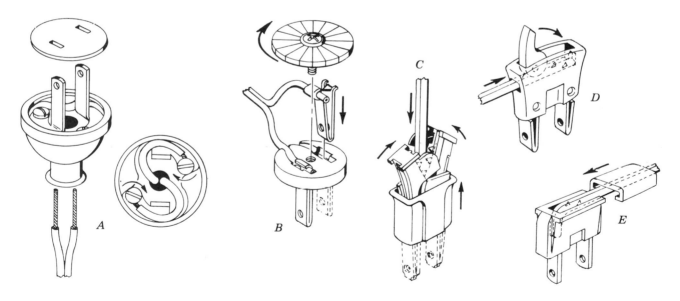

3-6. *Standard lamp-cord plug* (A) *is installed by securing the two stripped wire ends to the two screw terminals. The space-saving type* (B) *does not require wire stripping. Three snap-on types* (C to E) *are installed without tools.*

Bulb Sockets

The installation of wires carrying 120 volts, as described above, is to be used with 120-volt light bulbs, which are typically used in night lights. There are two kinds of sockets for these bulbs. Most common is the type that can be mounted on a flat base with the use of two screws or nails, and has two terminal screws which hold the wires. The wires are connected to the screw terminals as described above—the wire ends are first stripped of insulation, then twisted tightly. Each wire end is next formed into a loop with longnose pliers, and the loop is hooked clockwise under a terminal screw head. The screw is tightened securely. All bare metal (screw and wire end) is then covered with vinyl tape or, even better, with a 1/16-inch, or more, layer of epoxy putty, pressed firmly into place.

The second type of socket is an in-line, snap-on type. Instructions for its use are furnished with the socket. If the socket is mounted close to the end of the lamp cord, the cord end should be cut off square, with the insulation intact, and wrapped with vinyl tape or covered with epoxy putty.

LOW VOLTAGE WIRING

The wires leading *from* a transformer carry a low (10-, 12- or 16-volt) current that is not dangerous. These wires are normally very small in diameter, and all splices and connections must be well made so the current can travel through them without interruption. Splices can be made in any of the ways previously shown, but since the wires are too small to be used with wire nuts, every splice should be soldered. Taping such wires is neither necessary nor very practicable. Instead, all bare wires should be covered with Duco Cement, a silicone seal, or a thin layer of epoxy putty.

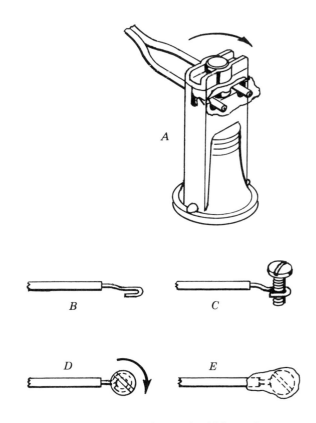

3-8. *Epoxy putty or vinyl tape should be used to cover wire ends when a snap-on, 120-volt bulb socket is installed at a lamp-cord end (A), or when a 120-volt wire is connected to a screw terminal on a bulb socket (B to E).*

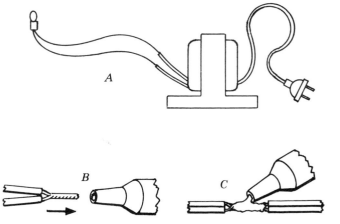

3-9. *Low voltage transformer wires (A) are not dangerous and can therefore be insulated after soldering with a sealant or household cement (B or C).*

THREE METHODS OF ROOM LIGHTING

As mentioned earlier, there are three methods of lighting a room: with lighted fixtures, with hidden interior lights, and with hidden exterior lights, the last usually located in channels outside the room.

In the writer's opinion, hidden lights, no matter where located, give the most subtle and effective lighting, and should therefore be depended upon to furnish the room's illumination. Lights from chandeliers and lamps should be so reduced in intensity that they do not obscure the details of the furnishings by shining too brightly in the eyes. A combination of two, or all three, of the lighting methods is probably the best solution to the problem of effective lighting.

Lighted Fixtures

Hobby shops that specialize in miniatures are carrying an increasing number of lighting fixtures, most of them on the 1-inch scale. These include battery-operated table and floor lamps as well as transformer-operated lamps, chandeliers, and ceiling and wall lights of many styles. Unfortunately, many of these are not detailed enough to belong in a carefully furnished miniature room, although some can be improved upon by the addition of "crystal" pendants, ornamentally curved brass wires, and so on.

Installing a battery-operated light can pose a problem. The battery pack that contains one or two D-size flashlight batteries is large and unsightly. Most of the lamps have a 6-inch cord

3-10. A miniature room can be illuminated by lighted fixtures (A), by hidden interior lights (B), by exterior lights (C), or by a combination of all.

with a plug on the end that fits into a socket in the battery pack, and the plug is too large to pass through a small hole. The battery pack must therefore be hidden in the room (inside a cabinet, behind a staircase, etc.), or the plug must be cut off and the wires fed through a small hole in the wall. The plug is then spliced back onto the wires, and the battery pack placed outside of the room. There is one alternative to the above method, however, which simplifies the work. Instead of a socket and cord plug, there are available in some hobby shops lamp sets with screw terminals on the battery pack. The wire can be fed through a hole in the wall or ceiling, and the battery pack attached wherever desired.

The 1 1/2- or 3-volt bulbs furnished with the lamps usually have a life of 1,000 hours or better, and while some are replaceable, most are not. The batteries, which are replaceable, will last 40 to 80 hours, depending upon whether they operate one or two lamps. An on-off switch on the battery pack is desirable.

Fixtures that operate from a transformer are always furnished with lead wires which can be passed outside the room through a very small hole that will be hidden by the fixture mounting plate. The transformer, which may be used to light one or more fixtures, is positioned outside, usually in a channel. Either 6- or 12-volt bulbs may be used. Both the number of bulbs to be lighted and the bulb voltages will determine the capacity of the transformer, and the method of wiring. This will be explained farther along.

Miniature fixtures that were manufactured a few years ago have bulbs that are a little large for the 1-inch scale. However, fixtures are now being produced with smaller, more suitable bulbs in both the grain-of-wheat and candle-flame shapes. Some have bulbs that are permanently attached to their wires. If such a bulb burns out, the fixture must be removed for rewiring. Much more desirable are those fixtures with bulbs that screw into sockets and can be easily replaced.

All miniature bulbs should be tested at the proper voltage for one hour. If the bulb does not burn out in that time, it will probably burn as long as guaranteed, which may be as much as 10,000 hours.

Concealed Interior Lights

Much concealed interior lighting is done by locating the bulbs behind the inner edge of the room's front frame, which must be widened to hide them. Lights can also be hidden behind natural obstructions, such as a slight projection of a front wall, either on one side or at ceiling level. A closet door can be left ajar, and the light placed behind it, or the space between a back wall and a projecting fireplace on a side wall can conceal a small bulb. A built-in alcove or window seat can be designed for the same purpose.

Interior lighting can also be provided by drilling small holes in the ceiling in which small bulbs are placed. The bulbs should be lifted high enough in the ceiling to be out of sight, and the holes should be drilled at a slant to direct the light where needed. If the holes are located at the front ceiling corners or behind a chandelier, they either will not be noticed at all, or, if seen, will not be objectionable.

The same bulbs used in lighting fixtures can be used in the ceiling holes. Both grain-of-wheat and candle-flame styles are available in either 6-volt or 12-volt types, and come either with attached wires ("pigtails"), or with a screw base (in which case, the wired socket must also be purchased).

3-11. A variety of miniature bulbs are available for use in lighted fixtures.

Somewhat larger but also more brilliant are Christmas tree lights, which are sold with from 10 to 36 bulbs on a string. Some have screw-base sockets, some, push-in sockets, and some are permanently attached to the wires, like the above pigtail lights. Old strings of lights can easily be cut apart, and the remaining good bulbs salvaged. The voltage at which one such bulb will operate is determined by the number of bulbs that light simultaneously when the string is in operation. That number is divided by 120. If 10 bulbs light simultaneously, for example, the voltage of each bulb is 120 ÷ 10, or 12. Various strings have 12-, 10-, 6- and 3 1/3-volt bulbs.

Wherever space permits, a bulb's luminosity can be increased by using a reflector. Reflectors can be made of tin or aluminum foil, cut to form a cone around the bulb base, and glued into place.

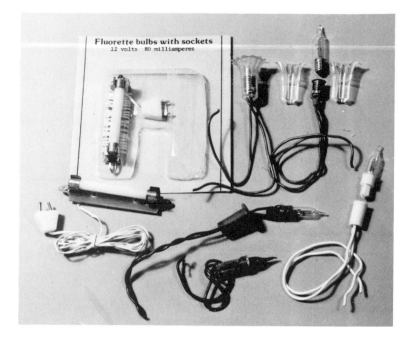

3-13. *Fluorette bulb or bulbs from a Christmas tree string can be used for hidden interior lighting.*

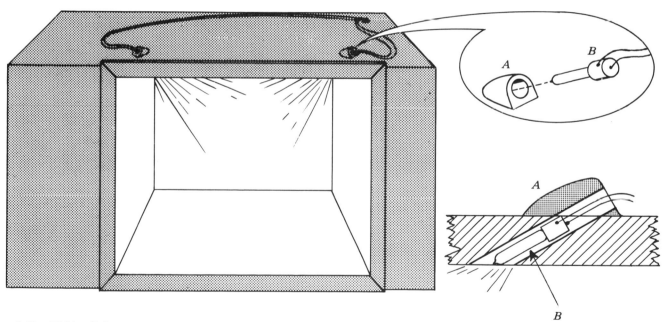

3-12. *Hidden lights in a ceiling illuminate selected areas. Epoxy putty (A) can be mounded on top, and a hole for the light (B) can be drilled as shown.*

61

Exterior Lights

Light bulbs, located in channels outside a room, can be placed to provide natural daytime lighting through windows and opened doors. Because high-voltage bulbs can be used, any amount of light desired can be introduced into a room, or used to light an outdoor scene in the channel. However, because all such light must shine through restricted openings, it is sometimes difficult to avoid contrasting light and dark areas in the room. For this reason, it is usually advisable to combine exterior lighting with one or more interior light sources.

For lights in the channels, a transformer and the low-voltage bulbs discussed earlier can be used. However, for stronger lights, it is better to make a selection from among the 120-volt candelabra screw-base bulbs. These include the familiar nightlight bulbs and the various bulbs sold for candelabra-type fixtures. They are preferred over standard-size 120-volt bulbs, because the sockets which hold them are much smaller and will easily fit inside a 2-inch-wide channel.

Nightlight-type bulbs are available with clear or frosted glass in 3-, 4-, 6-, 7- and 15-watt sizes. Candelabra bulbs range in size up to 60, or more, watts. For special effects, there are 7-watt Christmas tree bulbs in various colors. For all of these bulbs there are two types of sockets—a surface-mounting socket with two screw terminals and two holes for the mounting screws, and a small, round, snap-on socket intended primarily for adding lights to a Christmas tree string. All of these items are available at most hardware stores.

3-14. The 120-volt bulbs and accessories shown can be used for exterior lighting. Bulbs available range from 3 to 15 watts.

TWO WAYS TO USE LOW-VOLTAGE BULBS

There are two ways to connect two or more low-voltage bulbs to a transformer. The first way is *in parallel*. One wire from each bulb is connected to one of the transformer's low-voltage wires, and the other wire from each bulb is connected to the other low-voltage transformer wire. No matter how many bulbs there are, each will receive exactly the same voltage as any other, and this is the voltage that is provided by the transformer. For example, if there are four bulbs wired in parallel to a 12-volt transformer, each bulb will be operated at 12 volts.

The second way is *in series*. One wire of each bulb is connected to one wire of the next until all the bulbs are connected together, leaving only two unconnected wires, one from each of the two end bulbs. These two remaining wires are then connected, respectively, to the two low-voltage transformer wires. Whatever voltage the transformer produces is then divided among the bulbs wired in the series. For example, if three 12-volt bulbs are wired in a series to a 12-volt transformer, each bulb receives only one-third the total, or 4 volts.

A bulb can be wired to receive less voltage from a transformer than its own rated voltage, but if it receives more, it will burn out quickly. A 6-volt bulb, for example, may be wired to receive 5, but not 7, volts from a transformer.

A 12-volt bulb is designed to produce full brilliance when operated at 12 volts. At 10 volts, the light is dimmed slightly, but the bulb will last longer. Further reductions of voltage increasingly dim the light but increase bulb life. This same principle applies to any bulb that is given less voltage from a transformer than its designed capacity.

If the craftsman's purpose is to operate one or more bulbs and produce a good quantity of light, yet to keep the bulbs burning as long as possible, the best solution is to wire them in parallel to a slightly undersized transformer (use a 10-volt transformer to operate 12-volt bulbs, for example). If only half-bright or dim light is desired, it is better to wire the bulbs in series, using a transformer that will (when its voltage is divided by the number of bulbs used) give each bulb the desired reduced voltage.

It is possible to wire some bulbs in series, and some in parallel, to the same transformer. It is also possible to have more than one series of bulbs, with a different number of bulbs in each, connected to one transformer. This allows for a wide variance of bulb brilliance to give whatever lighting is desired. Bulbs of different voltages, however, should never be wired together in the same series or some might burn out.

TRANSFORMERS

To operate low-voltage bulbs, it is necessary to have a 120-volt transformer, which, when connected to a wall outlet, will produce the voltage (or less, but never more) required by the bulbs. Such a transformer has two "sides" named, respectively, the *primary* and *secondary* side. The primary side may have two wires for connection to an extension cord and plug, or it may be fitted with prongs, which allow it to be directly plugged into a wall outlet. The full 120-volt current flows through this side. The secondary side may have two wires, which are usually thicker than the primary wires, or it may be fitted with two terminal screws. Low-voltage current flows through the secondary side to the connected bulbs.

A transformer should be marked to indicate the approximate low voltage it will produce. Some will produce a voltage very close to that for which they are rated. Others, particularly toy-train transformers, may at times produce a voltage so much higher than the rated voltage that they will burn out bulbs not designed for the higher voltage. Transformers sold in hobby shops for dollhouse lighting, in electronic shops for professional use, and in hardware stores for use with doorbells and door chimes are usually reliable. Dollhouse transformers are rated at 12 or 16 volts, and the popular doorbell transformers are either 10 volts (an excellent choice for a few 12-volt bulbs wired in parallel) or 16 volts. Most electronic shops carry a range of ratings from 3 volts on up.

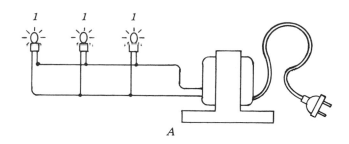

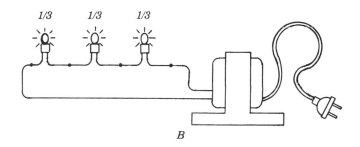

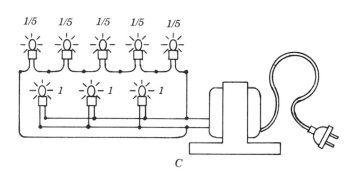

3-15. Bulbs in parallel (A) *receive one full share of power each. Bulbs in series* (B) *divide one share among them. Bulbs in parallel can be combined with bulbs in series* (C).

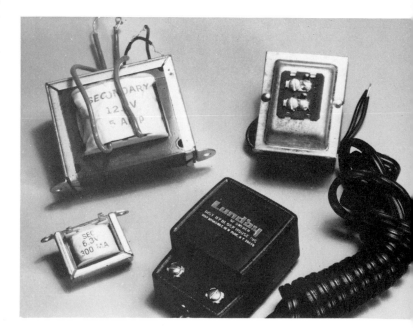

3-16. *A selection of low-voltage transformers is available.*

Two transformers of the same rating can be quite different in actual size. A small transformer may have the capacity to light only one bulb, unless two or three are wired in series, while a larger one may be able to light 10 or more bulbs in parallel and a great many more in series. The reason for this is that, according to its size, a transformer can produce only so much current without overheating and burning out.

Current is measured in milliamperes (MA) and dollhouse transformers are rated according to the number of MA of current they can safely handle. Bulbs for dollhouse use are rated as to the number of MA they require. As stated before, when bulbs are wired in parallel, their ratings must be added together. The total rating for a series of bulbs, however, is the rating of one bulb only. It works like this:

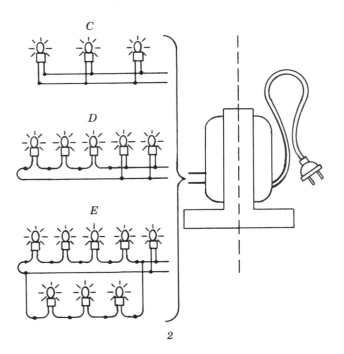
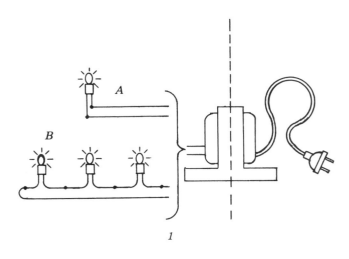

For 12-Volt Bulbs and a 12-Volt Transformer

No. of Bulbs	MA Rating	How Wired	Minimum Transformer MA
1	60	Alone	60
3	60	In Parallel	180
Any Number	60	In Series	60
1 plus	60	In Parallel	60
Any Number	60		60
in a Series			120
3 plus	60	In Parallel	180
4 in Series	60		60
3 in Series	60		60
			200

All bulbs in the foregoing table are rated 60 MA, but any other MA rating could be figured in the same way. However, all bulbs wired in the same series must have the same MA rating, or some may not light.

Some transformers are rated in amperes. To convert an ampere rating to MA, the amperes are multiplied by 1,000. For example, a 3 ampere rating is the same as 3,000 MA. Still other transformers are rated in watts. To convert the watts rating of a 10-volt transformer to MA, the watts are multiplied by 100, of a 12-volt transformer, by 83 1/3, and of a 16-volt transformer, by 62 1/2. For example, the MA rating for a 10-volt, 12-watt transformer is 12 x 100, or 1200 MA.

3-17. A small 60–MA transformer (1) can handle only one 60 MA bulb (A) or several MA bulbs (B) if they are in series. A larger 180–MA transformer (2) can handle up to three 60–MA bulbs (C) in parallel, or more (D and E) if some are in series.

INSTALLING 120–VOLT BULBS

Since 120-volt bulbs are too bright to be used inside a miniature room, they should be installed in a channel where the light will shine indirectly through windows and doors. Before attaching a bulb in place permanently, its lighting effect in the room should be tested, both for bulb position and bulb size (wattage). This can be done with a test cord made by cutting off the receptacle end of an extension cord and replacing it with a 120-volt snap-on socket (figure 3–18). By fitting bulbs of various wattage in the socket and holding each in different positions, the most effective intensity and position of the light can be determined.

For wiring, any covered wire from sizes 16 to 20 can be used, although the most readily available and easiest-to-handle wire is No. 18 vinyl-covered lamp cord. The 120-watt bulbs must be wired in parallel and be spliced to the plug-in extension at some convenient, enclosed location, preferably inside a channel. After having decided where the bulbs are to be located, a junction point, at which all wires inside the channel will meet, should be chosen. This is usually somewhere in the rear of the box where it will not be seen through a window or door. Next, an extension cord with a plug at one end is prepared, and a 1/4-inch hole for it is drilled in the rear of the box, near the junction point. (The hole should *not* be drilled in a removable panel.) The wire is then threaded through the hole, from the outside.

Next, the 120-volt bulbs are positioned permanently. If space permits the use of a surface-mounted socket, this should be secured to the floor, to the top underside, or to any channel wall other than a removable panel, with two screws or nails. Enough wire to reach the junction point is then attached to the socket, and the terminal screws are insulated with tape or epoxy putty as previously described.

If a snap-on socket is used, enough wire to

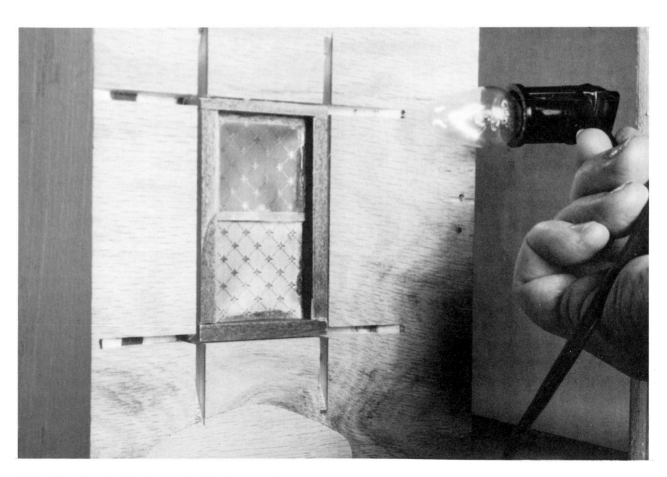

3-18. The effective illumination inside the room of an exterior bulb should be tested before the bulb is fastened in place.

3-19. This room is lighted by two 12-volt bulbs and two 120-volt bulbs. The junction where the 120-volt wires are spliced is at left.

3-20. Another view of the junction of 120-volt wires, showing also how the switch is installed to be accessible from the front.

reach the junction point is attached to it, then the socket is secured in position by stapling the cord (close to the socket) either to the wood, or to a piece of wood glued in place to serve the purpose.

When all the bulbs are permanently located, the lamp cord from each socket is fed back to the junction point. This can usually be done inside the channel, but if there is not enough space, it will have to be done on the outside of the box, across the top or along a side. In this case, additional 1/4-inch holes may have to be drilled for the wires to pass through. To repeat: the bulbs are wired in parallel by connecting one wire from each socket to one of the extension cord wires, and the other wire from each socket to the other extension cord wire.

A switch can be installed in one of two ways. The simplest method, but perhaps the most awkward to handle, is to install it in the extension cord line, as previously explained. The second method is to install the switch at the end of a separate cord extension that can be reached from the front of the room box. The other end of the cord goes back to the junction point, though a separate 1/4-inch hole in the side of the room box may be required. At this point the switch cord is wired to become a part of one of the extension cord wires.

INSTALLING A TRANSFORMER

If a transformer is to be used in addition to 120-volt bulbs, the primary side of the transformer is treated exactly as if it were another 120-volt bulb. That is, it is wired in parallel with the 120-volt bulbs. If there are no 120-volt bulbs, it is treated like a single 120-volt bulb. It should be located in a channel, fastened down with screws, tape, or nails as necessary, and be connected at the junction point with the plug-in extension.

If a plug-in type of transformer is used where no extension cord is needed on the primary side, the secondary (low-voltage) wires from the transformer can be used as an extension cord by extending them to reach the room.

INSTALLING LOW-VOLTAGE LIGHTS

The craftsman's own personal taste is the best guide for determining which light fixtures will be used, where they will be located, and how bright the lights should be. In turn, these decisions determine what voltage light should be used with what voltage transformer, and whether some or all of the bulbs should be wired in parallel or in series.

Wire-attached bulbs (or the sockets for screw-in bulbs) for miniature rooms usually have 6-inch-long wires, which are very fine (No. 32) and quite difficult to strip and splice to another wire. The insulation of this wire must be cut and/or stripped off very carefully. The wire ends should be threaded through a 1/16-inch-diameter hole in the ceiling or wall of the room, and the wires from each bulb (or group of bulbs, as in a chandelier) should be extended to reach the transformer as directly as possible.

If these wires are not long enough, they can be spliced to suitable lengths of No. 24 or 26 vinyl-covered, stranded copper wire. The latter wires are a little thicker and easier to handle than the very fine bulb wires. It is not necessary for every wire of each bulb to reach all the way to the transformer. The single wires can connect a number of parallel bulbs to the transformer, as long as the bulbs are connected in parallel to these two wires.

FINISHING THE WORK

It is not necessary to fasten down wires that are located inside a channel, but all exposed wires on the outside of the room box should be stapled or taped to the wood to prevent accidental damage and to make a neater appearance.

If, when the wiring has been completed, none of the bulbs light, the following points should be checked: There may be a bad connection between the plug, or the switch, and the cord. This is especially true if snap-on devices have been used, because the prongs sometimes fail to penetrate the insulation.

If some screw-in bulbs fail to light, they may not be seated tightly enough in their sockets. Troubles may also be caused by loose or dirty connections, by the shorting together of two wires at some point where both are bare of insulation, or by a fine wire that has broken inside the insulation.

WIRING ELECTRICAL FIXTURES

When attaching a miniature lighting fixture to a wall or ceiling, the most important problem to be solved is how wires, soldered joints, or other evidence of necessary electrical work can be concealed, or at least be made inconspicuous.

It is generally true that a miniature light bulb, with or without a socket, is easier to install if the shade is attached directly to the ceiling or wall plate than if it is suspended away from it at the end of a chain, cord, or rod. That is obviously because, in the first instance, wires and soldered joints will not show. The bulb need only go through a hole in the ceiling or wall, through the plate, and into the shade (figure 3-21). In the second instance, wires leading to the suspended bulb are visible, and must therefore be concealed or treated so as to become a planned part of the fixture design.

Although many full-size light fixtures have removable shades to facilitate the changing of bulbs, miniature shades need not be removable. A 1/4-inch hole, drilled through the ceiling or wall and through the plate, should be large enough to pass any in-scale light bulb, with or without a socket. If, in the future, the bulb should burn out, it can then be pulled through the hole to the outside for changing.

If the light fixture is to be dropped some distance below the ceiling, however, in most instances its bulbs will be accessible from the room. It is therefore only necessary to drill a 1/16-inch hole through the ceiling and plate, through which the wires alone can be passed.

There are several ways to treat the bulb wires between the ceiling and dropped fixture so that they become an integral part of the design. To make an informal fixture suspended by its own wires, the bulb wires need only be twisted tightly together and stretched to hang straight down. Other methods are to weave the wires through the links of a brass chain, or to braid them around a center core or wire that will help them to hang straight.

If a stiff support is required for the fixture, a length of hollow brass tubing can be used. Tubing is generally available in hobby shops, especially those that deal in model trains. To be correct for the 1-inch scale, the tubing should be no more than 1/16-inch in diameter, a size too small to contain two insulated wires. However, one wire, if small enough, can be passed through the tube, and the tube itself can be used as the second wire. To accomplish this, a short length of wire is soldered to the top end of the tube and another to the bottom end (figure 3-21). The tubing, with the two attached wires, then becomes the second wire.

If the wire that comes attached to the bulb or socket is too thick to pass through the tube, a length of No. 28 enameled copper wire (available at electronic shops) can be used instead. The bulb or socket is simply soldered to the enameled wire, which is then threaded through the tube. Care must be taken not to scratch the enamel, since the wire must remain insulated from the tube.

Sconce-type wall lights and multiple-armed chandeliers can be wired in similar fashion. The 1/16-inch brass tubing can be cut and bent to form shaped arms. Any number of such arms can then be soldered to a center tube with a suggested diameter of 1/8 inch. Soldering the tubes together allows them to serve as one of the bulb wires. Each arm can then be threaded with a length of enameled wire, which continues on up through the center tube and serves as the second wire for each bulb.

If desired, sockets, or bulbs without sockets, can be held in place at the ends of the brass tubes with the use of epoxy putty, molded to resemble fixture sockets. The putty can later be painted a brass color.

Because of the low voltage used, there is no danger in handling fixtures wired in any of the above ways.

Suggestions for making both lighted and unlighted fixtures will be found in Chapter 8.

3-21. *A few suggestions for lighting homemade fixtures:*
A — *The socket and bulb are inserted through the ceiling into a fixture glued to the ceiling.*
B — *Only the wires are passed through the ceiling when the fixture is suspended on chains. The socket can be lifted out when the bulb needs changing.*
C — *The two wires can be twisted, or, if a third dummy wire is added, they can be braided to form a cord for hanging the fixture.*
D — *A 1/16-inch brass tube can be used by passing one wire inside it and soldering wires to it, as shown. It will then serve as one of the two wires.*
E — *Three metal chains can be used to serve as wires for two bulbs in parallel, as shown. Or, instead of chains, wires covered with small beads can be used.*
F — *A four-light chandelier can be made with brass tubing (1/8-inch tubing at the center and 1/16-inch tubing for each bracket) to serve in place of one wire from each of the four bulbs. Epoxy putty (X) is used for shaping necessary parts, and the tubes and wires are soldered together, as shown.*

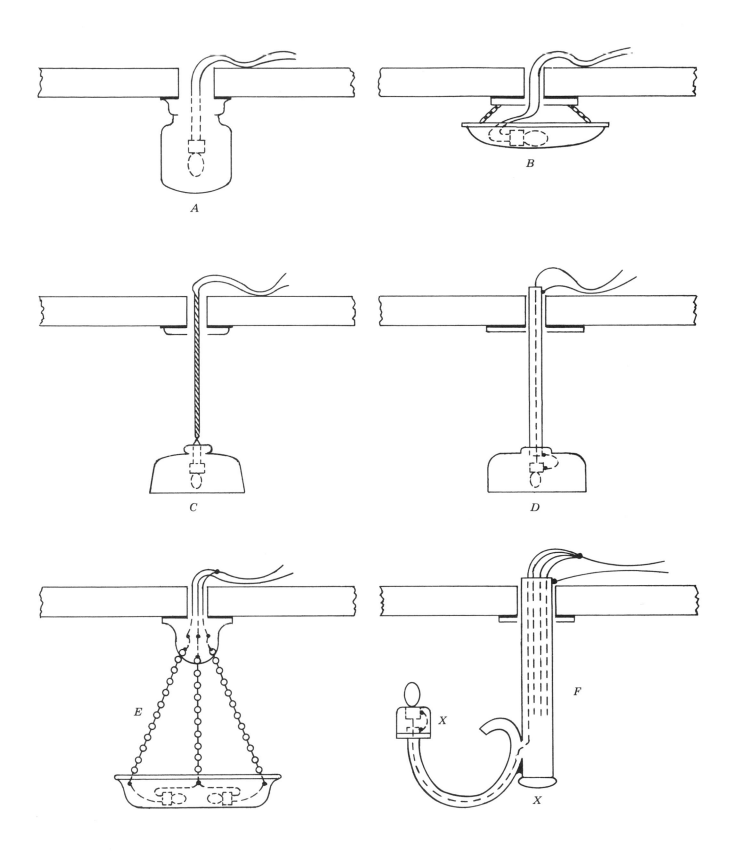

A

B

C

D

E

X

X

F

4.

Basic Tools and Supplies for Furniture-Making

Just as the quality of a photograph depends more on the photographer than on his camera, the quality of a piece of miniature furniture depends far more on the craftsman's skill than on the tools he uses. This does not mean, however, that the photographer can operate without a camera, or the craftsman without a few basic tools.

The necessary tools, and a few optional but useful ones, will be discussed here. There is little doubt, however, that as the work goes along, the craftsman's workshop will grow as does his enthusiasm, and as he runs across tempting equipment in shops and catalogs. Some of these tools will turn out to be useful, some not, but there has never yet been a true craftsman with such an iron will that he could resist buying an occasional, nonessential new tool.

In addition to the basic supplies discussed in this chapter, there will be a need for a small selection of assorted hand tools and materials, some of which may already be on hand.

It would not be possible, nor even desirable, to attempt to list all the nonessential equipment the craftsman may want to use. He will know, if he comes to a point where he wishes to bend some lengths of wire into intricate shapes, that he will need something to bend them with—either a pair of needle-nosed pliers or wire-bending pliers. If he wants to fasten the wires together, he will need an inexpensive soldering set.

In the writer's opinion, much of the pleasure of creating anything is lost if challenges do not continually arise and a way is not found to meet them. Equipping a complete workshop in advance to meet every possible contingency seems, to the writer at least, a very dull way to start a new project.

Skills that the craftsman may or may not need to learn are covered in sections throughout the book, and the equipment needed for such work is discussed in those sections. There seems to be little point, however, in listing them all here as a *sine qua non.*

TOOLS

Few of the tools discussed in the following pages are necessary for the craftsman to own. However, each will make his work a great deal easier and will widen the scope of the furniture styles he can make and of the details he can add to his pieces. (Instructions for using the tools are given in Chapter 5.)

The work of deciding which brand of tool to buy is made easier by the fact that the choice is limited. As far as the writer knows, there are only two or three brands of each of the electric tools listed here, so the choice narrows to which tool has the features the craftsman needs for his work.

As it is with most other things, the cost of the tool is an indication of its quality. A small lathe can be bought today for less than $50, and another for more than $200. The latter tool is probably the better one, but whether or not its higher quality is worth its higher cost to the craftsman is something he will have to decide for himself.

4-1. A small jigsaw is a most important tool.

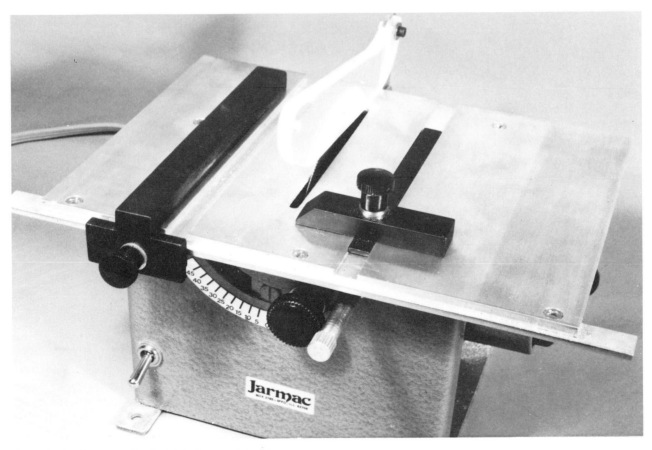

4-2. A circular saw cuts straight edges and bevels.

Jigsaw

A small jigsaw is the most important power tool the craftsman can own. There is no way a handsaw can be used successfully for intricate cuts, for mitering, and for other difficult operations that will be undertaken as the work goes along.

The two features necessary in the saw selected, in addition to the obvious one of general good quality, are a rotating, rather than a vibrating, electric motor (the latter does not cut smoothly) and a table that can be tilted so that beveled edges can be sawed. Since beveling is such an important operation when making furniture, the few dollars more that a tilting table costs will be money well spent.

Circular Saw

Until a few years ago, when a straight, sawed line was needed for a miniature piece, there was not much choice but to make the cut by hand or with a jigsaw. Only a considerable amount of luck prevented the resulting sawed edge from having minute imperfections in it, although these imperfections can be erased with the use of files, sandpaper, and wood filler. For the craftsman who does not wish to have to make these corrections, however, there are now on the market at least three miniature circular saws—one of them an attachment to a lathe—which will automatically guide the wood for making straight cuts. The most expensive of these saws costs about three times as much as the least expensive, and, as with most tools, the comparative price of the saw is an indication of its quality. However, any of the three will do a good job of making straight cuts on wood up to about 1/4 inch thick. The saw that is selected should be able to make mitered cuts, and the blade angle should be adjustable up to 45 degrees, so wood edges can be beveled.

Hand Drill

An electric hand drill is the second tool that, although not essential, will help to make the work more accurate and go more quickly.

Although many hand drills come in sets that include attachments, such as sanders, buffers, drills, bits, and the like, the craftsman should consider if he will have a use for most of them. If not, the drill itself, plus the separate accessories he will need, may be a more economical way of buying the equipment. In any case, it will be necessary to buy additional bits and drills, because those that come with the set do not include a good selection of the very small ones that will be needed.

The writer has found that the ball-shaped sander, called a "ball grinding point," is a time saver for the rough shaping of the surfaces of wood chair seats, which must then be hand-sanded for the final shaping and smoothing. Some of the drills and bits in the set are useful, but the rest of the accessories are not. The craftsman, however, may come to entirely different conclusions and find his whole set to be of value in his work.

The hand drill selected should have a variable speed. This is a most important feature that will greatly widen the drill's usefulness. If a drill with a set speed is already owned, it is recommended that a speed control attachment be purchased which will turn the tool into a variable-speed drill.

A selection of attachments for the drill will tempt the craftsman from time to time. Available are a stand, which will allow the hand drill to be used as a drill press, a router attachment, a stand to hold the drill at any angle (thus leaving the hands free), and so on. It would probably be wiser for the craftsman to become practiced in using the drill before considering the purchase of any attachments. He will then know better which, if any, he can use to good advantage.

Lathe

The third power tool on the list is an essential one only if the craftsman plans to make furniture with turned legs, rungs, posts, and so on. Since many styles of beds, chairs, and tables can be made that require only squared parts, the use of a lathe is optional. It will, however, widen greatly the range of furniture styles that can be made. Some craftsmen carve these turned pieces by hand, and while it can be done that way, to do it even acceptably well requires a great deal of work and a fair amount of skill.

The most important point to consider when selecting a lathe is how the left end of the wood piece to be turned will be supported in the tool. All lathes are alike, in that a holding device for the wood is attached to the left end of the lathe and is turned by the motor. Opposite, on the right end, is a "center," a small, pointed metal

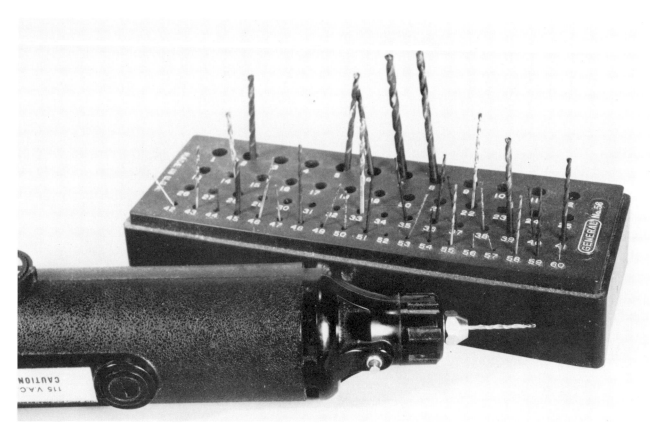

4-3. *A hand drill should have variable speed.*

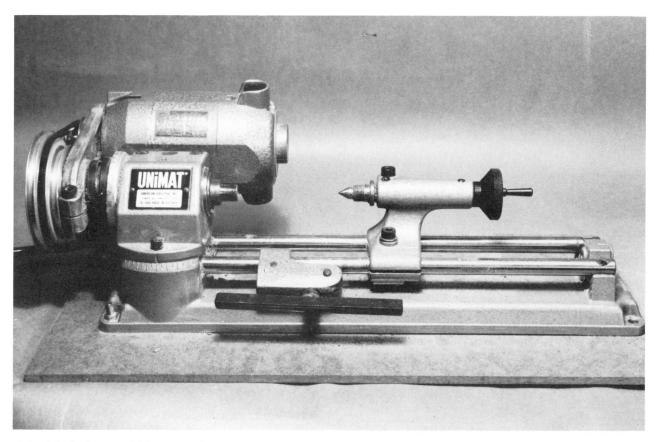

4-4. *A lathe is essential for turned legs and posts.*

piece, which supports, but does not grasp, the right end of the wood piece, allowing it to turn freely.

There is a variety of chucks, collets, and other holding devices that will hold the left end of the dowel in the lathe. Some are easier than others to use, and some will handle dowels in a wider variety of sizes than others. And some, alas, are a great deal more expensive than others!

The most expensive holding device, and the easiest to use, is the three-jaw chuck. As all three of the chuck's jaws close at one time with the use of a key, the wood workpiece is automatically centered.

Next in desirability, in the writer's opinion, is the four-jaw chuck. Each of the four jaws moves inward and outward separately, also with the use of a key, so the wood piece must be centered by hand. However, a square stick can be centered more easily in a four-jaw, rather than a three-jaw, chuck.

Both of the above chucks will hold a dowel the size of a toothpick on up to any thickness the craftsman is likely to use.

At the lower end of the cost scale are collets. These are very efficient little holding devices, but each will accommodate dowels in only a very limited range of diameters. Four or five collets of varying sizes should therefore be bought so the craftsman will be equipped to turn furniture parts in a wide variety of thicknesses.

By allowing the belt, or belts, to be moved to different positions, some lathes offer a choice of speeds. For making miniature wood pieces, however, a moderately fast speed will do for all the woodworking necessary, so there seems little need to keep changing belts. On the other hand, if the craftsman intends to use his lathe for metal as well as wood, the choice of speeds will be useful, since metal turning requires a slower speed.

Pin Vise

A pin vise is an inexpensive hole-drilling tool that is invaluable for miniature work. Although most holes will probably be drilled with an electric drill, the pin vise is excellent for situations where complete accuracy is of the utmost importance as, for example, when two holes in the ends of narrow dowels must meet exactly. A pin vise, especially if used without its handle, will fit into hard-to-reach places where the electric drill will not, and since it costs only a few dollars, it is a valuable adjunct to the larger drill.

Miter Box

Just as an inexpensive pin vise can drill some holes more easily than can the hand drill, in some cases an inexpensive miter box can miter wood ends more easily than can the jigsaw. In each case, the use of the smaller tool is limited, but of great value for certain jobs.

In general, the least expensive miter box is a small metal or wood box, open at the ends and the top, with slits down the sides into which the blade of a small handsaw will fit. (The purchase price usually includes the handsaw.) The wood piece that is to be mitered fits into a groove in the box (figure 4–6), and, depending upon which slit is used for the saw, can be cut at a 90-degree, or a 45-degree, angle toward the left or the right. It is not possible to be as consistently accurate when using the jigsaw for the same types of cuts.

More expensive miter boxes will cut wood at a wider variety of angles. The need for such angles is discussed in Chapter 6.

The only drawback to most miter boxes is that they will take only wood strips; the jigsaw must still be used to make mitered cuts for larger furniture parts. A miter box is, however, ideal for making mitered cuts at the corners of miniature picture frames, picture moldings, baseboards, door frames, and so on.

The bottoms of furniture legs can be made flat and even if trimmed in the miter box. Thin slices from the ends of square sticks and dowels have many uses and can be cut in the miter box more evenly than if done by hand or on a jigsaw. If a number of narrow strips are to be cut into short

4-5. Four- and three-jaw chucks.

sections of equal length, the miter box will do the job quickly and accurately.

Although owning and using a miter box is not a must for making miniatures, after having used one for a period of time, the craftsman will probably wonder how he ever got along without it.

WOODS
Hardwoods

Although it is possible to make miniature furniture reproductions of such softwoods as the much-used balsa or basswood, it is difficult to understand why any craftsman who owns an electric jigsaw would want to. The many available hardwoods have less tendency to split or chip along the edges during a delicate sawing operation. Less care is needed during sanding of hardwoods to maintain the clean, sharp lines of an intricately sawed edge. In addition, when the finished hardwood piece is stained and waxed, it has an indisputable look of elegance about it that even a dozen coats of shellac or varnish cannot give to softwood furniture.

Until a few years ago, it was very difficult if not impossible to find pieces of hardwood on the market that were sliced thin enough for use in miniature furniture. However, a wide selection of hardwoods were available in blocks that could be sliced and sanded in home workshops. Although many craftsmen still use this method to obtain a good wood supply, for those who are not equipped to saw the wood themselves, it is now possible to buy a limited selection of ready sliced hardwoods. Mahogany, walnut, and cherry are three that the writer knows are available nationally, and there may be others that have lately joined the list. The three woods mentioned, however, are sufficient to make almost any furniture of any style or period. Oak, the one popular wood that is missing from the group, can be simulated by giving cherry wood an oak stain. Since the marking in most oak is so large as to be conspicuous and the grain is far out of scale for miniature work, the use of cherry is preferable.

Rosewood is the only really excellent wood that, as far as the writer knows, is not yet

4-6. A miter box does small jobs quickly and accurately.

available in thin slices. It has a fine grain, is easy to saw and sand, and takes a beautiful finish with almost no effort. If the craftsman is equipped with a band saw and a belt sander, slicing a block of rosewood for miniature work will be well worth his trouble.

Almost without exception, any piece of miniature furniture can be made if there is a supply of hardwood on hand in the following fractions of an inch in thickness: 1/32, 1/16, 3/32, 1/8, and 3/16. In addition, a few sticks up to an inch square will be needed for sawing legs and posts.

It is a mistake to rely on only one or two thicknesses of wood to make most pieces of furniture. A table top alone may use three thicknesses, glued together, and a chair might need one thickness for its seat, another for the back splat, and a third for the railing across the top and down the sides. Using the same thickness for all these parts will spoil the chair's appearance. This is discussed in more detail farther along.

To find sources for ready sliced woods, and for other materials the craftsman may need from time to time, it is a good idea to subscribe to a magazine devoted to miniatures, or to a general craft magazine. If a full subscription is not desired, single copies are sometimes available in hobby shops, or from libraries. A careful reading of the advertisements will probably turn up many sources, not only for ready sliced wood, but for products the craftsman did not even know existed, but without which he will now be unable to function. Such are the trials, and the great joys, of having any hobby.

More and more companies are now offering catalogs for which a small charge is made, and on occasion the cost is returned to the customer if an order is sent. It is very helpful to be on the mailing lists of some of those companies, and most catalogs that cost a dollar or so are well worth the investment.

Softwoods

Although softwood is not recommended for use in the visible parts of miniature furniture, it has many uses in the workshop. It can be used for drawers and for the undersides and backs of cabinets, dressers, chests, and so on. Furniture that is to be painted, such as nursery furniture, can be made of softwood. Softwood is needed as a support for hardwood when using the jigsaw for special operations, for testing the accuracy of a pattern, and for other practice jobs. All of these uses will be discussed in more detail later.

Plywood is a softwood that the writer finds very useful. Because it is composed of separate layers, with the grain in one layer running crosswise to an adjacent one, it is far less likely to split or chip when sawed. It can be bought in some hobby shops, hardware stores, and art supply stores in the same thicknesses recommended for hardwoods above.

A 1/64-inch plywood has fairly recently come on the market. Thin as a playing card, it is useful, among other things, for backing pictures, mirrors, and upholstered sections of furniture. The wood can be cut in straight lines with scissors, but shaped pieces should be cut with a jigsaw, over a wood platform, to prevent splitting.

MISCELLANEOUS SUPPLIES

No matter what advice is given in this book about useful and less useful products, the craftsman is going to buy those materials that intrigue or look promising to him, which is as it should be. He will discover products in bottles, cans, and boxes, a few of which will work magic for him, and no doubt some of these will be things the writer has tried and judged to be of little value. On the other hand, products the writer recommends with enthusiasm may sometimes leave the craftsman cold. All of which indicates that it is not possible to be entirely objective about one's own discoveries.

As to the quality of the supplies all craftsmen accumulate, there has long been an educated suspicion on the part of the writer that many of the same products on the market are sold under different guises. For example, the material in a bottle of "plastic hinge," in jars of substances for stiffening cloth and repairing books, and in a container of ordinary white glue all look, smell, and feel suspiciously alike. At least, a little water added to the plastic hinge results in a very good cloth stiffener, and the original cloth stiffener, when allowed to dry partially, makes an effective adhesive.

Similarly, plastic-type sprays that ostensibly have such narrow uses as book-cover protectors, painted surface protectors, gloss-remover for photographs, and so on, all seem to have the same odor and to give about the same finish to wood as does a matte-finish, general-purpose plastic spray.

Caveat emptor? Perhaps, but finding useful materials is an important and personal part of the fun of making miniatures, and it becomes part of the game to evaluate the various products, to eliminate most of them, and to wax enthusiastic about what remains. Two of the latter products on the writer's shelf are worth listing here.

Polyform

Polyform, also sold for children's use under the name of Sculpey, can be bought in art supply and craft shops, as well as some hardware stores. Sculpey is sold packaged in two ways—the material alone, or in a box with a few paints and children's wood tools. The latter box contains less clay, and the tools would probably be of little use to the craftsman.

Polyform or Sculpey is a white, non-sticky, claylike material that can be molded to any shape, then hardened by baking for a short period in a kitchen oven set at a low to moderate heat. The material has so many uses, it would be impossible to list them all here. It can be shaped and finished to make a convincing substitute for wood, metal, pottery, brick, and stone. Clocks, statues, toys, and dishes can be made of it. It can be sanded and sawed. It can be painted or glazed and, as if all this weren't enough, it can be kept on the shelf indefinitely; it does not shrink or air dry.

The oft-read advice, "Follow the manufacturer's instructions," is often, but not always, the best procedure. Where Polyform is concerned, how long and at what temperature the material is baked depends upon what the craftsman is making. If it is the "tile" floor discussed in Chapter 2, which he wishes to remain white and flexible, baking at a very low temperature is best. If he wishes the material to darken, a longer baking is in order. (The writer once forgot a Polyform object in a low oven, and left it over-

night. It turned very dark and hard but did not crack or shrink. An excellent way to make slate or dark stone!)

Colors kneaded into Polyform give a different, softer effect than do those painted on the surface. Acrylic colors, worked into the material, turn it into an excellent clay for shaping pottery pitchers and bowls, foods, miniature soap, and so on. Metallic paste colors, kneaded into the clay, turn it into a usable material for plumbing fixtures and other metal objects that do not require a high shine.

In the writer's opinion, Polyform is second in importance only to wood when furnishing miniature rooms.

Epoxy Putty or Ribbon

Because it is basically an adhesive, epoxy putty (also sold as "epoxy ribbon"), is discussed under adhesives in Chapter 6. It is discussed here, however, because it offers so many other possibilities. Since epoxies in other colors do not seem to have the same elastic quality of the yellow-blue ribbon epoxy, only the latter is discussed in this section.

Like Polyform, epoxy putty or ribbon can be molded into any desired shape. However, it has a stretchy, leathery quality that is more suitable for some purposes and less so for others. As an excellent material for making ferns, palms, and other plant leaves, it is discussed in Chapter 8. Its use as leather upholstering material is covered in Chapter 7.

For making metal objects, a paste metal color can be kneaded into epoxy putty just as it can into Polyform. Since the most usable epoxy is green, the metallic colors worked into it lose much of their luster, but some very interesting effects can be produced in this way.

Although epoxy putty sets when left overnight, the curing process can be speeded up if it is left for a half hour or so in a very slow oven of about 200 degrees.

5.

Using Electrical Tools

One of the great pleasures in making miniature furniture is that such a wide variety of skills is involved. Not all of the skills used, or the necessary tools involved with those skills, will give equal pleasure to each craftsman. However, if one step in making a piece seems monotonous, it will soon be finished, and there is always the next one to be looked forward to.

The real enjoyment in using a tool lies in using it well, and it is almost impossible to use any tool, especially an electric-powered one, without at least a minimum amount of practice. Most of the practice will come as the work goes along, with the craftsman gradually using less effort to turn out increasingly better pieces. There should, however, be a short period of practice with each tool where the aim is not to make anything usable, but to get the feel of the new instrument. During those first few practice sessions, the quality of the work is relatively unimportant.

JIGSAW

The jigsaw is probably the one tool the craftsman will use more often than any other, so a great deal of the needed practice will come automatically. It is not a difficult tool to use, and after a time the craftsman will find his skills have increased so that he is no longer conscious of the tool itself, only of the work he is doing.

In setting up the jigsaw for use, there are only a few points to remember: the tool should be set on a flat, steady base, and at a level convenient for the craftsman to use. Since very small or intricate cuts are more easily made if they can be seen from above, it is advisable to place the saw on a table that is somewhat lower than the average workbench height.

Undue vibration or noise while the saw is running can be eliminated by setting the tool on a pad of heavy cloth or a rubber mat, such as those used under typewriters. A sheet of newspaper over the mat will simplify the removal of accumulated sawdust.

The blade must be attached to the saw with its teeth pointing downward; it will not cut at all with the teeth in the opposite position.

During the practice session, straight and curved lines should be drawn on scrap wood of various thicknesses, and the lines cut on the saw. The wood piece should be fed into the saw slowly and steadily, with the fingers pressing it down flat against the saw's table.

Since the saw blade is flexible, it will soon be obvious that the wood cannot be pushed straight in and held at one unchanging angle during the entire cut. How far out of line the blade will bend or twist will vary with the wood's thickness and density, and how fast it is fed into the saw. The only reliable way to cut accurately, therefore, is to focus attention on keeping the blade on the pattern line and to ignore completely the position in which the wood is held.

The simplest possible cut is one in which the blade enters the wood at one edge and follows a straight or gently curved line to another edge. However, when making miniature furniture, there will be many occasions when a sawed line cannot be made in a single operation; the wood must be backed out of the saw and the blade entered at another spot.

Backing Wood Out of the Saw

Even though a jigsaw blade is quite flexible, it cannot be made to turn sharp corners or to bend in small, tight curves. Not only is there a danger of the blade breaking, but also sharp turns cannot be made cleanly; the blade is apt to tear the wood as it turns. Furthermore, if an ornate edge is being cut, sharp turns can cause the blade to knock off points and tiny curves of wood that are a part of the design.

The problem is easily solved by making only short, straight, or gently curved cuts. When a point is reached where a sharp turn must be made, the wood is pulled away from the blade and turned to a new position, and the cut is approached from another angle. Using short, separate cuts in this way, and working from the outside edges inward, the most elaborate designs can be sawed with no difficulty.

To remove a partially cut piece of wood from the saw, the motor is left running and, as the wood is pulled backward, it is turned and manipulated so that the blade always stays in the path of the cut already made. For very shallow cuts, these instructions may seem to be elementary; the wood pulls away from the saw very easily. For longer cuts, however, when the blade is past a series of curves, it must be guided out carefully so that it never leaves the cut line. This is particularly important if the wood edges on both sides of the cut are to be used in the furniture piece being made, and must therefore remain clean and unchewed.

When cutting a very thick piece of hardwood, the blade will sometimes become so deeply imbedded in a curved cut that it cannot be eased out again. The problem can be solved by working the blade back to the first bend where it jams (at point *A* in figure 5-1). The blade can then be worked back and forth against the wood until the cut is widened a little, as shown in the shaded area. This will leave room for the blade to be worked back to *B*, where another widening is made. The blade can then be eased out of the wood at *C*.

When widening a path for the blade, care must be taken that the widening is done only in wood that is to be discarded after the cut has been completed. In the illustration, the wood should be pushed firmly to the right as the widened areas are being made so the edges of the piece to be used (in figure 5-1, a cabriole leg) remain undamaged.

If a small protrusion is left where two sawed lines have not met perfectly, such as at point *A* in figure 5-1, it can easily be sanded or filed away.

Illustrated in figures 5-2 and 5-3 are a few in-and-out saw cuts with suggestions on how they can be made.

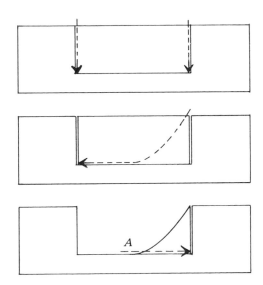

5-2. Four cuts remove a rectangular piece from a wood edge.

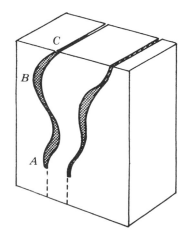

5-1. Widening the path for a saw blade to be backed out of the wood.

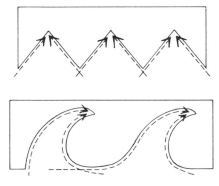

5-3. Starting each cut from the wood edge inward provides more accurate sawing.

Cutting Decorative Edges

There are times when very small cuts must be made, and the saw blade cannot be made to cut them in the usual way. This is especially true when an elaborate, decorative edge is being sawed. In such a case, the wood may be turned so that its edge is perpendicular to the blade. The wood is then worked back and forth against the blade, and the blade is used as a file.

Another way of making small shapes along an edge is to use a round or oval file as shown in figure 5-5. This method will result in two or more indentations that are exactly alike, something that does not easily result when a saw is used. The outline of the piece is cut with the saw, and the small indentations along the edge are made with a round or oval file, as shown, or with any file that will give the desired shape.

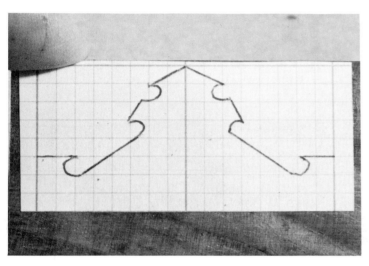

5-4. A pattern for a wood piece with small indentations along the edge.

5-5. The outline is first sawed, then a round file is used.

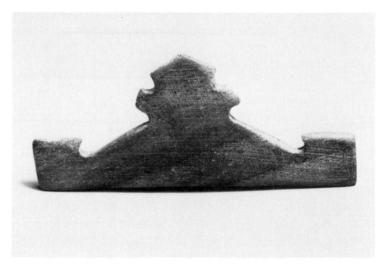

5-6. Indentations are more uniform than if they had been sawed.

Sawing on a Wood Platform

The craftsman will find that a piece of scrap wood, about 1/16 to 1/32-inch thick, will be an invaluable aid in his use of the jigsaw under certain conditions. The workpiece is laid on the scrap wood, and the sawing is done through both layers. The scrap wood platform can be used over and over for the same purpose until it has become so chewed up along the edges that it must be discarded and a fresh piece substituted.

Under the following conditions the extra wood support will be of almost indispensable help to the craftsman:

1. Sawing a Very Small Piece

When making miniatures, there are a great many occasions when the piece being cut is so small it will not straddle the opening for the blade in the saw's table. In such a case, the scrap piece used as a support need not be more than a few inches across. The tiny piece being cut is held near the edge of the support and can be manipulated separately from it.

2. Sawing a Narrow Strip

When a very narrow strip is being cut, the wood support underneath will prevent it from breaking or splitting during the operation. In this case, the support must be a little larger than the wood piece being cut.

3. Sawing Thin Wood

When sawing wood less than 1/16 inch thick, the extra wood platform will prevent possible cracking or splitting of the piece being sawed.

4. Sawing Decorative Edges

When an edge design includes small protruding points or curves, the danger of their being broken off during the sawing is greatly reduced if a supporting platform is used.

Inside Cuts

When it is necessary to saw an area that cannot be reached by sawing inward from an outside edge, an inside cut must be made. Such a cut is used to remove wood from inside a picture frame, for example, or to remove inside wood when cutting an openwork, decorative piece.

To start an inside cut, a hole a little larger than the end of the saw blade is drilled in the approximate center of the area to be cut. The upper end of the blade is then detached from the saw, slipped through the drilled hole in the workpiece, and reattached. The blade's lower end will not be disturbed if the blade is given a gentle pull upward when the upper end is detached. The workpiece can then be slipped down the blade to rest on the saw's table.

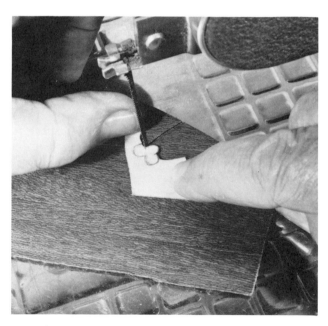

5-7. A tiny piece should be sawed on a wood platform.

5-8. Thin wood will not split if sawed on a wood platform.

Two inside cuts are shown in figures 5-9 and 5-10. The top diagram in figure 5-9 shows how a piece of wood is first removed by making a straight cut, *A*, from the center hole to a corner. Cut *B* swings up and along the curved edge to

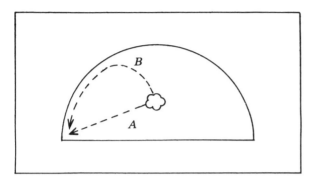

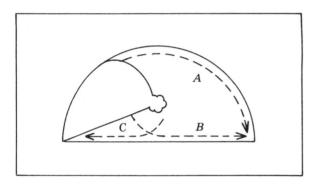

5-9. *Making an inside cut: 1. Wood is first removed as shown. 2. Three more cuts remove the remaining inside wood.*

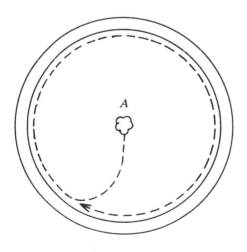

5-10. *Wood can be removed from a round pattern with one cut.*

meet *A* at the corner. A piece of wood will then fall out, leaving a wide space in which the blade can be manipulated in any direction. In the bottom diagram of figure 5-9, cut *A* completes the sawing along the curved edge. Cut *B* is made as shown, meeting *A* at the corner and removing all the wood but the small piece in the lower left-hand corner. Cut *C* completes the sawing operation.

Figure 5-10 shows how the wood from a circular frame can be removed. Since there are no corners, the whole cut can be made in one operation by spiraling out from the center hole, *A*, as shown.

Small Inside Cuts

The only limit to the size of an inside cut is that it must be large enough to take the end of the saw blade. Beyond that, the cut can be as large or as small as the craftsman wishes. If the cut is to be part of an openwork design, where each hole is quite small, the blade does not need to saw in the usual way. Just as an edge design can be made, as described earlier, by holding the wood perpendicular to the blade and moving it back and forth against the blade, so a small inside cut can also be shaped. In addition, as described for edge designs, the shaping of small inside cuts can be completed with the use of narrow files instead of the saw blade.

Shaping Four Sides of One Piece

The worker in miniatures will find many uses for the following method of cutting a chair or table leg or chair arm that is shaped on all four sides. If the wood piece were sawed in the usual way, one side at a time, it would soon become so lopsided that it could not be held in position for the last few cuts. Using the method described here, the wood piece retains its original shape until the final cut.

Like so many other instructions that must be put into print, the following may seem to be complicated and may make the operation seem to be more difficult than it really is. In practice, however, it is not at all difficult, and the craftsman is urged to try it.

A pattern for the desired leg or arm is first drawn on graph paper. If the piece is to be symmetrical, such as a cabriole corner leg, two patterns will be needed, each identical, except that one should face to the right and one to the left.

A stick of wood is then cut. It should be roughly square, and a little wider than the widest part of the leg to be sawed. Since more than one leg will probably be needed, the stick should be as long as can be handled easily, possibly 6 to 8 inches, so that more pieces can be cut from it later. Exact dimensions—length or width—are not important.

With the use of rubber cement, the two patterns are fastened, facing each other as shown in figure 5–11, to two adjacent sides of the wood stick. The tops of the patterns should be flush with the top edge of the stick, and there should be enough space on each side of each pattern so the saw blade can cut along the edges without cutting through the outside edges of the wood.

The leg is now ready to be sawed. Starting at the top edge of the wood stick, one edge of the leg is cut by following the pattern line to a short distance beyond the bottom of the leg. The stick is then backed out of the saw. Care must be taken that the blade does not cut through the side edges of the wood at any time. The second edge line of the same pattern is next cut, and the wood is again backed out of the saw. The stick is then turned so that the second side with a pattern is facing up, and the two leg edge lines cut as before.

The fifth and final cut is across the bottom of the leg (figure 5–13). This last cut will release nine pieces of wood, and the piece from the center of the wood block is the shaped leg.

This method of cutting odd-shaped pieces will solve problems for the craftsman that cannot be solved (short of hand carving) in any other way.

5-12. *The sides of the leg are cut with the saw.*

5-13. *The leg is sawed across the bottom.*

5-11. *To make a cabriole leg, two patterns are glued on the wood stick.*

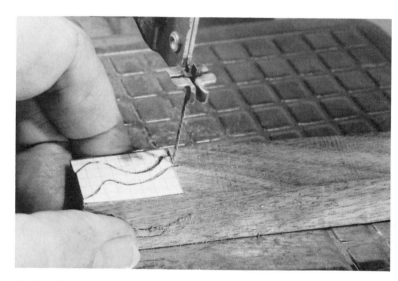

5-14. *In the foreground, the sawed leg ready for sanding.*

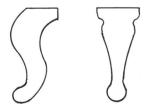

5-15. *Pattern for the nonsymmetrical center leg of a sofa.*

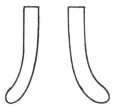

5-16. *Pattern for a chair arm with a two-way curve.*

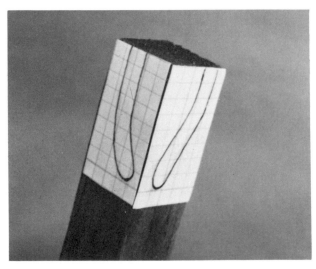

5-17. *Arm pattern glued to a wood stick.*

5-18. *The finished arm, made quickly and easily.*

Drawing Other Patterns

When drawing patterns for four-sides-at-once sawing, only two patterns are needed for each furniture part being made. As mentioned before, the two patterns for symmetrical parts are the same, but they face in opposite directions. However, if the part is not symmetrical, the two patterns will represent two different views. For example, the center leg of a sofa will match in design the two corner legs, but will appear to be flat when viewed from the front, and bowed out when viewed from the side (figure 5-15).

In the same way, patterns can be drawn for straight or curved legs that are tapered on all four sides, for the lower end of a stair railing that curves out where it meets the newel post, or for chair arms that sweep down from the chair back and, at the same time, curve out to the side (figures 5-16, 5-17, and 5-18).

A pyramid can be sawed by using this same method, although, since the piece, because of its shape, can always be held flat, the process can be simplified. The left-hand diagram in figure 5-19 shows the first two cuts to be made. Unlike other patterns discussed here, the saw is allowed to cut through the sides of the stick, leaving the house shape shown in the center diagram. Lines for the second cuts are then drawn on the "roof" as shown. The right-hand diagram in figure 5-19 shows the resulting pyramid, which can be cut off as shown on the dotted line, or farther down the stick if desired. This pyramidal cut is so simple that it can be done on very small sticks; the pyramid shape can be used for drawer pulls, the tops of posts, or, in a larger size, as the lid of a wind-up phonograph case.

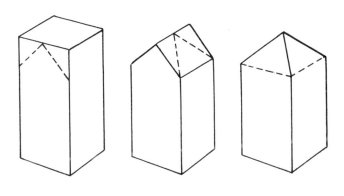

5-19. *Making a pyramidal cut.*

Unless the craftsman has a one-in-a-million talent for picturing just how a piece will turn out by studying two drawn patterns, he would be well advised to try them out on scrap wood. This is the right time to use softwood, such as basswood. The material is easy to saw, and the piece can be discarded after the pattern has been perfected.

When duplicates are needed for a fairly simple pattern, such as that for a straight leg tapered on four sides, they can be drawn with the aid of a ruler and graph paper. More complicated patterns, however, should be traced with the use of carbon paper. When the position of the second pattern needs to be reversed, as with a cabriole leg, for example, it can be done by placing the carbon face-up for the second drawing.

A word of warning: A spare pattern should always be kept on the graph paper sheet until all the needed pieces have been sawed. It can be most disconcerting, when a final piece has not turned out well and must be done over, to find that all the patterns have been used and that there is no way to make a duplicate. To draw an accurate pattern from an already sawed, fairly elaborate furniture piece can be very difficult.

Sawing Duplicate Pieces

When duplicate pieces must be sawed out, it is sometimes advisable to stack two or more pieces of wood, fasten them together with rubber cement, glue the pattern on top, and saw all the pieces at once. The cut pieces can then be separated, and the cement can be rubbed off with the fingers.

The number of identical pieces that can be cut at one time depends upon the thickness of the wood and how elaborate the pattern is to be. Some detail is apt to be lost along the edges if too many pieces are cut at one time, and of course it would be difficult to saw with much accuracy through four or five layers of fairly thick wood. However, when three or four identical legs for a pedestal table, or identical pieces of thin decorative trim are needed, this method of sawing can prove to be invaluable.

Mitering and Beveling

If a box, open on one side, were to be made, the edges of the box might be sawed at an angle so they would fit together with only a single seam showing at each corner. Cutting the box edges at an angle is called *beveling.*

If a frame for the open side of the box were being made, the ends of each of the frame's four sides would be cut at an angle so they would fit together at the corners. Cutting these ends at an angle is called *mitering.*

Mitering and beveling, then, are the same in principle; wood pieces are cut at an angle so they will fit together neatly. The difference is in the manner in which the cuts are made. A beveled edge is cut along the edge of a piece, as illustrated at the top of figure 20, and a mitered cut is made, as in the bottom of figure 5-20, at an angle across the surface.

To bevel an edge, the saw's table is tilted to the degree of angle desired, and the wood is fed to the blade at that angle. To make a mitered cut, the saw's table remains level, and the wood is held by hand at the desired angle as it is being sawed. A mitered cut can also be made in a miter box, which, in principle, is the same as working with a level saw table.

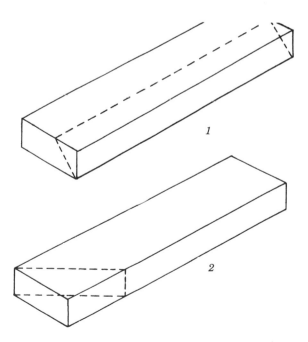

5-20. *1. A beveled cut. 2. A mitered cut.*

5-21. *Sawing a beveled edge.*

5-22. *Mitering a corner.*

In both mitering and beveling, the degree of the angle depends upon how many pieces are to be joined. If a four-sided box or frame is being made, each corner will be a right angle, or 90 degrees, and the angle of the two edges that will be joined to make the 90-degree angle will be half of that, or 45 degrees.

It is an easy matter to find the correct angle at which to tilt the saw's table for a beveled cut, or to slant the wood pieces for a mitered cut. The 360 degrees in a full circle are simply divided by the number of cut edges there will be. In the square frame illustrated in figure 5–23, there will be eight cut edges (one at each end of the four sides). The full 360 degrees are therefore divided by 8, equaling the 45 degrees mentioned above.

Similarly, there will be 12 cut edges in a 6-sided frame, as shown in figure 5–23, so the 360 degrees are divided by 12 to give 30 degrees as the slant of each cut. An octagon, or 8-sided figure would require 22 1/2-degree cuts, found by dividing 360 by 16.

Most jigsaws used for miniature work are not as accurate as the more expensive, full-size tools, but they are accurate enough to cut the bevels and miters mentioned above without being very far off the mark. Slight errors can usually be corrected with a file if they are not deep enough, or, if too deep, with wood filler after the pieces have been glued together.

When a front piece is desired for a boxlike piece of furniture, such as a chest or cabinet, the two side edges must be beveled, and the two cuts must be slanted inward, in opposite directions. If the piece being sawed has a top and bottom edge that cannot be reversed, the tilt of the saw's table must be changed for the second cut. However, if the piece can be turned after the first cut, so the top edge is now at the bottom, the table's tilt need not be changed.

When sawing a beveled edge, care must be taken to tighten the screw well that holds the table in position. There will be considerable pressure on the table during the sawing, and if it is not firmly fastened, the table may move and the angle of the sawing will be changed. Also, the workpiece must be held against the saw's table even more firmly than when a right-angle cut is being made. The table's tilt, along with the movement of the blade, tends to push the wood downward, which will produce a cut that is not straight.

Until the craftsman becomes practiced in knowing whether a cut will slant in or out when the table is tilted to the right or the left, he should lay the piece to be sawed on the table close to the blade and visualize what the result will be. If he finds this difficult, a practice cut should be made on scrap wood to make sure the desired angle will result.

Since mitered cuts are made on a flat table, the slanted sawing lines must be drawn with pencil on the wood, and the wood guided by hand during the sawing. This makes accuracy more difficult to achieve. However, a miter box will automatically guide the saw at the correct angle and should be used wherever possible.

When sanding both mitered and beveled cuts, care must be taken that the sharp edges are not rounded off. Sanding should be held to a minimum until the two edges have been glued together to form a corner, which can then be sanded and rounded off as required.

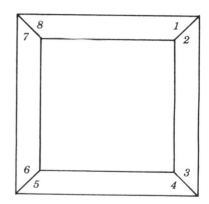

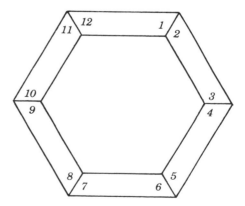

5-23. Determining frame angles.

USING THE CIRCULAR SAW

Like its full-size counterpart, a miniature circular saw is a no-nonsense tool that will make cuts with perfectly straight edges. With a simple adjustment of the blade, it will also bevel edges.

If the saw's cut is made along the length of a wood piece, with the grain, it is called a rip cut. If it cuts a piece in two crosswise, across the grain, it is called a "cross cut." When a cross cut is being made, or when an end is being mitered, the miter gauge is used to guide the wood. The miter gauge fits into one of two slots, located on the saw's table on either side of the blade. The slot to be used depends upon convenience.

When making rip cuts, the rip fence is used to guide the wood. The fence is adjustable so that it can be made to fit snugly against the piece being sawed.

When using the jigsaw to make a beveled edge, the saw's table is tilted so the blade cuts into the wood at an angle. When making a beveled edge with the circular saw, the table remains level, and the blade itself is tilted.

Before using the circular saw, adjustments should be made according to the manufacturer's instructions so that the blade and rip fence are exactly parallel. The miter gauge should also be squared by pushing it against the edge of the table and tightening the screw to hold it in position. If the miter gauge must be adjusted to any angle other than 90 degrees, a protractor should be used as a guide.

Most miniature circular saws offer, at the least, a coarse- and a fine-toothed blade. For the thicker wood of a room box, the coarse-toothed blade should be used. For making miniature furniture and doing other small work, however, the fine-toothed blade will provide smoother cuts.

The blade of a circular saw can be raised or lowered, and the safest cutting position for it is when the edge protrudes from the table just enough to penetrate the wood's thickness. However, the higher the blade is raised, the less strain there is on the motor. It is therefore advisable to start a cut with the blade set no higher than necessary, but if the motor slows and is

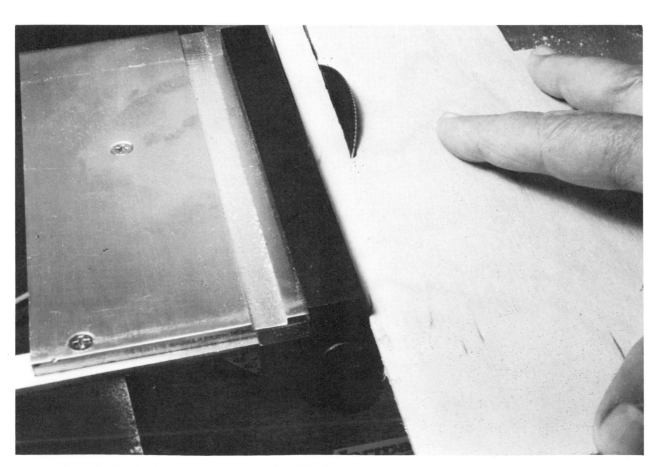

5-24. The blade of a circular saw tilts to make a beveled edge.

clearly laboring, the saw should be turned off and the blade raised. Obviously, the better the saw's quality, and presumably, the more powerful its motor, the less likely will be the need to raise the blade during a cut.

It should be emphasized that while a jigsaw is a relatively harmless tool, the circular saw can do serious damage to the fingers if the craftsman is careless. The guard should be kept over the blade at all times, except when a bevel is being made and the guard cannot be tilted with the blade.

USING THE ELECTRIC HAND DRILL

For doing miniature work, the craftsman will probably find that the two principle uses for his hand drill will be drilling holes and carving. He may also find useful some of the attachments that can be bought for the drill, such as a stand to hold it in position, a flexible shaft, a foot-operated speed control, and so on.

Some sanding and polishing can also be done with the drill, although the writer feels that for miniatures, these things can more easily and accurately be done by hand. An exception is the shaping of wood seats. Shaping seats is a tedious job if done on hardwood by hand sanding, a quick one by hand drill. Actually, seats can be rough-shaped so quickly with a ball sander grinding point in the drill that care must be taken not to allow the point to dig too deeply, or to indent one side of the seat more deeply than the other. With the rough shaping finished, the seats must still be smoothed, and the two sides evened up by hand sanding.

If the electric drill is used for nothing but drilling holes and carving, however, it will still be one of the craftsman's most important tools. Not until he has built his first room and has made the furniture for it, will he realize just how important the drill is.

Drilling Holes

When drilling a hole with an electric drill, the turning bit has a tendency to slip on the wood or metal surface until it has had a chance to dig into the material. By that time, the tip of the bit may be quite a distance from the exact place where the hole is wanted. A simple solution to this problem is to make a small indentation with a pin or any pointed tool at the spot where the bit is to enter. Even though the indentation might be quite shallow, it will catch the bit and allow the drilling to start at that spot.

Making small indentations before the drilling is started is particularly important when the ends of two very narrow sticks or posts are to be joined with a dowel. The holes for the dowels must be drilled in the exact centers of the post ends, and if the ends are only 1/8-inch across, or less, the indentations can too easily be made a little off-center.

There is a simple remedy for this mistake. The off-center indentation is widened until, no matter how large it becomes, it is now in the center of the end (figure 5-25). Since the indentation will be deeper in the center than at the edges, the bit will automatically slip to the center and start drilling the hole where it is wanted.

Unless an angled hole is to be drilled intentionally, the drill should always be held upright, at exact right angles to the work. This is an obvious point, but one that is too often overlooked until it is too late.

The correct speed to use when drilling a hole depends upon the size of the bit and the hardness of the wood. In general, however, a slow speed should be used at first, as the hole is being started. A fairly shallow hole, drilled with a fine bit, can be finished at the same slow speed. A wider bit and a deeper hole will require more speed. There are no rules to follow; the craftsman will know, if a bit is not drilling a hole quickly enough, that the drill speed must be increased.

It should be kept in mind, however, that the slower the speed of most power tools, the greater the control the craftsman will have over them. Most tools should therefore be run as fast as necessary, but no faster. An exception to this is a lathe; shaping is easier if the wood is turning quickly.

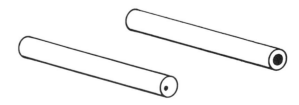

5-25. Correcting an off-center hole in a dowel end.

Controlling a Hole's Depth

Many times a hole is needed that will go only part way into fairly thin wood, such as when holes are being drilled for dowels that will attach arms, rungs, or splats to a chair, or legs to a chair seat or table. If the holes are not drilled carefully, the bit is likely to go all the way through the wood, leaving an unwanted hole in the surface of the furniture where it will show. Unfortunately, the turning bit has a way of cutting into the wood slowly until the opposite surface has almost been reached. Too often it then seems to jump suddenly through that last thin layer of wood, and the damage is done.

There is no easy way to avoid this mistake. It sometimes helps if the thickness of the wood is measured against the tip of the bit, and the bit is then allowed to go into the wood only as deeply as the measured point. Since it is not possible to mark the wood's depth on the bit, however, the depth must be judged by eye, and it is easy to err when one is trying to gauge a distance of 1/32 inch or even less.

It is almost certain, then, that until the craftsman develops an instinct for drilling holes only part way into thin wood, he will have to face an unwanted hole occasionally. Learning how to conceal the hole may be almost as important as learning how to avoid making it in the first place.

The hole may be filled with a paste wood filler mixed with a stain, filled again as the filler dries and shrinks, and again, if necessary, until the filler is level with the wood surface around it. It can then be finished along with the rest of the furniture piece.

Another method of camouflage is to fill the hole with a stick of wood. If the hole was drilled to hold a dowel, the dowel can be simply pushed and glued in the hole so that it sticks out, not only on the side to which another furniture piece will be attached, but also a small distance on the opposite side as well. On the latter side, the dowel end is sanded down until it is level with the wood surface. If the hole has been drilled in the wrong place, and is not to be used at all, both ends of the dowel are simply sanded level with both wood surfaces.

Using a Pin Vise

Although the electric drill can be used for drilling holes of any size, over the years the writer has come to use it for drilling larger holes only, and to rely on the pin vise for drilling very small ones. The pin vise is also more convenient to use in hard-to-reach places, and where a hole is needed in the end of a very narrow dowel, which is sometimes not much larger than the desired hole itself.

To drill a hole in such a dowel, a shallow indentation, as described earlier, is first made with a pin in the exact spot where the hole is to be. A very fine drill bit is then used to drill a hole, with

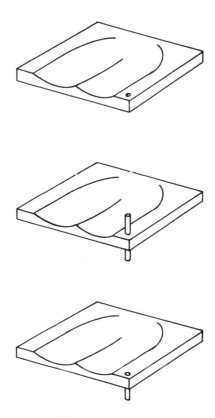

5-26. Filling an accidental hole in a chair seat.

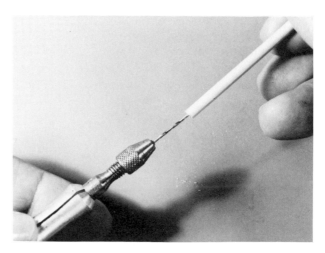

5-27. Drilling a hole in a dowel end with a pin vise.

care being taken to hold the pin vise at an absolute right angle to the dowel. If the bit enters the wood at even a slight angle, it will come through the side of the wood lower down as the hole is being drilled. If a larger hole is needed, a larger bit is used to re-drill in the same spot. Double-drilling provides the greatest possible accuracy when the area being drilled is very small.

Carving With a Drill

It has been mentioned that not all of the skills necessary for making miniature furniture will give equal pleasure to every craftsman. It is hard to imagine, however, how anyone could make a successful miniature carving and attach it to a piece of furniture without feeling something more than, "Well, thank goodness that's done!" To the writer, at least, carving is a much-anticipated step, the light dessert that follows a more solid meal of sawing and sanding, and the project is usually saved for a quiet evening when nothing pressing needs to be done.

Perhaps one of the attractions of carving is that complete accuracy is not essential. If a slip is made on one side of a symmetrical carving, the same slip can be copied on the other side and it will seem to be a part of the design. If the outline of a leaf or flower is not as intended, the craftsman's intentions can be changed after the fact and no one will be the wiser.

Perhaps an even more important attraction is that carving with a drill is so much easier than it looks. When a miniature carving has been smoothed and polished, it is hard for viewers to believe it was done in such a short time and that so little experience was necessary to do it.

Hardwoods should always be used for miniature carvings. When there is a choice, woods with a fine grain, such as walnut, cherry, or rosewood, are best, but more open-grained woods, such as oak and mahogany can also be carved successfully. Softwoods will not hold a clear pattern and are better used for other purposes.

There should be a selection of carving bits from which to choose as the work goes along, although the craftsman will probably find that two or three of them will become his favorites and will be used for most of the work. The writer uses a very fine router bit for outlining the design, and two or three small, ball-shaped bits of varying sizes for finishing the work. The craftsman may find, however, that other bits do the work better for him, and he should experiment with a few until he finds those that are easiest for him to use.

Carvings on full-size furniture are either part of the furniture wood itself, or are separate, smaller pieces that are glued to the furniture. It is not difficult to tell from a clear photograph of the piece being reproduced how the carving was done. For his first practice piece, however, the craftsman would be wise to do the work on a separate piece of wood. If it turns out well, he can find a later use for it; if it doesn't, it can be discarded.

5-28. *The more elaborate the pattern, the more a carving can be improvised.*

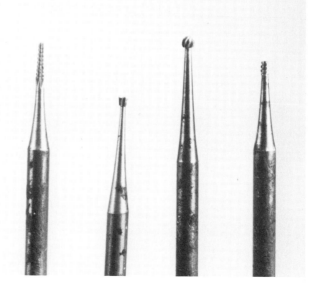

5-29. *Four useful carving bits.*

5-30. *A tentative design for the carving on the back of the chair.*

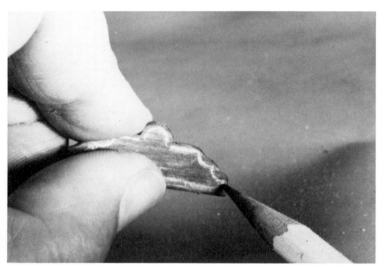

5-31. *The design's border is drawn on wood.*

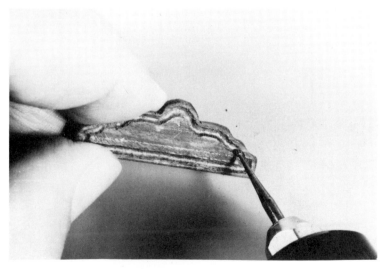

5-32. *The design is outlined with carving bit.*

Following are five suggestions for making a miniature carving.

1. Drawing the Design

If the carving is to have a border, or is to be outlined in any way, the border should first be measured against the wood piece to be carved and drawn on graph paper. Next, the important lines of the design are added. If the carving is to be of a simple flower or shell, the drawing can include all the lines. For a more complicated design, however, many of the small details will be improvised as the work goes along and need not be included in the drawing.

2. Copying the Design on the Wood

The border, if any, and the most basic lines of the design should next be drawn on the wood, using the paper drawing as a guide. These lines are then cut into the wood with the use of a narrow bit. A slow speed is best at the start, but the speed can then be increased gradually until the drill feels comfortable in the hand.

With the first lines outlined in the wood, the next few are pencil-drawn and cut in the same way until the whole design has been "drawn" on the wood with the bit. It is at this point that the craftsman can add to the design if he wishes. After the first cutting has been done, small, plain areas that showed in the original design are apt to have disappeared and new ones opened up. It is therefore better to make judgments about the next step after the amount of available space that is left can be determined. In this way, small details of the carving can be developed as the work goes along.

It can be said almost with certainty that with the first cutting of the lines of the first carving, the craftsman will think he must be doing something wrong and will feel discouraged. These first cut lines will look much like chicken tracks, thin and shaky, with no hint of the rich, finished carving that is only an hour or two away. This discouragement will pass when the craftsman is about halfway through the next step.

3. Deepening the Lines

One very important feature of a successful carving, full-size or miniature, is the depth to which the lines have been cut. The outlining of the pattern with a bit was just a beginning. The same lines should now be deepened, widened, and smoothed into grooves with the use of a tiny, round bit. As they are being widened, they can easily be straightened where necessary. The craftsman can hardly go over the lines too many times; the more he retraces the original pattern, the deeper, smoother, and more professional the carving will become.

At this point, the work can be left as it is, or the background can be routed out with a router bit, or with any bit the craftsman prefers. The background should be made as smooth and flat as possible so the design will stand out clearly in relief.

It is strange but true that the more elaborate the carving, the easier it is to do. A very plain pattern, such as a straight border, must be done carefully, since the eye will quickly pick out any irregularities in it. On the other hand, a pattern that fills the entire space need not be done so perfectly; the eye will receive an impression of the whole design and is not apt to see the details. Therefore, if a first carving has started with a line too crooked to be straightened by deepening and smoothing, the day may yet be saved by adding a matching line opposite it and by filling in the space between with leaves, grapes, or whatever is suitable to the whole design. In this way, the finished carving may turn out to be even more successful than it would have been if no mistakes had been made.

4. Sanding and Filing

Once the design has been deepened and smoothed with the drill as much as necessary, the carving is next smoothed with sandpaper and small, shaped files, if available. Small pieces of sandpaper can be folded to give sharp edges for getting into tiny indentations, and a fine-grit paper can be used to round the outside edges of the carving and to smooth its surface. The finished carving should then be thoroughly cleaned with tack cloth.

5. Finishing

A final step is required to give the carving the same finish as that of the furniture piece of which it will be a part. If an open-grained wood has been used, it can be filled with a paste filler, wiped off, then waxed and polished. A light spraying of Krylon instead of a filler will help to fill the pores of the wood if they are not too prominent.

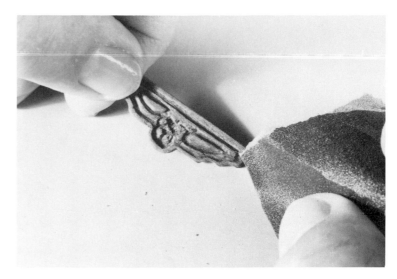

5-33. The pattern lines are deepened.

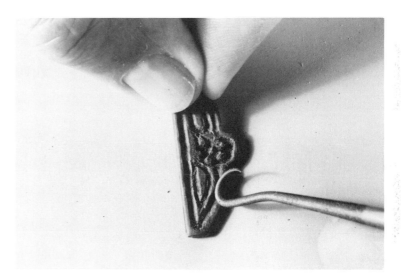

5-34. The carving is smoothed with sandpaper and files.

5-35. The waxed carving, ready for the chair back.

Additional Carving Hints

When very small, decorative carvings such as tiny shells or rosettes are being done, they can first be sawed to shape, then fastened temporarily to a larger piece of wood so they can be carved more easily. If rubber cement will not hold them steady enough, white glue can be used. The carving can later be cut from its wood base with a razor blade.

A second method of making an extremely small carving is to do the carving first and the sawing of the outline afterwards. For carvings with irregular outlines, such as those on a cuckoo clock (figure 5-36), this method works very well. For geometric designs, however, this method is less desirable. Even when extreme care is taken when sawing, the carved pattern is very apt to be close to one edge of the tiny sawed piece instead of in the center where it belongs.

A suggestion for adding to the richness of a carving without cluttering the design too much: very thin pieces of wood are sawed to match the shapes of the open areas in a carving. These pieces are sanded smooth, their edges are rounded off, and the wood is finished to match the finish of the carving. They are then glued to their matching areas in the carving. These plain, raised pieces, surrounded by the carved areas, give a rich, three-dimensional effect, as can be seen in figure 3-37.

5-36. For extremely small pieces, the carving can be done first and the outline sawed last.

5-37. Glued-on wood shapes enrich a carving.

A last suggestion for enriching a carving: The outline of the wood piece that is to be carved is first sawed into two (or more) separate pieces, with the cut following a line in the carving (figures 5–38 and 5–39). The carving is done, and the pieces glued back together, but on slightly different planes than before, so that one piece is attached just barely in front of, or barely behind, the other. The resulting carving seems a great deal richer and fuller than it would if done on a single, flat plane.

5-38. A carving can be sawed apart and pieces reglued on slightly different planes.

5-39. The resulting carving has been given an added depth.

LATHE WORK

Unlike other electric-powered tools, the lathe defies the craftsman to make a mistake. There is not much he can do to spoil his first piece as long as the dowel is centered exactly so that it does not wobble as it turns. With that done, and with the machine turned on, all the craftsman need do is press a cutting tool, or an abrasive tool such as a file, against the smoothly spinning dowel and watch it take shape.

Later, with the machine turned off again, he will find he has made a perfectly symmetrical newel post, pedestal leg, vase, lamp base, or other turned item. His first piece may not conform exactly to the shape he had in mind when he started, but it will probably be attractive and usable.

Later on, with practice, will come increased skill. The craftsman will then be able to control the shapes he is turning, so he can make a set of table legs that match, or turn his own hardwood dowels from square sticks.

The craftsman should select a chuck or other holding device that will handle a variety of dowel sizes from 1/2-inch or so, down to 1/8-inch or even less. Without these extremes, the miniature room will lack some of the small details that may not be missed, but if present will add a great deal to its charm. Examples of one extreme are thick columns for doorways and mantel supports, and heavy pedestal legs for tables. At the other extreme are thin, decorative posts on furniture, turned handles on small household tools that traditionally have them, and turned legs that are in scale for small pieces such as stools, delicate side tables, fireplace screens, and so on.

Supplies and Shaping Tools

To start, there should be on hand a supply of ready-made dowels of diameters that can be used in the lathe. Because these dowels are usually light in color, and because they do not absorb dark stains very well, the craftsman will later learn to make his own, turning them from the same hardwood he is using for his furniture. For many pieces, however, the light color is no handicap, so until he has become acquainted with his lathe, it would be better for him to use commercial dowels.

In addition to the dowels, all that will be needed for starting the lathework are a few shaping tools. Other craftsmen may disagree, but it has been the writer's experience that, although one or two of the tools in a wood-turning set were helpful when making dowels from square sticks, the rest were of little use for shaping miniature furniture parts on a lathe.

A set of small, shaped files, such as an X-Acto set, a larger flat file or two, a package of emery boards, such as those used for manicuring, and a sheet of medium-fine sandpaper will do most of the miniature shaping needed.

Centering a Dowel

When fastening a section of dowel in the lathe, the manufacturer's instructions should be followed for using the holding device the craftsman has purchased. To prevent the dowel from wobbling as it turns, the two ends must be fastened in the lathe on their exact centers. If a chuck or other holding device centers the dowel's left end automatically, only the right end need be centered by hand. Otherwise, both must be.

There are mechanical ways of finding the center of a dowel end automatically, but in the writer's experience, the only way to find it in a narrow dowel suitable for miniature work is to judge the center by eye. Using a very sharp pencil, a mark is made in what appears to be the exact center of the dowel end. If the mark then seems to be a little off, it can be moved as necessary. Using a sharp instrument, such as the point of a large safety pin, an indentation is then made on the pencil dot. The indentation does not need to be deep; the lathe's center will fit into, and be held by, even the shallowest hole.

Learning to Turn

With the dowel fastened in the lathe and the motor turned on, the first practice piece can now be made. The craftsman should experiment with whatever turning tools or files he has, holding each against the spinning wood in turn and noticing the shape it makes.

At this point, a mistake can hardly be made. As mentioned earlier, the shaped dowel will probably be attractive and will automatically be symmetrical. The only thing that could go wrong is that a thin place in the dowel might break if too much pressure is applied. This is discussed more fully farther along.

Making two or more shaped pieces that match is a little more difficult. A pattern should first be drawn on graph paper. Short pencil dashes are then marked on the wood dowel to correspond to the narrowest part of each shaped area (or to any easily distinguishable area of the pattern). When the dowel is turning in the lathe, these dashes will show up as solid lines.

Next, the pencil lines should be cut into the turning wood with a sharp-edged knife or file, and should be recut from time to time as the progressing work threatens to obliterate them. These lines are necessary as a guide for correct spacing of the pattern parts on the dowel, but the details of the shape itself must be copied by eye from the pattern or from an already finished piece.

Although it is theoretically possible to turn two miniature pieces on the lathe that are identical, the craftsman will need not only skill, but also a great deal of luck to do it. The bright side, however, is that very small differences in a pair of legs or posts are not apt to be noticed when the pieces are fastened to the furniture. Also cheering is that small differences in turnings on full-size antique furniture are marks of distinction and prices go up accordingly.

When shaping the first pair of legs or posts, it is a good idea to remember which file or other shaping tool was used for a particular area, and to use the same tool when working on a matching area in the next leg.

Another aid in making matched pieces on a lathe is to shape two or more at the same time on a single dowel. The pieces being turned must be short, or the dowel will necessarily be so long that it will sag under pressure as it is being shaped. The length of a dowel on a lathe depends upon the dowel's thickness and the hardness of the wood. A very thin section will probably bend under pressure if it is more than 2 1/2 to 3 inches long, but a thick dowel may be twice that long, or longer, without giving any trouble.

When shaping two or more legs on a single dowel, a small part of the pattern should be completed on both legs before the next part is started. Working on each leg in turn in this way simplifies the problem of making them match.

It is not possible to describe in detail how to shape on the lathe any pattern that might be wanted. The shaping tools the craftsman has should be held in turn against the spinning wood and the results noted. A practice session or two, far more than words, will show which of his files or other tools will give him the results he desires.

Removing the Finished Work

When removing a shaped dowel from the lathe, the motor can be turned off and the dowel taken out by loosening the chuck on the left end. The wood ends can then be trimmed off with the use of a small handsaw or, better still, a miter box. The latter will assure that the ends will be trimmed at exact, 90-degree angles.

Another method of removing a dowel from the lathe is to use a sharp-edged file to cut through the turning wood at one end of the shaped section. This will produce a small, pointed knob that can be used at the top of a post. When the dowel has been cut through, the other end that is still fastened in the lathe can be removed by loosening the chuck as described above.

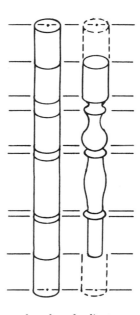

5-40. Marking a dowel to duplicate an already turned leg.

5-41. A partly shaped matching leg.

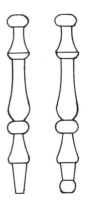

5-42. *The leg on the left can be shortened more easily.*

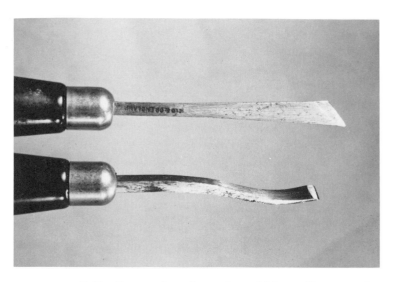

5-43. *Two wood-turning tools useful for making a round dowel from a square stick.*

5-44. *The chisel should be held at right angles to the wood and a little above the center.*

When drawing the design for a set of table or chair legs, thought should be given to shortening the legs later if it becomes necessary. If the pattern includes knobs or other shapes at both ends of the legs, filing one end to shorten it may change the design conspicuously. If the leg is shaped as shown in the left side of figure 5-42, however, it can be shortened less noticeably.

Hardwood Dowels

As far as the writer knows, hardwood dowels of such popular woods as mahogany, walnut, cherry, and so on, are not yet available on the market. If the craftsman has now begun to feel at home with his lathe, it is time for him to learn to turn his own dowels.

Square sticks, a little larger than the diameter of the desired dowels, are first sawed from the hardwood to be used. Great accuracy in cutting these sticks is not necessary; the turning lathe will ensure perfectly round dowels, even if the sticks are not symmetrical. The length of the stick is immaterial as long as it is short enough to withstand the pressure of the tool against it without sagging.

The stick is fastened in the lathe and can now be turned into a dowel in one of two ways: (1) the unwanted wood can either be filed away, a method that works but is time-consuming, or (2) it can be cut away with a wood chisel similar to those shown in figure 5-43. The second method requires a little practice, but it so speeds up the work that it is well worth learning.

The chisel should be held at right angles to the wood with the cutting edge just slightly above the center of the dowel. If the chisel is held in the center of the dowel, or slightly below, the spinning wood will grab the tool and throw it downward.

The chisel is then moved evenly to the right and left as it smooths the wood. It will be easier to keep the diameter of the dowel uniform if its whole length is worked on at once, in a sweeping motion, instead of working on a short section at a time.

Words of warning: the roundness of a shaped dowel should never be judged while the wood is spinning in the lathe; it can appear to be perfectly round but, after the motor has been turned off, can be found to be slightly square.

When the dowel has been reduced to the desired diameter, a piece of fine-grit sandpaper should then be held against the turning wood to smooth its surface.

If very narrow dowels are wanted, wood chisels cannot be used to make them. Rather, small wood sticks should be rounded off with sandpaper, emery boards, or small files.

After successfully making his first few dowels, the craftsman will find them so easy to make that he will probably not want to buy the more expensive hardwood dowels when and if they do appear on the market.

Shaping Tiny Dowels

It has been said before, but bears repeating, that the small details of miniature reproductions are their most important feature. Lathe-turned legs on a table or chair whose period or style requires them are admirable, but not surprising, features. It is the unexpected, unnecessary, and usually very small additions that distinguish the best miniatures from the merely good ones. Very tiny, turned furniture parts usually fall into the "unexpected" category.

When making such parts, it is almost impossible to fasten both ends of a very thin dowel in a lathe. A suitable chuck will grasp the dowel's left end, but split wood is the usual result when the right end is pushed onto the metal center.

There are two solutions to the problem, but both call for very short dowel sections, pieces that extend not more than an inch or so beyond the chuck. The tiny dowel, which can be as thin as a match or toothpick, is fastened in the chuck on the left, and the right end is left free. Since the right end is unsupported, pressure of the shaping tool on the dowel must be very light, or the wood will be pushed downward and the finished piece will not be symmetrical. With care, however, short pieces can be turned very successfully in this way.

A hand drill can also be used for turning a tiny dowel. The dowel is fastened, just as a drill bit would be, in the chuck of the drill and shaped with small files, using light pressure.

When a dowel is supported on one end only in either a lathe or hand drill, the section that extends out from the chuck should be quite short, but the other end should be as long as the chuck, or other holding device, will allow. The extra length, fastened tightly in the chuck, will help to hold the shorter, protruding length steady as it is being shaped.

Broken Dowels

It was mentioned earlier that a turning dowel sometimes breaks when the pressure of the tool against a thin area becomes too great. Unfortunately, there is no way of telling the craftsman when such a break may occur, or how to avoid it. The best warning system he can have is to acquire a feeling that will tell him when he has gone far enough, and that further turning on a weakened spot will probably result in a break. Such a feeling will come only with practice.

If a break does occur, all is not necessarily lost. The broken ends can often be fastened together with the use of drilled holes, a tiny dowel, and an adhesive. If the broken pieces are quite thick, a strong adhesive, such as an epoxy glue or Scotch's Super Strength Glue, can be used alone.

If the damaged dowel represents a great deal of work, it would be wise to attempt to repair it. Otherwise, it is usually easier just to throw it away and start over.

5-45. *Shaping a small piece with only one end supported.*

6.

Making Furniture

As this book progresses, it seems to the writer that each step ahead is more pleasurable than the one just passed. Perhaps that thought has occurred now because the making of the furniture seems to be the nucleus of the entire project. Beautiful miniature furniture, even if it stands alone on a shelf, is an end in itself; an empty room is not.

When making any furniture pieces, the general sequence of steps is the same:
1. Drawing the pattern
2. Selecting the wood
3. Fastening pattern parts to the wood
4. Sawing furniture pieces
5. Thoroughly sanding and filing
6. Gluing
7. Filling and staining

(Numbers 5 and 6 above sometimes change positions, as explained farther along.)

DRAWING THE PATTERN

Although a number of commercial patterns for making miniature furniture can be bought individually or in book form, it is hoped that the reader will make his own. The most important reason for using homemade patterns is that there will then be an almost unlimited choice of furniture styles, so the craftsman's furnished rooms will be a reflection of his own taste and personality.

Because the Victorian period seems to have universal appeal, the majority of commercial patterns are for Victorian furniture, with a scattering of other styles mixed in. While there is nothing wrong with these styles, or with any other tastefully executed furniture style, there is

hardly a soul alive, especially a craftsman, who does not wish to be original. Selecting one's own furniture pieces to reproduce, and making one's own patterns, is a good way to begin.

The second reason for using homemade patterns is that all important details on the full-size model, some of which are likely to have been omitted in a commercial pattern, can be included in the miniature copy. It cannot be emphasized too strongly that the details make most of the difference between fine reproductions and toy furniture. That is not to say, however, that details cannot be changed to suit the craftsman's own taste, or that some may not be omitted and others added. It is only important that nothing be omitted simply because it would be easier to use someone else's pattern and not to do the extra work. If historical accuracy is not the craftsman's aim, he may make any changes in design that he wishes.

For drawing a pattern, graph paper should be used, and an inexpensive calculator will greatly speed up the work of reducing full-size measurements to the craftsman's scale.

As an illustration of pattern drawing, an "inexpensive chifforobe" (and indeed it was—only $17.65!) was selected from the 1927 Sears, Roebuck catalog. In this case, the important measurements were given in the catalog, but if they had not been, they could have been estimated rather accurately by guessing the height of any chest of drawers with a mirror above it. Measurements for the rest of the piece could then be estimated by relating them to the height.

The chifforobe measurements as given in the

catalog are: Height, 66 inches; width, 40 inches; depth, 18 inches. Mirror, 12 by 16 inches. Converted to the 1-inch scale by dividing the figures by 12, measurements for the miniature copy become: Height, 5 1/2 inches; width, 3 1/3 inches; depth, 1 1/2 inches. The mirror is 1 by 1 1/3 inches.

Front- and side-view drawings are next made on graph paper with 12 squares to an inch (figure 6–2). Although the right side of the chifforobe cannot be seen in the advertisement, similar furniture pieces on the same page show each tall side panel edged with wood strips, and one crosspiece in each center, but none on the shorter left side panel.

The two drawings will not be used for sawing furniture parts, but for reference from time to time. The craftsman will find such drawings of his own useful for obtaining measurements, and they should not be discarded until the furniture piece itself is completely finished.

Although, in this case, it was necessary to draw all the pattern pieces at one time, in practice they would be drawn a few at a time as the work goes along. In this way, measurements for the next ones can be taken from the furniture itself rather than from the drawings. This step-by-step method of building a furniture piece will ensure greater accuracy.

Although there are no hard-and-fast rules about which parts should be drawn and sawed first, in this case the first logical step would be to cut the top and bottom pieces of the right-hand wardrobe. These should be thick enough (perhaps 3/16 inch or so) to support the sides, and since they will be glued between the sides and will not show, can be made of plywood or any scrap wood.

The tall sides should be cut next, and the four pieces glued together. Since, as the drawing shows, the right side of the dresser shares a common wall with the wardrobe, only the left side need be cut. The top and bottom pieces of the

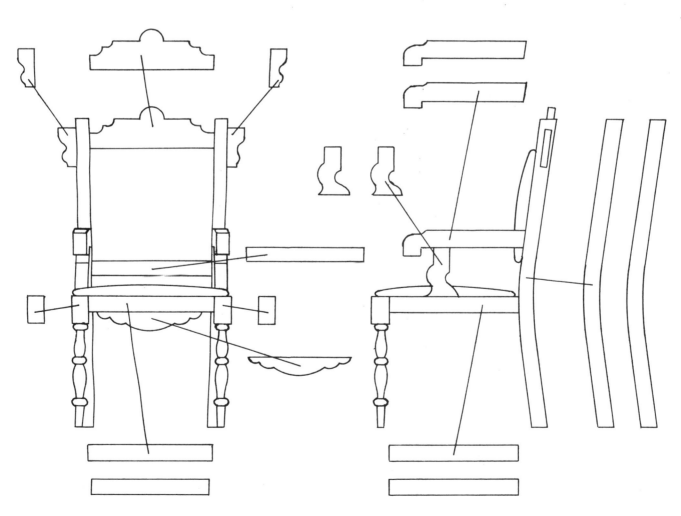

6–1. Pattern for "The Chair."

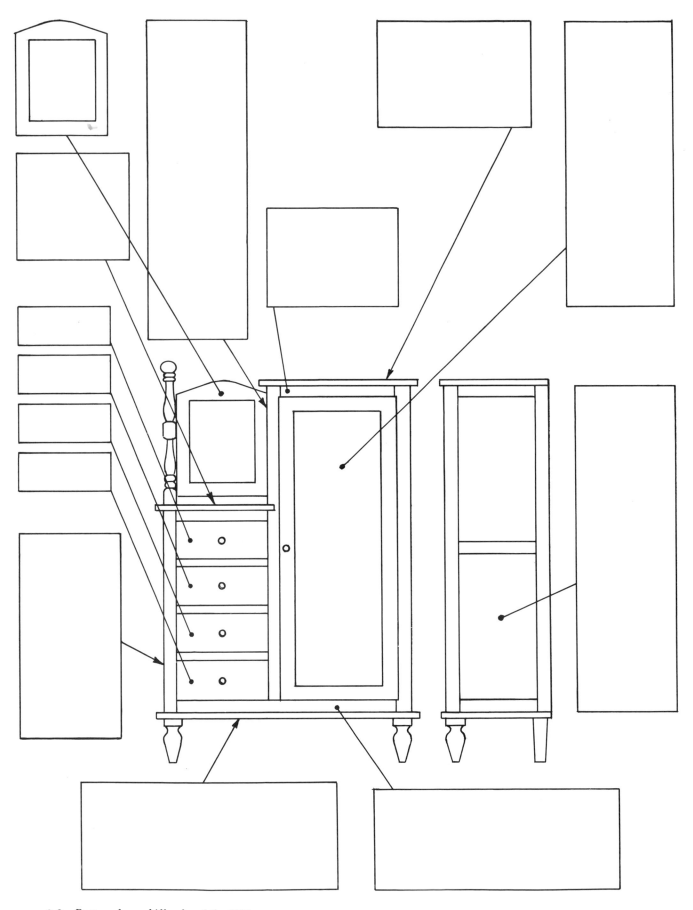

6-2. *Pattern for a chifforobe of the 1920s.*

dresser, which will also be glued between the sides and will not show, should be cut next.

When all of these pieces have been glued, the framework of the chifforobe will have been completed. From here on, it will not be difficult to add, piece by piece, the thin tops, the wardrobe door, the drawer dividers, the drawers, and so on.

This particular furniture piece requires a great many trimming strips. They are used to edge both sides, the front, and the wardrobe door. Since all of the strips are the same width, it is not necessary to draw patterns for them. A supply of strips should be sawed and sanded. The individual pieces are then cut to length in a miter box and glued in place as needed.

Figure 6-4 shows the pattern parts for a gas stove from the same 1927 Sears, Roebuck catalog. Although the details on the stove give the impression that it is a complicated piece, basically it is quite simple, and was chosen as a contrast to the chifforobe.

Unlike the chifforobe's drawers and door, which can be opened, the drawers and oven door of the stove do not open, so the stove is basically made of three solid blocks of wood—the oven on the right, the taller, two-door section on the left, and the low, one-drawer center piece. The blocks are made from softwood scraps, and since several thick coats of paint cover the whole stove, plywood was used for the rest of the piece.

It is the porcelain-like finish and the details of the stove that make the whole effective. Thorough sanding and several sprayings of white enamel give the effect of metal. The gray enamel trim was applied with a brush.

The burner handles are plain pins, cut short and bent at right angles. Polyform was then molded around the pinheads to shape the handles, and the cut ends of the pins were inserted into holes, drilled with a pin vise into a length of 1/8-inch dowel. Burners were made from the thinner halves of oversized dress snaps, bought at a dime store.

The above sample patterns and accompanying descriptions are not intended to be complete instructions for drawing and making these particular pieces, but to suggest to the craftsman methods by which any chosen furniture piece can be drawn, cut, and assembled. Few pieces of furniture, no matter how small or simple, should be made without first making patterns for them. With the exception of straight strips, which can be sawed by following pencil lines ruled on the wood itself, all sawn parts—irregularly shaped in particular—should be cut by following a paper pattern.

Although some craftsmen draw around a paper pattern on the wood, then follow the drawn lines when sawing, it is not possible to be entirely accurate using this method. Some of the lines are sure to be a small fraction of an inch or so larger than the pattern, and when these fractions are added up in the finished piece, there is almost surely to be trouble in fitting together and gluing the various parts.

6-3. A chifforobe made from the illustrated pattern.

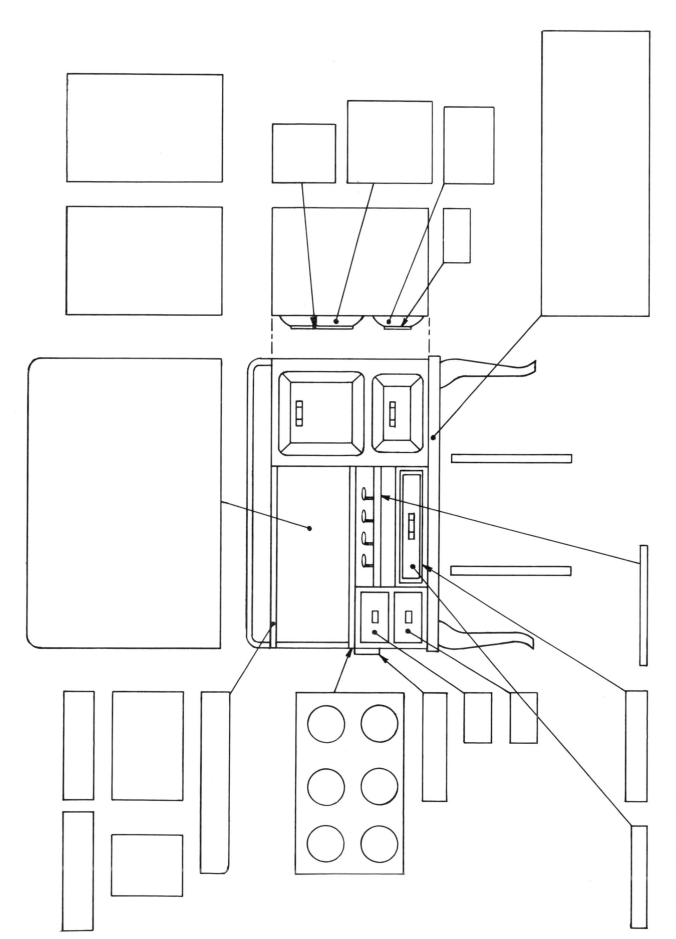

6–4. *Pattern for a porcelain stove.*

SELECTING THE WOOD

Assuming there is now a good supply of thin wood on hand, pieces that will be used for the new pattern are selected according to their thicknesses. As mentioned earlier, a variety of wood thicknesses is an important feature of carefully made miniature furniture. The craftsman need only look at full-size furniture pieces in his own home to see how much this variety contributes to the whole design. Some parts, such as legs and corner posts, are usually cut from one thick piece of wood, but as a rule, tops of tables, dressers, chests, and so on are made of two or three thinner layers glued together. The layers are usually of slightly different sizes so that they will form a shaped edge (figure 6-5).

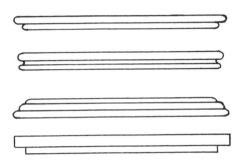

6-5. *Gluing wood layers together shapes the furniture edges.*

Of the miniature furniture the writer has seen, if any error at all has been made in wood thicknesses, it has nearly always been on the side of wood that is too thick rather than too thin. When selecting the wood for the furniture piece to be made, a ruler should be used frequently. If the pattern calls for three layers of wood glued together, the chosen pieces should be stacked and their total height measured. Strict adherence to scale is of first importance, so if the three layers will be too thick, one of the layers should be omitted, or thinner wood should be used.

FASTENING PATTERN PIECES TO WOOD

The paper patterns are next glued to the wood with rubber cement. Careful attention should be given to the direction of the grain, which should run with the length of each part. Grain should go up and down on perpendicular pieces, such as legs, posts, and cabinet ends, and across on pieces where the length is horizontal, such as drawer faces, and table and cabinet tops.

It is also important to pay attention to the direction of the grain of two pieces of wood that will be placed side by side on the finished furniture. Many woods have a way of catching light that can change their colors when they

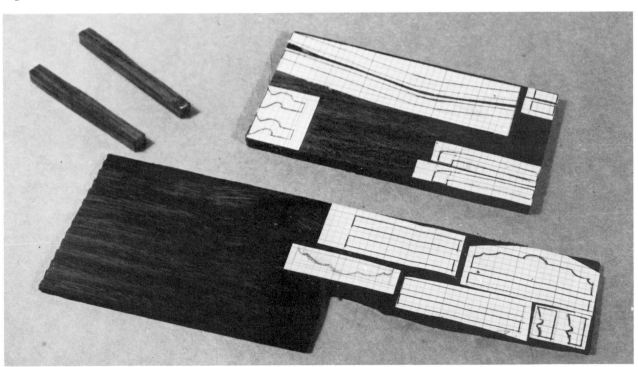

6-6. *Paper pattern for "The Chair" glued to rosewood. The two sticks will make the legs.*

are viewed from different angles. The two halves of an extension-top table, for example, can be cut from the same piece of wood, yet can look entirely different if the grain of one half runs from left to right, and of the other from right to left. It is therefore important that two such parts be cut, not only from the same piece of wood, but with the grain running in the same direction. If the wood piece being used is large enough, the safest way to avoid trouble is to cut the table top in one piece, then to saw it in half.

When sawing, it is easier to follow pattern lines if a slight margin of paper is left all around them. However, since thin-sliced hardwood is such a precious commodity, the margins should be kept narrow, and the pattern pieces should be glued to the wood as closely together as possible. On straight edges, the margin can be cut off altogether and the pattern glued on the straight edge of the wood.

SAWING FURNITURE PARTS

Just as it is usually advisable to draw only a few pattern parts at one time, so also is it better to saw only a few wood parts at a time and glue them, or at least measure them for fit, before sawing the next few. This is more a safety measure than a rule, but it does minimize the

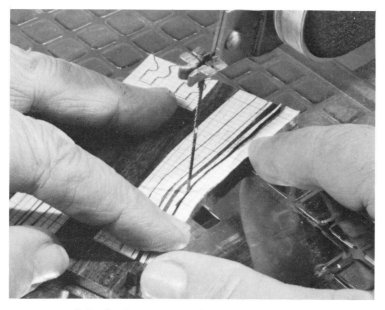

6-7. *Sawing on pattern lines.*

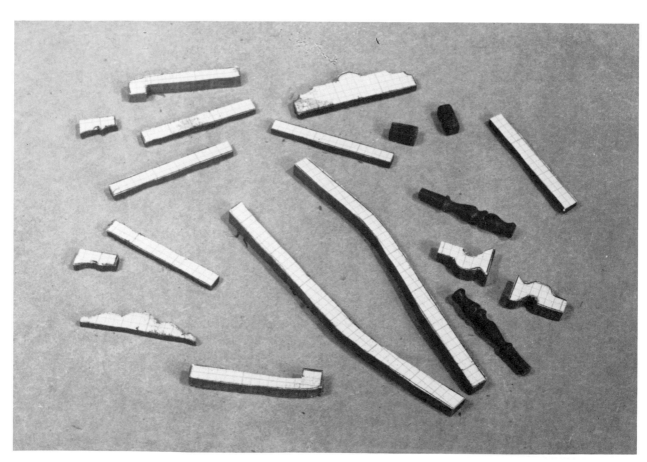

6-8. *The chair pieces sawed and ready for sanding.*

106

chances that the parts will not fit together neatly. Common sense should, of course, dictate which pieces of furniture can be done all at once and which should be sawed a few at a time.

Chair rungs, for example, whose exact fit depends upon the distances between the legs, should be cut after the rest of the chair has been glued and measured, while a simple table consisting of a top and four legs can be done all at once, because its parts are more or less independent of each other.

When the furniture parts have been sawed out, the patterns can be peeled off and discarded. Briskly rubbing the wood with the fingers will remove all traces of rubber cement and leave the cut pieces perfectly clean.

SANDING AND FILING

When making full-size furniture of wood, sanding surfaces smooth and straightening edges are most important steps, but in miniatures they become vital ones. Small flaws are apt to seem larger when on miniature surfaces, and since there are no automatic controls on a jigsaw, very few edges will be cut so perfectly that they will not need some finish work. This is particularly true of straight edges that have not been cut on a circular, or similar, saw. Fortunately, however, small mistakes that are so easily made can also be easily erased.

Edges that are to be glued together should be held in position and viewed in front of a light so that any areas that do not touch can be seen. Perfectly cut and filed edges will show no light at all, but a few small spots that do not touch are not major flaws; the joint can be glued and then filed smooth. If any small holes are still visible in the glued joint, they can be concealed with paste wood filler, a material that will be discussed later.

If there are fairly large areas where two wood edges do not touch, a file should be used to straighten them until they can pass the light test.

Once the edges are as straight as possible, the surfaces can be sanded until they feel perfectly smooth to the touch. If they are very rough at the start, a fairly coarse grit sandpaper should be used, followed by medium-fine, and then fine grit papers. If the wood is already fairly smooth, only the finer grit need be used. Sanding should always be done with the grain of the wood; sanding across the grain will leave visible scratches that are very difficult to remove.

The fine dust, some of it invisible, that is left by sanding should be removed before the surface is finished. An inexpensive package of tack cloth—a cheesecloth-like, tacky material available in paint and hardware stores—is almost a must for the worker in miniature wood pieces. A small square of it can be used over and over to make wood surfaces perfectly clean, as they should be before they are stained. The cloth is also useful for keeping saw and workbench surfaces clean.

GLUING

It is usually easier to stain and fill furniture parts before they are glued together. When working with miniatures, there are many areas in glued pieces that cannot be reached easily and which therefore make the job of finishing a more difficult one. Also, if gluing is done first, any squeezeout of the adhesive around a joint will prevent the stain from reaching the wood underneath. The result will be a permanent light area, which can mar the beauty of the finished piece.

On the other hand, there are advantages to gluing the furniture before finishing the wood surfaces. The joints will be much stronger, since the adhesive will be able to penetrate raw wood. In addition, if a filler is used after the joints have been glued, the filler will erase some of the cracks in the joints and minimize others. The result will be a much smoother-looking job.

Having given both sides of the question, and having no single answer to give, the writer will now withdraw and leave the craftsman to solve the problem as best he can. Actually, there *is* no single answer. Where the strength of the joint is of secondary importance, or where a dowel will be used in addition to an adhesive, the wood can be filled and stained first. (Dowels are explained later in this chapter.) If an adhesive is being used that gives very little squeezeout, the furniture piece can be put together first. Each situation should be evaluated individually.

Clamps may be of any style that will hold the glued pieces together. Figure 6–9 shows C-clamps, spring clothespins, and spring paper clips. For most miniature gluing jobs, any of them will exert enough pressure to make strong bonds.

If two wood pieces are to be glued at right angles to each other instead of being pressed flat, holding the joint steady while the adhesive dries or sets will be a problem. Since even the slightest shifting in position of the wood pieces will prevent a strong bond from being made, the hands cannot be trusted to do the job alone.

There are two reliable methods of holding right-angle wood pieces steady during gluing. One is the use of a wood block, two to three inches square, with exact right-angle corners, kept in the workshop for the purpose. Adhesive is applied to the gluing surfaces of the wood pieces, which are then firmly pressed together and held against two adjacent sides of the wood block until the adhesive dries.

A second method is to make a gluing jig by gluing or nailing fences on two adjacent sides of a square or rectangular wood platform. The two pieces to be glued are then held together at the corner of the jig and pressed against its sides. This will prevent the wood pieces from shifting until the joint is firmly bonded.

There is available on the market an ingenious variation of the above jig. The platform is made of iron, the two fences of aluminum (figure 6–10). Very strong magnets are supplied with the jig, and these do an excellent job of holding the wood pieces steady as the adhesive dries. The advantage of this jig is that any adhesive can be used, since the pieces being glued can be left overnight to dry.

FILLING AND STAINING

The importance of giving miniature furniture wood a beautiful finish is clearly demonstrated when one examines the surfaces of manufactured pieces. Although, as far as detail is concerned, the quality of such furniture continues to improve, one rarely, or never, sees manufactured furniture that has a really nice finish. No doubt the reason is that miniature wood pieces must be finished by hand, and the extra hours this takes adds too much to the cost. Whatever the reason, the value and beauty of such furniture would be greatly increased if the buyer himself would take the trouble to improve its finish.

Handmade miniature furniture, increasingly seen in shops today, usually has a better finish than manufactured pieces. Some pieces are excellent. Others, however, have been given too many coats of shellac or varnish. Although such treatment fills the pores and leaves the surface smooth and shining, the finish is not a natural one and robs the wood of its character. There is a great difference between a shining and a gleaming finish; wood furniture, full-size or miniature, should gleam.

There is no substitute, then, for a good hand finish on wood, and since producing one in miniature is a simple process requiring little skill and no great amount of time, nearly all miniature wood furniture pieces should be given one. (Exceptions are painted furniture and reproductions of some very early pieces that may require a rough, unfinished look.)

Some woods have a more open grain than others. Of the hardwoods most popularly used

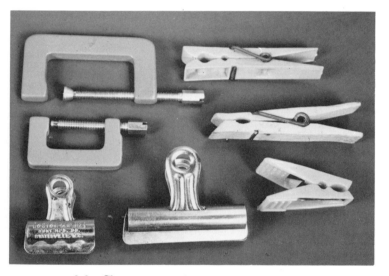

6–9. Clamps, paper clips, and clothespins are useful for gluing.

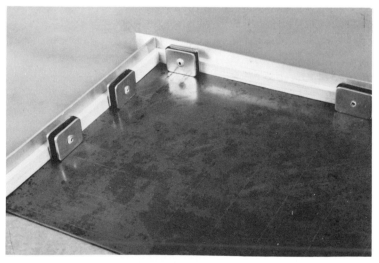

6–10. Gluing jig with magnets to hold the glued wood in place.

for miniature furniture, cherry, maple, walnut, and rosewood have a fine grain, while the grain of mahogany and oak is more open.

No matter what the size of the grain, the appearance of a piece of miniature furniture will be improved if a filler is rubbed into its pores. If, on the coarser-grained woods, a first filling does not do the job, a second application should be given and, if necessary, a third. Wood has been filled sufficiently when no open grain at all can be felt or seen on the surface. However, this is the ideal condition, and the craftsman may come as close to it as he wishes in filling his own woods.

Although there are many products on the market for filling woods, or for filling, staining and varnishing them in one step, a simple, paste wood filler is recommended. Some of the newer products may save time, but, where finishing the small surfaces of miniature furniture is concerned, time is not an important factor.

Similarly, a penetrating oil stain is recommended, not one combined with varnish or any other material. Stain may be applied to the furniture before the filler is added, or it may be mixed with the filler and applied at the same time. Depending upon the effect desired, however, some woods do not need to be stained at all.

As examples, the writer is partial to heavy oak furniture, but because of that wood's open grain and coarse streaks, most oak is not suitable for miniature pieces. A good substitute for dark oak is cherry wood with an oak stain. Cherry with no stain at all, but filled and waxed, could easily pass in miniature for light oak. Similarly, unstained rosewood when polished has a beautiful rose color; with a walnut stain, it becomes rich and dark.

So many interesting effects can be obtained by experimenting with various stains and mixtures that it is a good idea to save some hardwood scraps to test colors before they are used on a furniture piece.

Using a Filler

Filler should be mixed with the thinner in the can until it is the consistency of thick cream. If a stain is to be used, a little of the pigment from the bottom of the stain can be mixed with a small amount of the filler at this time. Working across the grain, the filler is then brushed or rubbed into the pores of the wood with a stiff brush or piece of cloth. The material should be applied thickly, so a thin layer of it stands above the surface.

At this time is the opportunity—for which even the most skilled craftsmen are occasionally grateful—to conceal past, minor mistakes. The furniture should be examined for gaps in glued joints and for any small holes or irregularities that would mar the finished appearance of the piece. These should be filled along with the wood surface.

When the filler has lost its surface shine, usually after five to ten minutes, a cloth is used to wipe the excess off, working always across the grain. Wiping with the grain is apt to gouge the filler out of the pores. The wiping should be thorough so that the wood surface appears to be perfectly clean and unclouded.

The filled piece is then allowed to dry overnight, after which it is examined for any imperfections. If a large gap in a joint has been filled, the filler may have shrunk, or there may be pores that still show on the surface. If so, more filler should be applied until the surface is as smooth as the craftsman wishes it to be.

If not done earlier, holes should be drilled now for hinges, drawer pulls, and dowels where posts or other pieces are to be attached. All surfaces should be then cleaned thoroughly with tack cloth.

Finishing the Wood

The wood is now ready for the finishing coat. A light coat of wax (paste shoe polish does an excellent job) can be applied, left to dry, and rubbed

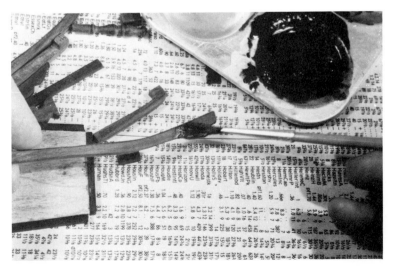

6-11. *Filling the wood of the chair.*

briskly. A thin coat of shellac may be given, or a very light coat of matte-finish Krylon, Deft, or similar material.

Although the plastic-type sprays are excellent for light finish coats, care must be taken if they are sprayed on a painted surface. If the paint underneath is not thoroughly dry, the finishing spray may lift and bubble it. The entire wood piece will then have to be cleaned and finished again.

Paint should be allowed to dry at least twelve hours (longer, if a fairly thick layer of glossy enamel has been applied) before Krylon or other material is sprayed on. The spray should then be applied thinly. If a thicker coat is desired it should be built up with two or three thin coats.

TYPES OF ADHESIVES

Although special uses for the various adhesives are covered, where appropriate, in other parts of the book, a general discussion will be helpful here. The writer admits to a great weakness for trying any adhesive product that is advertised as being stronger, longer-lasting, or easier to use than anything ever before offered. The result is a shelf in the workshop stacked with almost-full adhesive containers, and some notes which indicate that not all of the products are as effective as advertised.

Many of the adhesives on the market will, however, do an excellent job of holding things together, and those which have been found to be especially useful for working in miniature will be

briefly discussed in this chapter. It is by no means necessary for the craftsman to buy more than two or three types of adhesive, but there are others that do a special job so well, he may want to know about them and try them as special needs arise.

White Glue

White glue is probably every craftsman's most-used adhesive. It handles easily, can be used on almost any material, and forms a strong bond. It should, however, be used on raw wood if possible, and since it has less body (thickness) than some other adhesives, is not the most effective type to use for gluing small metal or glass surfaces.

To obtain the strongest possible bond with white glue, the material should be spread thinly on both gluing surfaces and allowed to stand for a few minutes until it has almost dried. A second thin coat should then be spread on one of the surfaces and the two pieces clamped or pressed together as tightly as possible.

If there is any squeezeout, it should be wiped away immediately. This holds true for any adhesive being used. Despite the claims of some manufacturers, no adhesive is completely invisible and most are quite glossy. There is, therefore, no adhesive that will not show if the excess is not removed.

White glue can be thinned with water and used as a stiffener for miniature curtains, bedspreads, and tablecloths, which can then be draped more realistically. This is discussed more fully in Chapter 7.

When more body is needed, the glue can also be thickened by pouring a small amount in a shallow bowl and allowing it to stand uncovered for a half hour or so until it reaches the desired consistency.

Rubber Cement

A can or jar of rubber cement kept on the workshelf is almost a must for the careful craftsman. Rubber cement is a temporary adhesive whose most important job is the fastening of paper patterns to wood for accurate sawing. It is also useful for gluing small pieces of wood together so they can all be sawed at once to produce identical shapes.

Rubber cement can fasten wood pieces, too small to be handled easily, to larger pieces, so that carving or other work can more accurately

6–12. Every craftsman has his favorite adhesives.

be done. The material is extremely useful for other purposes as well, many of which are covered in appropriate sections throughout the book.

To remove rubber cement from hard surfaces, the material can be rubbed briskly with the fingers, or with an art gum eraser. The small balls or rolls that result can then be brushed away easily.

Rubber cement thickens rather quickly in a half-filled jar, so a can of rubber cement thinner should be kept on hand and poured into the jar as necessary to keep the adhesive soft and usable.

Epoxies

All epoxy adhesives are composed of two parts — the epoxy and a hardener — which are mixed together just before use. Within a given period of time, ranging from five minutes to twenty-four hours, the material sets chemically. The resulting bond, if the adhesive has been used on clean, porous material, is permanent and stronger than the material itself.

The writer is familiar with three types of epoxies that are sold in tubes and with an epoxy putty, which is discussed separately in the following section. These epoxies, under a variety of brand names such as Scotch, Duro, and Devcon, can be found in any large hardware store.

Two of the three epoxies differ only in setting times; one sets within twenty-four hours and the other in five minutes. The latter is therefore excellent for use on small, irregularly shaped pieces that must be pressed together with the fingers and held until the adhesive has set.

The third epoxy must also be allowed to set overnight, but differs from the others in that it has a great deal more body, a quality that simplifies the gluing of pieces that cannot be clamped together. Also, the extra body lessens somewhat the possibility of a squeezeout of excess material.

Epoxy is an excellent adhesive to use where a very strong bond is needed and where the gluing surfaces are adequate. It is one adhesive that will permanently hold flat two pieces of wood that have warped out of shape. In such cases, however, the wood pieces must be clamped tightly together; pressing them under weights alone will not do the job.

Epoxies, and the five-minute epoxy in particular, should be used as soon as they are thoroughly mixed. Even though the material may seem to be workable for quite a while, if it has stiffened noticeably, it will not be able to penetrate the wood, and the bond may not be a good one. Epoxy should therefore be mixed in small batches and the excess discarded after each use.

Epoxy Ribbon or Putty

Epoxy putty is newer than the epoxies discussed above and is therefore not as well known or as widely used for miniature work. It has so many advantages when used for working in miniature, however, that the writer feels it will become popular once more craftsmen have become familiar with it.

The most widely sold epoxy putty comes in the form of a ribbon about an inch wide, composed of yellow and blue colors running side by side. A short length of the strip is cut off crosswise with scissors, and the two colors kneaded together thoroughly until the material is a green color, with no streaks showing. Small pieces are then pulled off for use.

Similar putties come in other colors, such as gray and tan, which mix to an aluminum color. However, it has been the writer's experience that these become brittle when set, and are therefore recommended only as adhesives, and not for the other uses described in this book.

There are many advantages to epoxy putty for miniature work. Following are those the writer has found. The reader will no doubt find more as he becomes better acquainted with this excellent material.

1. If the amount used is small enough, there will be no squeezeout at all. The material is as thick as clay and is not sticky. If a very thin roll of it is placed on one of the gluing surfaces, and the other surface pressed lightly against it, the craftsman can judge if he is using too much epoxy for the job. If so, some can be removed before the second surface is pressed permanently into place.

While the above method of gluing joints makes certain gluing jobs easier, it is not recommended for all glued furniture joints, particularly those with long seams. The squeezeout from other adhesives, such as white glue, will help to fill a very fine crack between the two wood pieces being joined. Epoxy putty, on the other hand, is a claylike material that tends to enlarge the crack in the joint. Such a crack should later be filled with a paste filler.

2. Although epoxy putty should be left overnight to set, it is so thick that it has immediate holding power, a quality that is of inestimable value to the miniaturist. A fairly heavy chandelier can be pressed to the ceiling, using a small ball of epoxy putty, and the chandelier will remain in place, if it is not jarred, until the adhesive has had time to set.

This same holding power makes epoxy putty an ideal adhesive for gluing such things as beads and small metal pieces. Although the putty will not penetrate glass or metal (no adhesive will), its thickness forms a bed for the material being glued. It should be remembered, however, that the putty is green, and must be painted to match whatever is being glued.

3. Epoxy putty is the only adhesive the writer knows of that will make a fair bond between two very small gluing surfaces, such as the ends of two thin dowels in a chair leg. It is also very useful for gluing the end of a thin arm to a chair back. In both of these cases, reinforcing dowels should be used, but if they are not, epoxy putty is the best hope the craftsman has that the bond will be strong enough to hold.

4. Epoxy putty has been found useful for holding stiffened curtains in place if they tend to balloon out from a window frame. Tiny balls of the material are pressed against a sill or frame, and the drapery or curtain is pushed against them. If the curtain is transparent, the balls must be placed where they will not show, such as along the edges of the frame close to the wall.

Other, nonadhesive uses for epoxy putty, such as making green plants and upholstering a "leather" chair, are discussed in appropriate sections in this book.

Duco Cement

Duco Cement is an old and versatile adhesive that can be used on both porous and nonporous materials. Since it is quite thick, it will hold small metal and glass pieces, such as metal trim and beads, fairly well by forming a bed around them.

Although cloth is not listed on the tube as a material for which Duco Cement is recommended, the writer prefers it for nearly all upholstering jobs, because it tends not to soak through the material and leave stains on the surface.

Scotch Super Strength Adhesive

Scotch Super Strength Adhesive has many of the qualities of contact cement, although it is not so advertised. It is a fairly new product and because of its instant holding quality, has proved to be excellent for working in miniature.

The adhesive is spread on both gluing surfaces and allowed to dry for about 30 seconds. The pieces to be glued are then pressed together and left to dry overnight.

The material has two advantages that some of the other adhesives do not: after it has been spread on the gluing surfaces, the craftsman can take a reasonable length of time to complete the operation. There are occasions when that extra 30 or 60 seconds can be very welcome.

The adhesive will also hold pieces to be glued, such as a series of stair posts, in an upright position as soon as they are pressed into place. The hand rail can then be glued across the posts, and the whole assembly left to dry overnight. There are few adhesives that will do such a job so easily.

The adhesive has one disadvantage—it spins fine threads, which must be pulled and brushed from the work after the gluing operation is finished.

Contact Cement

Contact cement, a type of adhesive that is sold under various brand names which may or may not contain the words "contact cement," joins two objects as soon as they are pressed together. Although the material has a strong holding quality, it is difficult to use for very fine work because it spins fine threads, and is quite sticky and messy to use.

All contact cements have the same quality: Large surfaces, once they have been pressed into contact, cannot be repositioned even slightly; smaller glued joints can be shifted a little, but it is always advisable to use the material carefully.

In spite of its handicaps, contact cement can do special jobs better than any other adhesive. One of them is the laying of a miniature floor that might otherwise buckle when glued. In addition, since objects glued with the adhesive do not need to be clamped together for long periods, the material is useful for working in tight or awkward places where such clamping is not possible.

DOWELS

When joining thin ends or edges of wood, the importance of using dowels in addition to an adhesive can hardly be overemphasized. There are many occasions when an adhesive alone cannot possibly do the delicate work that dowels make possible. It is therefore important that the craftsman learn how to use them.

The writer is moved at this point to deliver a sermon. No craftsman should ever say of any new operation, "That sounds too hard or too complicated," until he has tried it. The imagination has a way of complicating things that the hands find fairly simple to do. And so it is with using dowels.

When used for miniature work, a dowel is simply a tiny, short stick of wood whose two ends are pushed and glued into opposing, matching holes drilled into the two pieces of wood being joined. In some instances, a strong joint cannot possibly be made without the use of a dowel, as, for example, when the ends of two very narrow posts are being joined. In other cases, a dowel, while not essential, will serve to strengthen a joint that will be given extra pressure in future handling.

Holes into which the dowels will be glued should be exactly opposite each other in the two pieces being joined and must, of course, be of the same size. The larger the dowel, the stronger the joint will be, so the bit chosen to drill the holes should be as large as the wood pieces being joined will take. However, since dowels are usually used to join very thin pieces, the drilled holes must sometimes be so small that the craftsman may wonder how dowels can ever be made to fit them.

There can be a dowel to fit any hole drilled to receive it, from barely visible slivers of wood to round sticks as much as 1/8-inch across. The dowel should be long enough to fit the combined depths of the drilled holes, but not so long that the two surfaces being joined will be held apart.

Any wood scrap can be used from which to cut bits of wood to be used as dowels, but the simplest source is a toothpick, either a round or flat one. The end of the toothpick can be shaved with a razor blade, or sanded, until its diameter is small enough to fit into the drilled holes. It can then be cut to the needed length.

The end of a dowel is dipped into an adhesive (white glue works very well) and pushed into one of the holes. Adhesive is then applied to the protruding end of the dowel, and to both gluing surfaces, and the two pieces being joined are pushed together. When the adhesive has dried, the joint should be so strong that it will never come apart, either by accident or design.

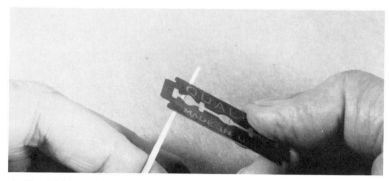

6-13. Making a dowel from a toothpick.

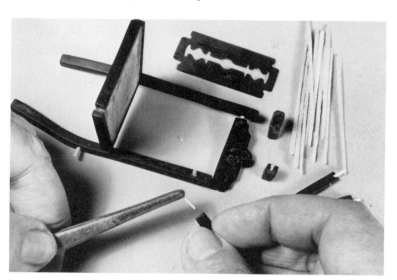

6-14. Gluing dowels to the chair.

6-15. Adding the arms. The gluing is almost completed.

113

A pair of tweezers will be of great help in handling dowels if they are very small and difficult to pick up with the fingers.

The smaller of the two almost-matching Victorian chairs shown in the color pages was put together with 14 dowels. Parts of the chair were quite delicate, and although the number of dowels used could very well have been reduced, the chair is so strong that it probably could be dropped onto a hard floor and not come apart. Although it is entirely unnecessary for all miniature furniture to be reinforced to this extent, there is a certain satisfaction in knowing that a miniature piece is much sturdier than it looks.

BENDING WOOD

There are occasions when it is necessary to curve a piece of wood. Curved wood, for example, might be used as a sofa or chair back, the arch over a grandfather clock, or a facing strip to cover the unattractive edge of a round or oval table. Basically, all curved wood pieces are treated the same way; they are softened in water, then fastened around a curved mold of the correct diameter, such as a glass or bottle, and left to dry.

Most softwoods are easier to bend than hardwoods, but the extra care needed to bend hardwoods is effort well spent. Thin plywood is probably the easiest of all the woods to bend without breaking, because it is strengthened by the layers that run at right angles to each other.

The wood should be soaked in cold water until it is thoroughly saturated. Some woods reach this point sooner than others, but any wood will be ready for bending if it is soaked overnight. Wood should not be boiled in an effort to speed up the softening; the surface can too easily become rough and pitted, and difficult to finish.

The bending process sounds simple, and it is, with two exceptions. The wood may snap in two if it is curved too much too fast, and it is not always easy to force the ends of a piece of stiff wood, even when wet, to hug the curved mold tightly.

There are two things that can be done to lessen the danger of breaking. First, the wood to be curved must be cut with the grain running lengthwise, along the desired curve. Wet wood, with the grain running up and down, across the curve, is sometimes so fragile that a thin piece can be snapped in half with the fingers. Second, if the desired curve is deep, the bending should be done by degrees. The wood should be tied in a soft curve, and allowed to dry. It is then wet again, without being removed from the form, and the curve deepened a little more. In this way the curve can usually be made without a break in the wood.

The problem of bending and tying the wood so that its ends hug the mold is easily solved. The wet wood is first tied to the glass with several strands of heavy twine. A thin metal rod, such as the filler of a ballpoint pen, is next slipped between the glass and twine, and used to twist the twine slowly, until the string is tightened enough to bend the wood against the curve of the mold. If necessary, the tightening can be done over a period of a day or two, with the wood being re-soaked as it dries. To prevent the twine from unwinding, the rod end is held against the glass with a heavy rubber band (figure 6–17). If the wood piece is too wide to be held in place by a single group of twine strands, a second group, and, if necessary, a third, can be added below the first. Each group should be tightened against the glass by a separate metal rod.

If the desired curve is irregular so that a round mold, such as a glass, cannot be used, a form can be made by sawing a wood block in two, following the lines of the desired curve. The wet wood to be shaped is pressed between the two cut halves of the block, which are then clamped together tightly, or tied with heavy twine or wide rubber bands.

When a desired wood piece simply cannot be curved successfully (because it is too thick, or the curve is too elaborate), it can be sawed from a thick block of wood (figure 6–19). The curved side of the grand piano shown in the color pages was sawed in this way from a thick rosewood block.

6-16.   Bending wood. Wet wood is tied to a jar.

6-17.   Strings are tightened by twisting metal rods.

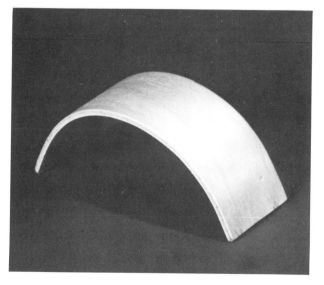

6-18.   Dried, bent wood will hold its shape permanently.

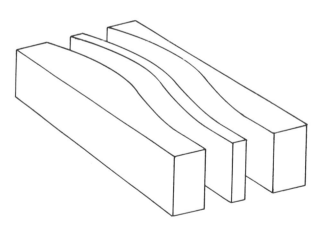

6-19.   A curved wood section can be sawed from a wood block.

6-20. The seat of the chair is edged with hardwood strips.

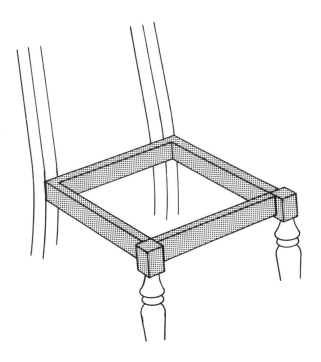

6-21. The tops of the front legs usually protrude a little beyond the seat edges.

FURNITURE DETAILS

Most of the work of sawing miniature furniture parts and fastening them together presents no special problem. At this point, if the craftsman has learned to handle his jigsaw and other tools with reasonable ease, and to use dowels in addition to an adhesive when assembling the furniture, most of the remaining work will require more time than experience.

However, in constructing miniature furniture, special problems may occasionally arise, the solutions to which are not immediately obvious. The writer has tried to anticipate some of these in the following paragraphs:

Chair Seats

If a chair seat is to be upholstered, only the top and side edges of the wood will show. Valuable hardwood will be saved if the seat itself is made of basswood or plywood and hardwood edging strips are glued all around. Wood saving, however, is a secondary benefit. An across-the-grain wood edge does not take a finish as nice as one cut with the grain. Obviously, a chair seat cut in one piece will have two with-the-grain sides, and two across-the-grain sides. If the seat is fairly thick, the poorer finish on the across-the-grain sides will show. If the seat is edged with four with-the-grain wood strips, the appearance of the finished chair will be greatly improved.

This same principle applies to other furniture pieces. If a table top has thick edges, the piece will look better if the edges are faced with wood strips, although, in such a case, the strips should be as thin as possible. Chair seat facings should be thick, so the upholstery will cover the line where the hardwood and softwood meet.

Chair Legs and Stretchers

If the entire length of a chair leg is round, the leg should be attached to the bottom of the seat, either with glue and a dowel, or with glue and a large hole drilled part way into the seat bottom to accept the chair leg. However, if there is a squared section at the top of a front leg, the leg is usually attached to the front corner of the seat, with its top even with the seat top. A small square is sawed out of the seat corner to make room for the leg, which usually protrudes a little from the seat edge on the front and side (figure 6–21).

If stretchers are to be used between round legs, leg areas where the stretchers will be attached are usually left square (figure 6–22). If the chair style is such that squared areas in the leg would be inappropriate, the stretchers should be thin, usually tapering at the ends, and should be inserted into holes drilled into the legs.

When gluing particularly troublesome stretchers, usually thin ones, in place, it is a help to cut them a little longer than needed and to enlarge the gluing surfaces by filing the ends to a slight taper. The stretchers are then pushed tightly into place and glued. The taper of the ends should not be so radical as to be obvious after a stretcher has been glued into place.

Cabinets, Dressers

The front edges of all cabinet-type furniture pieces should be mitered. The back of the cabinet, which will not show, can be sandwiched between the sides (figure 6–23).

If the wood being used is fairly thick, there will be no problem in gluing the pieces together along their edges. However, thin wood will need additional support to make the furniture sturdy enough to withstand future handling.

If the piece being made is a cabinet with a door and no drawers, the sides and back can be reinforced by gluing them to square posts located at the inside back corners, where they will not show. The same result can be gained by using thick wood for the back of the cabinet, thereby giving ample gluing surfaces for holding the sides in place.

If there are to be drawers instead of a door, the inside of the cabinet must not only be hollow, but also its sides should be lined with softwood where necessary so that the drawers cannot jam sideways as they slide in and out. Figure 6–24 shows the positioning of softwood pieces on each side of the cabinet.

If there are to be shelves instead of drawers, the shelves can be supported from below by thin wood sticks, stained and then glued to the inner walls of the cabinet. Such supports for shelves cannot be used, however, if there are to be drawers that will rest on the shelves; the supports will occupy space needed for the drawers. Instead, the shelves are measured and cut carefully so they will fit tightly, and are then glued to the cabinet walls.

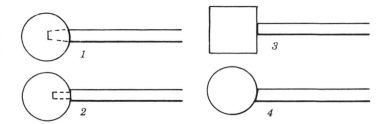

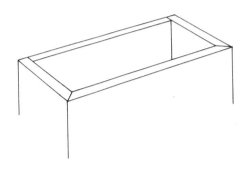

6-22. *Bird's-eye view of the chair leg with the attached stretcher.* (1) *The stretcher end is tapered and inserted into the drilled hole in the leg.* (2) *A dowel fastens the stretcher to the leg.* (3) *The stretcher is glued to the square section of the leg.* (4) *The stretcher end is filed to a taper and glued a little in front of the leg's center.*

6-23. *The back of the cabinet is sandwiched between the sides; the front corners are mitered.*

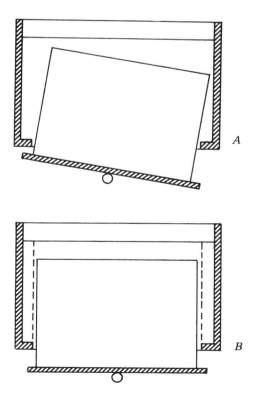

6-24. (A) *Without guides, the drawer is apt to twist when pulled out.* (B) *Wood strips inside the drawer space keep the drawers straight.*

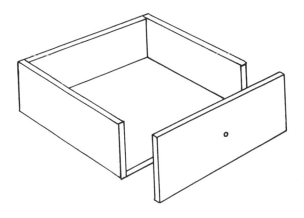

6-25. *A simple box drawer is easily made.*

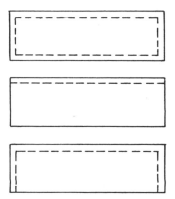

6-26. *The drawer faces can extend beyond the drawer on all four sides, on the top only, or on the top and sides.*

Drawers

Drawers are simple to make. Four pieces of wood (softwood, usually) are glued to make a frontless box (figure 6-25). Some purists dovetail the rear joints, an impressive but nonessential touch. The face is made of hardwood to match the furniture piece. Depending upon the design of the piece being copied, the face may be the same size as the drawer, a little larger all around, a little larger at the top only, or flush at the bottom and a little larger on the sides and top.

Holes for drawer pulls should be drilled before the face is glued into place. The faceless drawers should then be put into the cabinet and the faces glued on. In this way, the faces may not line up exactly with the drawers, but they will line up with the cabinet, which is the important thing.

Whether all the drawers in a piece of miniature furniture can be opened, whether only some can, or whether none can, is entirely between the craftsman and his conscience. The writer's feeling is that only a sinner would make a chest of drawers out of a solid piece of wood, and that only a saint could furnish a dozen or so miniature rooms without making at least one fake drawer. In between are all the craftsmen, including the writer, who feel that if most of the drawers in any miniature piece can be opened, it is a forgivable sin to cheat and use one or two nonopening drawers occasionally.

Corner Posts

So many chests and dressers have corner posts that a word should be added here about preparing them. As a rule, the posts extend below the cabinet to the floor and become the legs. Although most corner posts extend only slightly beyond the sides and front of a cabinet, they can be made flush with those surfaces, or they can be extended prominently beyond them.

Figure 6-27 shows small pieces sawed from the corners of the cabinet base to make room for the posts. The depth of these cuts, if they are needed at all, depends upon how far out the posts are to extend, and upon the thicknesses of the sides, the back, and the wood strip in front (above which a door, or drawers will later be added).

To clarify: if a 1/4-inch post is to extend beyond the cabinet surface by 1/16 inch, 3/16 inch of the post must be covered. In the unlikely event that 3/16-inch wood is used for the sides, the back, and the front wood strip, there would be no need to saw out the corners of the base at all; the post would extend the desired 1/16 inch. However, if 1/8-inch wood is used, the corners of the base would have to be cut to a depth of 1/16 inch, to total the needed 3/16.

When working with such small measurements, it is not a good idea to go by figures alone. As the work goes along, measuring the wood pieces against each other, as well as against the ruler, will provide greater accuracy.

Before assembling the cabinet, a top piece is cut that is large enough to cover the tops of the posts and extend a little beyond. The top and base are then glued to the sides and back, and to the front strip (or to both strips if there is one at the top.) The corner posts are then glued in place.

As mentioned earlier, corner posts usually extend to the floor to become legs. Where a cabinet is designed with only front posts and none at the back, tapered back legs are glued to the underside of the base, at the back corners.

Extending a Pedestal Table

Even in miniature houses, more guests are occasionally invited for dinner than can be seated at the dining table without extending it. A simple maneuver for the semi-purist, who wants his pedestal table to look as if it can be extended, is to saw the table top in half, then either glue it together again, or glue the halves, with the cut edges touching, onto the pedestal.

For the total purist, however, the table halves must really slide apart, and a leaf or two must be kept nearby for use at the next miniature party. Although sliding mechanisms vary with furniture manufacturers, the procedure for making one is not difficult. The diagrams in figure 6–28 can be followed, or the craftsman can lie face up under his dining table, as did the writer, and study it firsthand. Possibly a combination of the two will make the arrangement easier to duplicate.

First, the table top must be composed of two layers. The bottom layer, which must be at least 3/16-inch thick, is sawed in half. A rectangle is then cut out of each half (figure 6–28). Next, the top layer, which should be slightly larger and a great deal thinner than the bottom layer, is

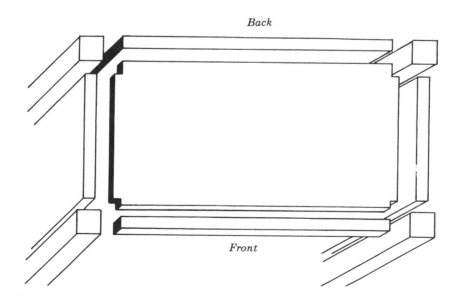

Back

Front

6-27. *The bottom of a cabinet with posts showing the arrangement of the parts.*

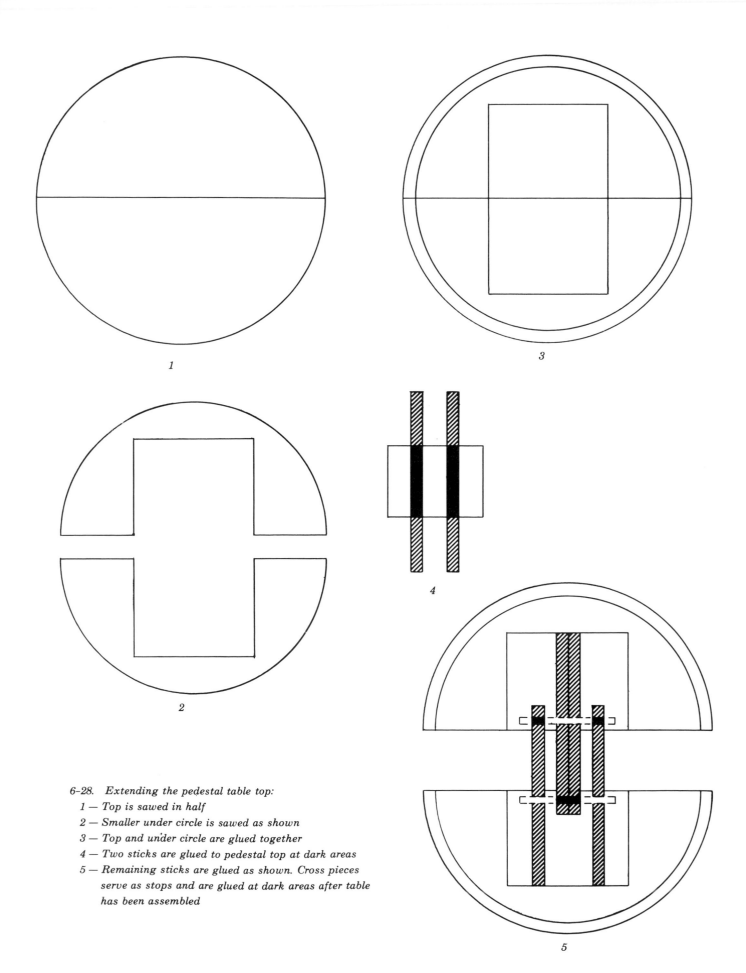

6-28.   *Extending the pedestal table top:*

1 — *Top is sawed in half*

2 — *Smaller under circle is sawed as shown*

3 — *Top and under circle are glued together*

4 — *Two sticks are glued to pedestal top at dark areas*

5 — *Remaining sticks are glued as shown. Cross pieces serve as stops and are glued at dark areas after table has been assembled*

sawed in half (carefully!). The bottom halves are then glued to the top halves. The sliding mechanism will fit into the rectangular, cut-out area on the underside of the table.

Before gluing the mechanism together, the table's pedestal must be completed. It should be at least 1/2-inch thick, preferably more, so that its top will afford a good, wide gluing surface.

The only supplies needed for making the mechanism are two flat toothpicks, a small piece of 1/32-inch plywood (or other thin wood), and a piece or two of square stick, 1/8-inch across and totaling about 18 inches in length. The wood stick can be found in most craft shops where small wood pieces are sold. If he prefers, the craftsman can saw his own stick, but the manufactured ones are inexpensive and, more important, accurately cut. The leftovers, if any, will come in handy for other purposes.

To start, a small rectangle of plywood, 7/8 by 3/4 inch, is glued to the top of the pedestal. If the pedestal is square, a straight edge of the plywood should line up with a side of the pedestal. Next, with the two halves of the table laid upside down and with their sawed edges touching, the length

of the rectangular cutout is measured. Six pieces of the square stick are cut to that length, preferably in a miter box, and sanded smooth.

The sticks are then glued to the table in pairs, a pair to each table half, and a third pair to the plywood piece on the pedestal (figure 6–29). The latter pair should be glued parallel to the shorter side of the plywood piece.

The short lengths of toothpicks serve as stops to prevent the table halves from separating completely when they are pulled apart. Although the stops have been laid in place for the illustration, they cannot be glued permanently in place until all the sticks have been glued on, and the table top has been put together and closed.

When gluing the stops in place, care must be taken to glue each to the ends of the proper two sticks, and to those sticks only. Even with the table closed, this is not difficult to do if small balls of epoxy putty are used as the adhesive.

With the table halves pulled apart as far as they will now go, the space between them is measured for a leaf. The leaf should be of the same thickness as the table's top layer, and finished to match.

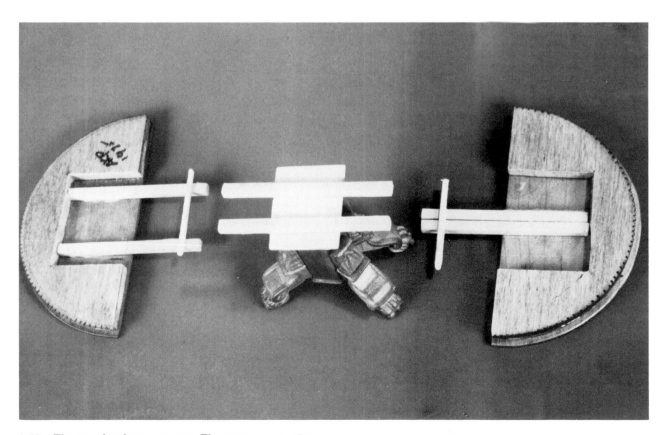

6–29. *The completed arrangement. The narrow cross pieces will not be glued on until after assembly.*

Cane Seats and Backs

The first and major problem to be faced when making a miniature chair with a "cane" seat and back is to find materials that can be substituted for miniature cane. This is not always easy to do, but they do exist, and with a little luck and persistence, can be found.

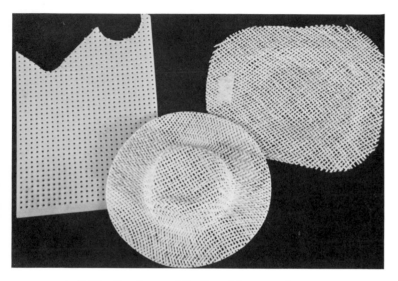

6-30. *Toy hats and Perfboard from a radio supply store furnish straw and cane for chair seats and backs.*

The plastic "straw" shown in figure 6-30 is sold in some dime stores in the shape of a toy Mexican hat, and in others as a farmer's hat. Pressed flat between newspapers with a warm iron, it can be used for chair seats and backs.

On one occasion, an old straw hat with an in-scale straw band was found in a Goodwill store. Unexplored sources are the doll clothing to be found in toy stores and, as a last resort, the usable straw toys taken from one's own children by force.

Two methods for using straw to make "cane" seats and backs, one legitimate and one not, are described here. The latter method is the easy one, since the chair seat and back are actually made of wood, cut to fit loosely into the chair's frames. The straw is laid over the wood pieces, bent down sharply along their edges, and glued to them. The straw edges are then trimmed back to the wood, and the finished pieces glued into the frames of the chair seat and back. Although this is an easy and neat way to do the work, the straw is backed

6-31. *The seats of the chairs to the left and right are backed with wood. The straw in the center chair has no backing.*

with wood and the seat would therefore be uncomfortable, and light cannot be seen through the straw, which prevents the chair from being a true copy of a full-size piece. This is a flaw detectable by only a few viewers.

The cane in the seat and back of a full-size chair is usually fastened to wood frames, which are then fastened into the chair's frames. In a miniature chair, however, space inside the frame of the seat is limited, and since the straw is stiff enough to be shaped to fit the seat and back areas, the extra frames can be omitted. In this method, the wood shapes that fit loosely into the chair's seat and back are cut as before. However, they will be used only as patterns this time, to be later discarded, so they may be made of heavy cardboard or scrap wood of any thickness.

Pieces of straw are then cut to the shapes of the pattern pieces, but a little larger all around. White glue should be applied to the edges of the cut straw to prevent the material from becoming unwoven as it is being worked. The straw pieces are then creased around the edges of the pattern pieces, removed from them, and creased even more sharply. White glue is next applied to the turned-down straw edges, and, when it has dried, the edges are cut off almost entirely. The straw seat and back, without any backing, are then glued into the chair's frames.

It is possible that some straws will be so soft that the above method of shaping will not work, but it has worked quite well for the few miniature straws with which the writer is familiar.

BENTWOOD FURNITURE

In the more than a century since bentwood furniture was first introduced into America and England from Austria, its styles have changed very little. The most popular bentwood pieces today are the rocking chair, with its many elaborate curves, and the cafe chair, with its small, round seat and simple, curved back. The latter is still one of America's most-used occasional chairs and is often seen not only in informal homes, but in public places as well.

Every craftsman who has made bentwood furniture in miniature has devised his own way of bending the material used, keeping it in position until dry, and fastening the pieces together. The writer is no exception. The method described here was used to make the chairs shown in figure 6-43.

Materials

Any type of round or slightly flattened basket reed can be used for making miniature bentwood pieces, as long as its diameter conforms closely to scale. If such reed cannot be found in a craft shop or one that specializes in weaving materials, it is suggested that the craftsman buy an inexpensive basket that has been woven with usable reed, and take it apart. The reed can be straightened by soaking it in water.

Basket reed has one drawback: it has very fine hairs along its surface, and these tend to stick out when the reed is bent. The reed can be sanded after it has been bent to shape and the pieces are ready to be glued together, but it is possible that another material, such as wicker, would be preferable. If the reader has access to a source of weaving materials, it is suggested that he experiment with whatever is available and offers possibilities.

Most bentwood chairs have cane seats, and electronic supply shops can furnish a convincing substitute for the material in the form of "prepunched Perfboards." The boards are an excellent material, not only for cane seats, but for other miniature pieces as well.

Perfboards can be cut easily with a jigsaw. To make the slight curve in the seat, which many rocking chair seats have, the sawed piece can be dropped into boiling water, lifted with tweezers, and bent while it is hot. The process can be repeated until the desired curve has been made.

6-32. A basket can be taken apart to furnish reed for bentwood furniture.

123

Drawing Patterns

Cafe Chair

Since the cafe chair is so simple in design, drawing a pattern for it presents no problem at all. Only a back-view pattern need be drawn. This will establish the desired height and width of the chair, the curves and lengths of the back legs, which are in one piece with the outer curve of the back, and the inner curved piece of the back. Only the length of the front legs needs to be established on the pattern. Although some bentwood cafe chairs have straight legs, while others are curved, the curves are so slight they can be made by either of the methods described farther along, without the use of a pattern.

6-33. Only the back view of the cafe chair need be drawn.

Rocker Pattern

In contrast to the simple pattern for a cafe chair, it is chancy to plan a whole, elaborate rocker in advance. The exact shape of each new reed piece in a bentwood rocker depends upon the shape taken by the one just finished. The work is therefore easier if the rocker is built a few pieces at a time, with the craftsman and his plans remaining as flexible as the material he is using. It would therefore be a waste of effort to draw a pattern for the whole chair at one time. Too many adjustments would have to be made as the individual pieces were curved and glued together. Instead, only a side view of the chair need be drawn. This drawing can then be used as a reference for shaping each curve individually.

Curving the Reed

Since basket reed varies in thickness, only those pieces should be selected for use that are of about the same diameter. The reed is then soaked in water overnight. The next day it is shaped and held in place until dry by using one of the two following methods:

If a two-dimensional curve is needed (as in the back of a cafe chair, which curves upward and back down to the seat, and at the same time curves from back to front to conform to the shape of the sitter's back), a rather stiff wire is coiled around the wet reed. The reed is then shaped as desired, and when it has dried, the wire is removed. When using this method, care must be taken not to wrap the wire so tightly that it will leave marks on the wet reed.

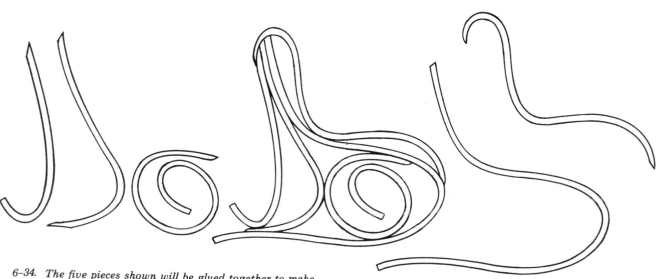

6-34. The five pieces shown will be glued together to make a side of the rocker.

The second method, used for any flat piece, such as a side of a rocking chair, is to press the wet reed into a rolled-out layer of Polyform, or any putty-like material that will not air dry. Patterns for the desired curves are first made by using carbon paper and a softly pointed instrument, such as a ballpoint pen, to transfer the curves from the drawn pattern to a piece of cardboard. These curves are next cut out with scissors. Only the curved edges are important; the rest of the cardboard pieces can be of any shape.

Each cardboard piece is then laid flat on the clay, and its edge is pressed down into the material so that the desired curve shows clearly. Starting at one end, a length of wet reed is then fed, slowly and carefully, into the surface of the clay, following the pressed-in pattern line. Where there is a tendency for the reed to straighten out, particularly at the ends, the clay should be pushed up and around it as much as necessary to hold it firmly.

If the reed ends will not stay in position one of two other methods can be used. If the pattern will allow it, a reed piece is cut an inch or so longer at each end than the pattern indicates. When the curved reed has dried, these ends are cut off and discarded. The second method is to handle an end that is curved in a tight spiral that the clay will not hold. The spiral is coiled with wire and shaped, as described previously. The wired end and the rest of the reed piece is then pushed into the clay and left to dry.

6-36. *Shaped back of the cafe chair.*

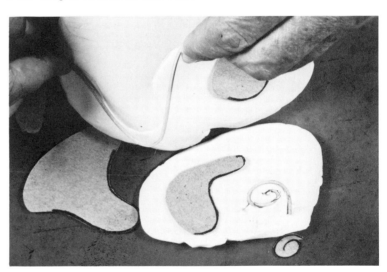

6-37. *Cardboard patterns, with the edges darkened to show the desired curves, are pressed into Polyform.*

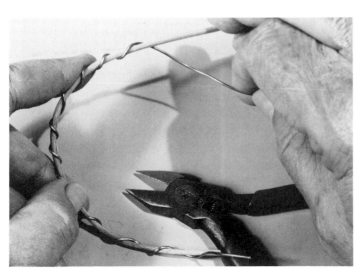

6-35. *Wrapping reed with wire preparatory to shaping.*

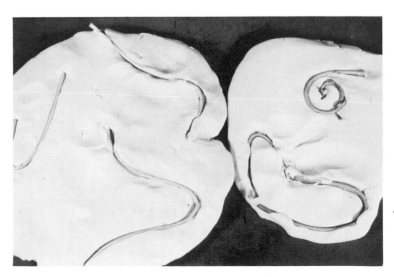

6-38. *Following the pressed-in lines, the wet reed is pushed into Polyform.*

125

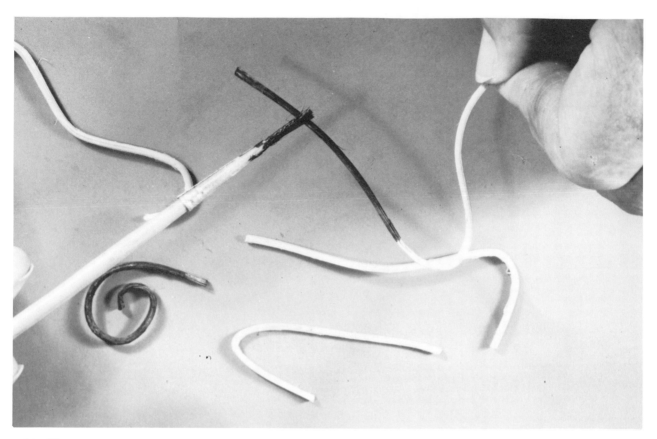

6-39. *The curved reed pieces are painted.*

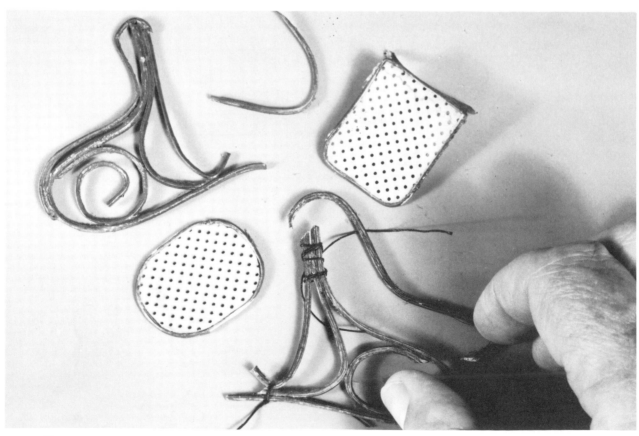

6-40. *Gluing the chair together.*

Making Cane Seats and Backs

The cane seats of most bentwood cafe chairs are round, or nearly so, while the seats and backs of most rockers are rectangular, with rounded corners. Pencil lines of the shapes wanted can be drawn directly on the Perfboard, or on the other material being used as cane, and sawed out.

Both the seat and back should be edged with curved reed. Since the reed used for the chair will be too thick to use as edging, the wet reed is sliced in two lengthwise with a razorblade or sharp knife. The sliced reed, while still wet, is then shaped around the seat or back edge and held in place with rubber bands. When it has dried, it can be sanded and painted, then glued permanently in place. (Warning: The reed must be painted before it is glued around the seat or back. The writer once made the mistake of reversing that order, and had to apply the paint later with a fine brush and take painful care to avoid smearing the seat.)

Sanding and Painting

When all the pieces for a bentwood chair have been shaped, dried, and trimmed to length, they are sanded smooth, then painted. Unfortunately, wood stain will not penetrate reed, so it is necessary to use a wood-colored, opaque paint. Later, when the chair has been glued together, a light, finishing coat of varnish or Krylon can be applied if desired.

Assembling the Chairs

Gluing

Any all-purpose adhesive can be used to glue the shaped reed pieces together. However, with so many joints to be glued, Scotch Super Strength, with its instant-hold quality, is probably the best choice.

The flexibility and light weight of reed, although disadvantageous in some ways, allow the craftsman to alter the shapes of curved pieces during the gluing. If two pieces do not meet exactly at a joint as planned, they can be pulled together and glued, and the joint can be wrapped with thread to hold it until the glue dries. If the joint is so located that it cannot be tied, a small spring-type paper clip or other clamp will hold it, although care must be taken that the holding device does not mar the reed.

Assembling the Rocking Chair

The two matching sides of the rocker are first assembled by gluing the curved reed pieces together. If there are places in the pattern where one reed piece overlaps another, the end of the overlapping piece should be tapered with a file or sandpaper (figure 6–42).

Next, one of the completed sides is laid flat and the seat and back, standing up at right angles, are glued to it. The second side is then laid flat, and the glued section is turned over and glued to it.

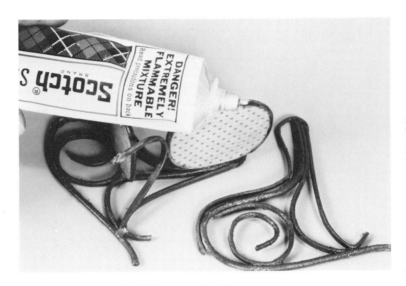

6-41. *The back is glued between the sides.*

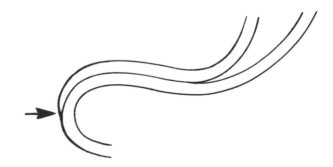

6-42. *The end of top piece is tapered where the two reed pieces join.*

With the body of the chair assembled, it is not difficult to measure, shape, and glue into place the small, finishing pieces, such as the stretchers, the arched pieces that are fitted below the back and seat of some chairs, and any other parts showing in the model being copied.

Assembling the Cafe Chair

The cafe chair is much simpler to make than the rocking chair. The front legs are usually curved slightly, and the back legs and the outside curved back section are in one piece. This latter piece, and the inner curved section of the back, are wired and given matching two-dimensional curves as described previously.

Since shaped reed is very light and easy to glue, the front legs need only be glued directly to the underside of the seat; it is not necessary to use the supports or dowels required if the chair were made of wood. The two back pieces are glued to each other at the top and to the seat edge below.

Miniature bentwood cafe chairs, while strong, are so light in weight that they tend to tip over easily. It is therefore recommended that they be fastened lightly to the floor with tiny dabs of rubber cement.

LATTICE WORK

The following is a simple way to make perfectly even lattice work for a trellis, baby gate, fence, or trim for a house foundation. Because of the ease with which it can be cut, balsa wood is recommended, particularly since nearly all lattice work is painted, and the material used will not show.

First, a pattern is drawn. The outer edges and angled, crossed lines of the lattice are drawn with a ruler on graph paper proper for the craftsman's scale. Careful attention should be paid to the graph-paper lines, so the angled lines cross each other at the same point horizontally all the way across the lattice.

Next, narrow strips of 1/32-inch balsa are cut with scissors, razorblade, or sharp knife. The

6-43. *Completed bentwood chairs.*

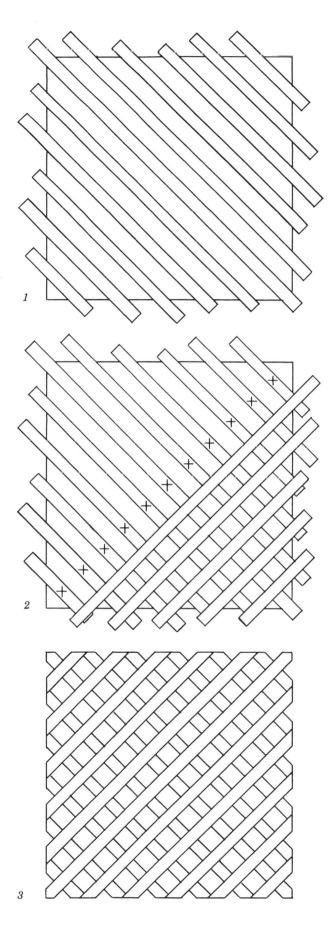

strips needn't be of the same length, but they should be at least one inch longer than the length needed for the lattice.

White glue, or other adhesive, is applied to both ends of one of the strips, which is then laid on the pattern so that it covers an angled line. The ends are pressed to the paper and glued in place outside the drawn lattice area. The strip itself, inside the area, is not glued down.

The above system is continued until all of the lines angled in one direction are covered. The first strip to go in the other direction is then fastened in place by putting small dabs of white glue on the lower strips in an angled line, and pressing the top strip down firmly (figure 6-44). Following the pattern lines drawn on the graph paper, the rest of the cross strips are glued in the same manner until the lattice is completed. It is then removed from the paper by using scissors to cut along the border lines, leaving the lattice piece free and the glued tips of the under layer of strips still adhering to the discarded paper.

To make the finished piece more realistic, tiny dots, representing pins or nails, should be pressed into the wood at each cross point with a sharp pencil point.

6-44. *Making latticework:*
  1 — Ends of balsa strips are glued to graph paper
  2 — Cross strips are glued at each cross point
  3 — Ends, attached to paper, are trimmed away leaving completed lattice.

7.

Cloth, Glass and Metals

WORKING WITH CLOTH

Finding Materials

When upholstering, and when making miniature curtains, draperies, bedspreads, and tablecloths, the first step—finding just the right fabric with which to work—is by no means the easiest.

One feature that catches the eye in many dollhouses is the quality and treatment of the cloth that is used. The material of some curtains is thick and stiff, bedspreads and tablecloths stand out at the corners, and draperies do not drape. Yet, the dollhouse tradition goes back so many years that even flaws have a nostalgic charm that might be lessened if too much importance were placed on realism. Rooms reproduced in miniature, on the other hand, should be made to look as real as possible. Finding and handling the fabrics that are used in them is an important part of that reality.

The weave and thickness of the material used in miniature rooms is most important. Although to count the number of threads in an inch to make sure the cloth being considered conforms to scale would be overzealous, the rooms should *look* as if that has been done. Even more important, the print or pattern of the material must also conform to scale.

To find fabrics of the correct weight, weave, and pattern is not easy to do, especially when a fourth criteria—color—is added to the list. Since color has no scale, however, and since it can be changed by dye, it should be considered last.

Suitable materials are so difficult to find that the craftsman should not wait until a particular piece is needed before a search is made for it. In addition to the more obvious places, such as yard goods and drapery departments, usable pieces may sometimes be found in attic trunks, in boxes stored on closet shelves, in antique and junk shops, and at garage sales. Such places will sometimes offer old clothing—yellowed silk or cotton, or fine old velvet dresses, worn and split in places—items of the sort that cause casual shoppers to pause and wonder who would buy such things. Makers of miniatures would, and happily!

Old materials are more valuable than new for more than one reason. Not only do the faded colors complement the furniture in a way that new materials cannot, but old cloth is likely to be fine and sheer. There are exceptions, of course, but the writer has yet to find new lace, lace edgings, or velvet ribbon anywhere today that is as thin and delicate as pieces bought, even in dime stores, many years ago.

Softening and Coloring Materials

When new material is used, and if it is washable, it can sometimes be softened and the filler removed by boiling it in soapy water for a while. If, after drying, the material still feels stiff, the process should be repeated once or twice in the hope that the stiffness is caused by filler, which must eventually wash away.

It is easy to change the color of small pieces of fabric, but since one color is nearly always present at the start, changing it to another of the exact shade desired can be difficult. Colors that are too bright can be toned down with coffee or tea;

the same liquids will turn glaring white to beige, ecru, or eggshell. Fabric dyes can be used, of course, but almost any liquid, such as inks, food colors, and vegetable juices can be used to obtain something approximating the desired colors.

Since there are so many unknowns when working with already dyed cloth, the only possible way to find a usable color is to make tests on scraps of cloth, and always to wait until the material has dried before making judgments.

Stiffening Cloth

It seems strange, after having worked so hard to remove the stiffener from the fabric being used, to have to stiffen it again. However, this is usually the case. For example, the craftsman is about to make draperies from a sheer red jersey blouse. When he holds the blouse up, the material drapes beautifully, falling straight down from his hands like a fiery waterfall. Then he cuts a three-inch square from it, and what happens? The law of gravity has ceased to function, and the little piece of fabric, balanced on a finger, stands out as stiffly as if it were made of cardboard.

Although small pieces of cloth, no matter how thin and soft, refuse to obey nature's laws, they can be made to look as if they do. The folds and draped lines that appear naturally in full-size curtains when they are hung can be reconstructed in miniature by first stiffening the material so that it has something of the quality of thin paper. Gathers and creases can then be pressed in with the fingers. Those that tend not to stay in place can be encouraged to do so by the judicious use of small dabs of adhesive where necessary.

Of the materials that can be used to stiffen cloth, the most widely used is probably white glue diluted with water. Many of the commercial stiffeners sold in hobby shops are apt to be that same mixture, bottled and given a brand name. Some craftsmen stiffen their fabrics with ironing aids such as spray starches and fabric finishes.

The writer's preference is a plastic-type spray such as Krylon No. 1311 or Deft. These materials do not thicken the cloth noticeably, nor do they tend to fill the spaces between threads, as white glue sometimes does.

Since Krylon is transparent, it can be sprayed heavily on both sides of the material, which is then smoothed on a flat surface and allowed to dry. After pleats have been creased into the material, a second spraying, if needed for any reason, can be given without flattening out the work already done. This cannot be done with a water-soluble stiffener.

Instructions are sometimes given for pinning pleats or fixing gathers in cloth while it is still wet with a stiffener. For large pieces of cloth, this method works, but for small pieces it does not, or at least it has not for the writer. Since the stiffener becomes effective only after it has dried, cloth that is wet with it behaves no differently than cloth that is wet with water, and small pieces of wet cloth are hard to pleat and drape.

Unfortunately, it is not possible to have miniature curtains and other fabric accessories that both look and feel soft. The more naturally they hang, the likelier they are to feel like boards to the touch. In miniature rooms, however, appearance is the important thing, and visitors who must finger the contents—and loosen chandeliers in the process—deserve to be disappointed with what they find.

A useful tip that will speed the work of handling cloth and adhesives, and will help to keep the material clean: A board, about 12 x 10 inches, or large enough to provide a working area, is covered with Saran Wrap. The edges are brought to the underside of the board and secured with adhesive tape. Materials, wet with stiffeners and adhesives, will not stick to the Saran Wrap as they dry or are being worked. In addition, if a small wad of Saran Wrap is used, instead of the fingers, to press glued pieces flat, and if the wad is turned frequently to a clean area, the adhesive will not smear on the material as it frequently does when the fingers are used.

Curtains and Draperies
Hemming and Gathering

When making miniature curtains, or when working with cloth for any purpose, it is best to do as little sewing as possible. Machine stitching is too stiff, and hand stitching cannot possibly be fine enough to be in scale. Hems, where they are necessary, should be pressed into the stiffened material with the fingers, then glued flat with the smallest possible amount of either white glue or Duco Cement. On semitransparent material, it is important that the width of the hems be in scale. One too often sees miniature hems that, if full-size, would be as much as six inches deep, and this small detail helps to detract from the credibility of the whole room.

7-1. *A variety of curtain styles for miniature windows: (1) Priscilla, (2) cafe, (3) tier, (4) panel, (5) cottage.*

If the material used is fairly heavy, it is sometimes possible to omit hems altogether. This is especially true if there is a print with a border that can be used on the inside and bottom edges of curtains or draperies, or if the material is very rough or nubby. It is the craftsman's decision to make in each case, but where hems can be omitted, the material can be pleated or draped more easily. The stiffener, by the way, will prevent unhemmed edges from raveling.

One exception to the general rule of not sewing curtains: Where gathering is needed, it is usually necessary to use a needle and the finest thread possible. Even though the stitches will not show after the material has been gathered to fit the length of the curtain rod, they should be made as short as possible so that the gathers will be in scale.

The width of a curtain or a drapery panel depends upon the material used and how it is to be styled. A fine net panel that is to be gathered and will cover half the window should be about 1 3/4 times the width of the area it is to cover, and an inch or so longer. Heavier drapery material can either be cut in panels that will not be gathered at all, or, if they are to be gathered, in pieces only slightly larger than the door or window openings. Just a suggestion of fullness can be worked into the material by gathering it with needle and thread. If fuller draperies are desired, the craftsman should first make sure the material used can be stiffened and made to hang realistically. This is not easy to do with such materials as velvet and brocades, even if thin.

To make a typical sheer curtain, either to hang at the window or to be stretched between two rods on a door, the side hems are first creased in the stiffened material, then glued flat. The top edge is folded back and creased, and a tiny running stitch is sewed about 1/12 inch below the crease to make a heading. If a heading is not wanted, the stitching should be on the crease, through a single layer of the material. In either case, enough material should be left below the stitching line to go around the rod. The material is then gathered to fit the length of the rod, and the thread end is secured by whipping. When gathering the fabric, if the curtain is to go around the corners of the rods to the walls, allowance should be made for the extra width needed.

With the rod temporarily in place above the window, the curtain is next measured against it to determine the needed length, including an allowance for a hem, to the sill or floor. The material is then trimmed and a hem glued in.

Whether soft folds or sharp pleats are desired, stiffened materials can usually be shaped without the use of pins or other holding aids. Whether or not such aids are used, miniature pleats or gathers tend to spread apart and to fan out when the curtains have been hung. If the spread is only slight, it can be ignored, since full-size curtains do the same thing. However, if the spread is too wide to look natural, it can be controlled with the judicious use of very small amounts of white glue or Duco Cement. Since gathers and pleats should hang straight but should not appear to be flat, the adhesive should be used only to tack the inner, back edges together, leaving the front edges free.

If curtains and draperies still do not hang closely enough to window frames and sills, small balls of epoxy putty or other claylike material can be used to hold them in place.

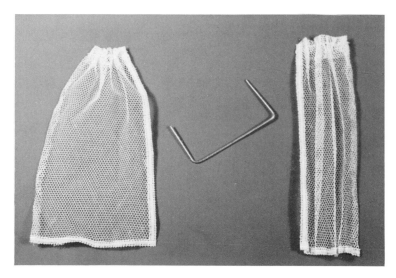

7-2. Unstiffened curtain (left) can be stiffened and shaped into natural folds.

Attaching Curtains to Rods

At best, attaching miniature curtains realistically to a rod is a delicate, and sometimes exasperating, operation. Following are three methods that have worked for the writer, although the craftsman may find a fourth or fifth that works as well or better. They can be used to hang any style of curtain.

The first, and probably the easiest, method is to use an adhesive putty to fasten the curtain to the rod. A very thin roll of the putty is pressed against the front of the rod, and the curtain is pressed against the adhesive. With this method, the curtain does not go over the rod, so the extra material that was left for the purpose can be trimmed off.

If the curtain material is sheer, a white putty, such as Holdit, sold for hanging posters and holding shelf paper, should be used. For heavier, opaque material, epoxy putty is preferred because its hold is stronger.

The second method of attaching curtains to the rod consists of making a second row of stitches below the first, leaving a tube into which the rod is slipped. The stitches must be very short and close together so they will barely show.

The third method is to omit the bottom row of stitches, but to give much the same effect by pulling the short piece of material, left under the heading in back of the curtain, over the rod and gluing it to the rod. Its edge is then glued to the curtain just under the rod (figure 7–3).

Bedspreads and Tablecloths

Once the right fabric for a bedspread or tablecloth has been found, the material needs only to be sprayed heavily with Krylon or similar stiffener, the hems turned up and glued flat, and the piece laid in place on the bed or table. The final step is to fold the corners so the material hangs realistically, or, if the table is round, to shape ripples all around, and to crease the cloth at the table edge so the overhang will be almost vertical. As with curtains, a cloth can be held in place at trouble spots with an adhesive such as white glue or Duco Cement, or with tiny balls of epoxy putty.

In-scale prints, suitable for spreads and tablecloths, are hard to find; even when they are found, the designs are often poorly suited to the purpose. Flowers in calico prints, for example, are usually small enough for the one-inch scale, but in other respects, the typical calico pattern does not look right when used for a tablecloth or spread.

One good source for in-scale prints is a patchwork-printed fabric. The patterns in the individual squares are quite small, and squares that are large enough can be used to cover beds and tables. Many such squares have their own borders, which makes them even more desirable as miniature covers.

A thin, worn washcloth, heavily sprayed with a stiffener and flattened with a hot iron makes a convincing candlewick spread, as well as a bath

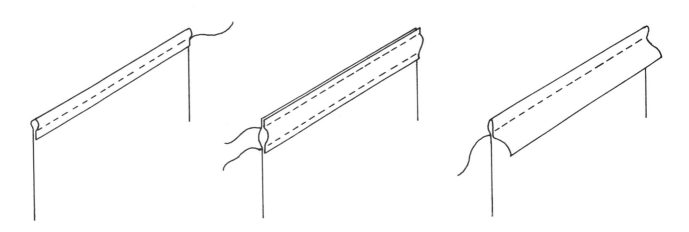

7–3. *Three ways to prepare the tops of curtains for the rods.*

mat or towels. Sheer linen handkerchiefs make excellent dining tablecloths, sheets, and pillow cases.

Purists are advised not to read the rest of this section. All others may find the following idea useful: paper products can be used, not only for tablecloths and spreads, but for curtains as well. Many paper napkins and towels have interesting, fine textures that can be Krylon-sprayed and, if flattening is needed, pressed with an iron. Stiffened Kleenex can be used for curtains if fabric that is thin enough cannot be found.

In the writer's opinion, the only requirement for the materials used for miniature tablecloths, bedspreads, blankets, and so on, is that they look real. Bedspreads and blankets edged with lace are for dollhouses; fringed or hemmed bedspreads and blankets edged with matching bands are for miniature rooms.

When putting a tablecloth or spread in place on the furniture, the overhang should be lightly creased at the edge so that it will fold down and hang almost vertically. A flare to the material is permissible, but it should be very slight. If the overhang tends to flare out more than is wanted, a few dabs of rubber cement or glue, or a few tiny balls of epoxy putty along the furniture edge will hold it in place.

With the cloth piece shaped along the edges, the corners are next folded down and creased. The extra material can be shaped in either of the ways shown in figure 7–5 and held in place with an adhesive.

Making a Crazy Quilt

A crazy quilt is one accessory that appeals to nearly everyone. It also goes well with a wide variety of bedroom styles, and can be used in rooms of periods separated by hundreds of years.

Many dollhouse quilts have been made by sewing colorful fabric squares together in the style of full-size patchwork quilts, but again, the ever-present problem of scale arises. Even if the patches of material are in scale, the stitching and thickness caused by the doubling of cloth at the seams makes the finished quilt seem too puffy and stiff for a miniature bed. In the following method for making a quilt, no stitching is needed and no folds are made in the material. The result is most convincing.

To start, the Saran-wrapped board mentioned earlier is almost a must for the work ahead, as are a few wads of Saran Wrap for pressing the glued pieces in place. Also needed are a small bowl of white glue, thinned slightly with water, and a stiff brush, the tin-handled kind that often comes with a jar of paste. There should also be on hand a good selection of fabric scraps, both plain and printed. The prints should be as small as possible.

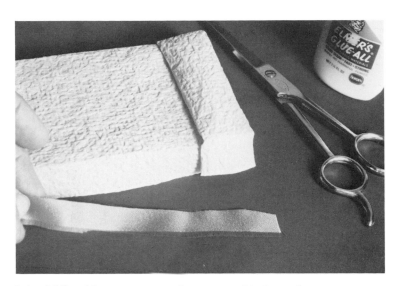

7-4. *Adding fringe to a textured paper-towel bedspread.*

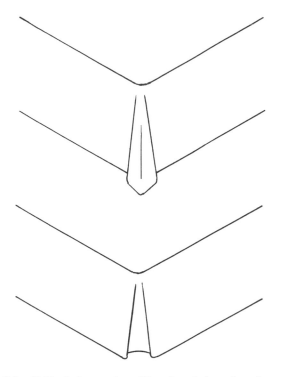

7-5. *Tablecloths can be stiffened and shaped at the corners.*

135

7-6. *Making a crazy quilt. The background material is taped to a Saran-wrapped board.*

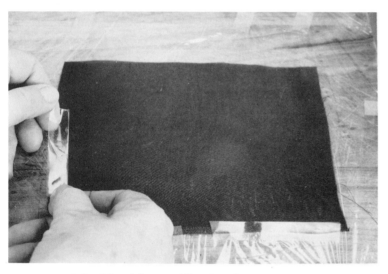

7-7. *Materials are stiffened with Krylon.*

7-8. *Bits of material are glued to the background.*

The scraps of material should first be stiffened with Krylon, then cut into small squares, rectangles, and odd-shaped triangles. Again, the scale should be strictly adhered to. Since full-size quilt pieces are usually no more than six inches on a side, and often less, no miniature piece to the one-inch scale should be larger than a half inch on a side, and a good number of smaller pieces will make the quilt even more convincing. These small cut pieces are laid aside, with each print pattern and each solid color being kept in a separate pile.

A piece of background material is next cut at least a half-inch larger all around than the finished quilt is to be. Recommended is a thin rayon or synthetic lining material of a not-too-bright color, such as navy, gray, brown, or off-white. The background material will show here and there, and will set the color tone of the whole quilt.

The background piece is next sprayed generously with Krylon or other stiffener, dried, and Scotch-taped along the edges to the Saran-covered board. The outer edge of the background piece will later be trimmed away, so the taping should be confined to that area.

The small cut pieces of cloth are now glued to the background by brushing them with the glue and pressing them into place. It is easier to end with an attractive balance of colors and prints if the fabric pieces are scattered evenly one group at a time over the surface. A little water should be added from time to time to the glue in the bowl to keep it from becoming too thick.

As the work goes on, the empty spaces between the color patches will become smaller and smaller, until there are only a few left. These last spaces should be filled with small fabric pieces cut especially to fit as needed. The craftsman will find that complete accuracy is not necessary when making this patchwork quilt. Tiny areas of the background material showing along the edges of some of the patches add to the effectiveness of the whole.

When all but the outer edge of the background piece is completely covered with small fabric patches, the quilt is taken from the board and trimmed to the desired size. A border is then added by gluing lengths of hemming tape of a matching or harmonizing color to the underside of the quilt, leaving about 1/16 to 1/8 inch of the tape showing along the edges.

As a finishing touch, tiny stitches along the edges of some of the patches can be marked with a fine brush or ballpoint pen. The ink will not run, since the sprayed-on stiffener has made the material nonabsorbent. Gluing tiny cutout flowers and leaves on some of the plain patches will also add to the attractiveness of the quilt.

Since the glue will have stiffened the cloth, the quilt will be more convincing if it is used on a miniature bed with a foot and headboard, so that only the side edges will need to be folded down and creased. It is difficult to drape the quilt at the corners.

7-9. Edges are trimmed.

7-10. A border is added.

7-11. The finished quilt appears to have been sewed.

UPHOLSTERING

The upholstering methods described here are those that have been worked out and used by the writer. They are not rules, by any means, and if the craftsman can think of a better or easier way to do the work, he should certainly try it out.

Basically, the upholstering of miniature furniture consists of gluing the edges of fabric pieces around the edges of backing pieces, which are then glued to the furniture. The backing can be made of paper, cardboard, or thin wood, as discussed farther along. It sounds fairly simple, and it is, with one exception: the gluing can be difficult.

Gluing

While gluing upholstery, accidental spotting of the fabric with adhesive is difficult to avoid. Since it is almost impossible to wipe any adhesive from most fabrics without leaving a stain, glue must be used with great care if the work is to be a success.

That only the edges of the fabric are glued around the backing pieces is of great help in keeping the work clean. If the adhesive penetrates the cloth in places and comes through to the right side, it will at least be on the under edges where it will not show.

Three precautions that can be taken to minimize the chances of spotting are:

1. An adhesive with body should be chosen. Although white glue is the popular material for doing miniature upholstering, the writer prefers Duco Cement, because it not only takes hold more quickly, but also it is thicker and is less likely to soak into the cloth.

2. Some fabrics spot more easily than others. Satin and velvet, for example, are more difficult to work with than are fairly hard-surfaced materials, such as some wool, cotton, and synthetic fabrics.

3. It seems elementary to mention that the hands should be kept clean, but when work is in progress, it is sometimes hard to stop often and clean the fingers before going on to the next step. Wiping is not enough; if white glue is being used, the fingers should be cleaned with water; acetone will remove all traces of Duco Cement.

Spraying fabric with Krylon or a similar material before cutting it will help to prevent an adhesive from penetrating the cloth too deeply, but it also stiffens the fabric and reduces its stretchiness. For simple, flat chair seats, this does not matter, but for more elaborate upholstered furniture, it may.

Backing

In addition to keeping the work clean, using a backing for pillows makes it easier to shape fabric sections accurately, no matter how elaborate the pattern, and to keep them from stretching out of shape as they are being worked on. Turning fabric edges around a backing is much easier work than making and gluing a hem.

The stiffer the backing, the simpler it is to cover with fabric. Therefore, when the area to be upholstered is perfectly flat, 1/32- or 1/64-inch plywood should be used. If the area has a slight curve in it, such as the gentle upward slope at the head of a couch, cardboard can be used. If the fabric must be curved deeply, as in the arms of the Sears, Roebuck sofa in figure 7-13, a heavy paper can be used.

The backing piece should be cut a little smaller than the area to be upholstered so room is left for the fabric edges to be glued around it. Obviously, the thicker the fabric, the more the space that must be left for it.

Time will be saved if, for all but the simplest straight-edged areas, paper patterns are first made for the backing pieces. This can sometimes be done by measuring with a ruler, but for more elaborate sections, patterns must be cut on a trial-and-error basis.

Padding

There are two basic types of padding that can be used for miniature furniture—hard or soft. The choice of the craftsman depends upon which is more important to him, reality or the convincing appearance of it.

A miniature chair with a soft, smoothly rounded seat that gives at the touch of a finger can, if made carefully, be a perfect reproduction of a full-sized chair. On the other hand, if the small chair looks well used, as if someone had just walked away from it after having enjoyed a good rest, should it matter if the obviously comfortable seat feels hard to the touch?

The craftsman who answers "Yes" should pad his chairs in the conventional way, using sheets of cotton, facial tissue, or other soft materials. A pair of foam rubber innersoles from the dime store will furnish enough padding material for many miniature chairs. Those to whom the comfortable look of age ranks first can shape their cushions realistically, using Polyform or any other claylike material.

Whatever padding is chosen should be used sparingly. If there are to be separate cushions, most should be a little thicker at their centers than around their edges. The exceptions to this are "saddle seats," which are used on some styles of chairs. As the name implies, saddle seats are a little higher along the edges than in the centers.

The padding should be attached to the backing piece with a few dabs of any adhesive to keep it from slipping until the upholstery fabric holds it in place permanently. If Polyform or a similar clay material is used for the padding, it should be molded on a stiff backing piece. Any desired shape can be formed, including asymmetrical

7-12. *Backing pieces are cut for The Chair's pillows.*

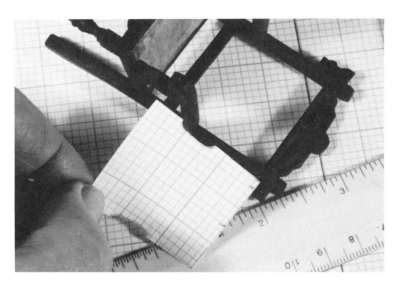

7-14. *Paper patterns for pillows make work easier.*

7-13. *Heavy paper was used as a backing in the curved arms of the sofa.*

7-15. *The Polyform-padded pillows of the chair are ready for the covering of old velvet.*

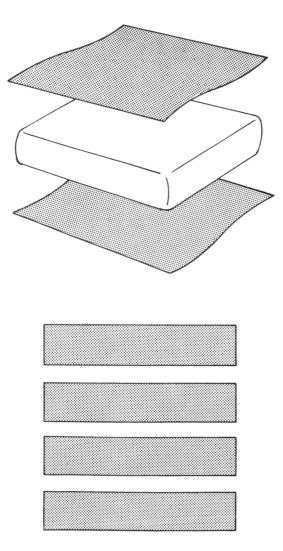

pillows, such as those sometimes used on Victorian sofas, or seats with cut-out spaces for the arms.

If air-drying clay is used for the padding, it should be left to dry according to the manufacturer's instructions. Polyform, along with the backing piece on which it rests, is baked in a 300-degree oven for about 25 minutes. After baking, if the clay padding does not adhere to the backing, it can be glued in place.

A third useful material for making some padded cushions is balsa wood, which can be cut with a jigsaw and quickly sanded to shape. The wood is excellent for fairly thick pillows with softly rounded corners and edges, but it is less desirable for those with more intricate shapes. Balsa pillows do not need a backing piece.

Adding Upholstery Fabric

Upholstery fabric should be added to the furniture in sections that correspond to seams or corded lines in the full-size piece being reproduced. For example, a boxy cushion should be made of a top square or rectangular piece, a matching section for the bottom, if the cushion is to be loose, and either four short strips for the sides, or one long piece that will go all around.

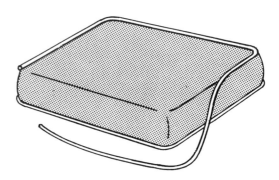

7-16. *Covering a boxy pillow in sections that correspond to seam lines.*

Even if a single piece of fabric can be handled in such a way as to cover neatly two or more furniture sections, for realism the cloth should still be cut into pieces to correspond to the full-size upholstering, and the pieces backed and glued on separately.

The upholstery fabric is first cut to shape, using the backing piece as a pattern but leaving a wider-than-needed margin around the edges. Fabric can always be trimmed later; it cannot be added to. The fabric piece, with its wrong side facing up, is then laid on a flat surface, and the backing piece, with the padding underneath, is laid on the fabric. Care should be taken to center the fabric pattern, if used, and to ensure that the weave of the cloth runs parallel to one side of the backing piece.

One edge of the fabric is next trimmed to within about 3/8 to 1/2 inch of the backing piece, pulled up tightly around the backing, and glued in place almost to the corner. The opposite edge is then trimmed and glued in the same way, and the other two opposing sides trimmed and glued next. Last, the corners are trimmed and slashed, pulled smoothly around the backing edges, and glued.

If a backing piece is round, or of any irregular shape, the fabric edges should be slashed where necessary, and the corners of the slashed edges trimmed off at an angle (figure 7–18). The material is then pulled over the edge and glued to the backing all around.

If the pillow is padded with Polyform, and if the fabric material is heavy enough so the adhesive will not soak through, it is usually easier to cover the whole surface of the padding with adhesive and glue the fabric to it. It is then not necessary to pull and glue the fabric edges to the underside; the material can be trimmed almost to the edge of the backing and be pressed under with the fingers. Treated in this way, the pillow is quite flat on the bottom and can be glued more easily to the furniture.

If a chair is to be fully upholstered with no wood showing, the above method of covering backing pieces with fabric can still be followed. The furniture is still covered in separate sections, which correspond to those on the full-size piece, and the backing pieces are padded as necessary to follow the padded areas of the model.

If made accurately, a chair back can consist of an open wood frame, and of a separate pillow of the correct thickness, flat on one side, padded on the other, and upholstered on both sides. The pillow must be made to fit the opening in the chair back as exactly as possible. It is then glued in the frame. Any small spaces that may show along the edges can be concealed with cording.

The advantage of the above chair-back treatment is that the pillow can be made as thin as desired. For certain chair styles, a solid wood back, covered by a padded pillow in front, and a backed and hemmed fabric piece on the back can sometimes make the total thickness more than is wanted.

7-17. *The edges of the material are pulled around the backing piece and glued.*

7-18. *Slashing the edges of a round pillow covering.*

Cording

There are so many useful threads and strips that can be used for edging miniature pillows and covering upholstery seams that the craftsman should experiment with some of the promising materials he has on hand. The writer has two favorites. The first is embroidery thread, sprayed heavily with Krylon and stretched straight as it dries. If a strand is thicker than necessary, some of the threads can be removed. Embroidery threads come in such a wide variety of colors that it is most unlikely the exact color and shade wanted cannot be found.

A second useful edging is made of epoxy putty. The two colors are first kneaded together thoroughly. A piece of the mixed putty is next rolled, as thinly as possible, between the palms, then stretched and pulled into a thread as thin as desired. The finished threads should be allowed to set overnight on Saran Wrap before being glued to the furniture. They will remain flexible permanently and will be useful wherever leatherlike edgings are needed. If the epoxy's green color is not wanted, a paste color, such as Rub 'n Buff, can be kneaded into the putty, or the threads can be painted with oil colors before use.

Gluing Edgings

When gluing a narrow edging to a pillow edge or over a seam, the problem, discussed earlier, of keeping the fabric clean can be serious. Luckily, the two cordings described above are fairly stiff, and therefore do not need to be glued along their entire lengths. Using the point of a rounded toothpick, tiny dabs of Duco Cement can be placed at the front corners of the chair seat, and two or three more spaced evenly along the front. The edging, with the two front corners pre-creased into right angles, is then pressed into place. When the adhesive has dried, the sides and back are glued, one at a time, in the same way. Since Duco Cement dries quite fast, it is necessary to work quickly and glue one side at a time.

Scotch's Super Strength Glue can be used instead of Duco Cement and will give the craftsman more time in which to work. However, the stringiness of the material makes it more difficult to apply in small, neat dabs.

MAKING A LEATHER CHAIR

By pure serendipity, an unusual method for making a convincing leather chair with a tufted back has been developed, and the craftsman may wish to try it. Although the Morris chair shown in figure 7-24 is part wood and part leather, the following method can be used for making an all-leather chair or any other leather-covered furniture desired.

To start, chair pillows that will be covered with leather are made as described in the preceding pages on upholstering. Polyform or a similar material is shaped on plywood backing pieces and baked or air-dried.

The pillows are then covered with a thin layer of epoxy putty. The putty's green color makes a most attractive leather, but if another color is wanted, it can be kneaded into the material. The writer has tried Rub 'N Buff, oil-based house paint, and the thick pigment from an oil wood stain. All three blended with the putty successfully, and no doubt there is other coloring matter that will work as well. It is probably safe to assume that working colors into the putty will weaken its adhesive quality, but this point is unimportant when the material is being used for upholstering.

Before the blue and yellow sides of the putty strip are kneaded together, it is recommended that a very thin strip between them be cut out with scissors and discarded. The two colors sometimes partially set at the point where they meet, and the resulting hard line can mar an otherwise smooth mixture. When the putty has been kneaded so the color is a solid green without even a trace of blue or yellow showing, it is ready to use and will remain usable, although it will stiffen gradually, for about 20 to 30 minutes.

The Saran-wrapped board described earlier will also be useful in the work ahead. The epoxy putty is gently pulled and stretched into a not-too-thin sheet of even thickness, about 1/16 inch, and cut with a razor blade or sharp knife into pieces to fit the pillow being covered. If the pillow is box shaped, separate pieces should be cut for the top and sides; a single piece will do for a rounded pillow. The cut pieces should be just a little smaller than the areas to be covered, since they will stretch slightly as they are being applied.

One by one, the pieces are put into place on the pillow, and their edges rubbed gently with the thumb to make them meet at the seams. The lower edges of the seat cover are smoothed and stretched so they are carried a little distance around the bottom edges of the pillow. The edges of the back pillow are treated in the same way. If the back of a pillow will show, it must, of course, be covered with a separate sheet of putty.

The tufted lines are made by pressing the edges of a piece of thin, stiff material (a plastic playing card is excellent) into the putty while it is still workable. The desired pattern should first be drawn on graph paper, since it is next to impossible for even the most careful craftsman to do perfect tufting without a guide. The playing card or other stiff piece is then cut into strips whose widths match the lengths of the various lines in the pattern. The ends of these strips are next used to press the pattern deeply into the epoxy-covered pillow (figure 7–23). The drawn pattern should be held next to the pillow as the work is being done and followed as closely as possible.

7-21. *Covering the back pillow.*

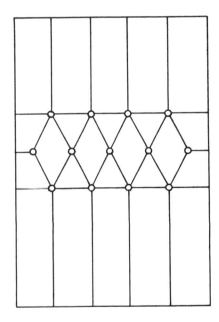

7-22. *A typical upholstering pattern for a chair back.*

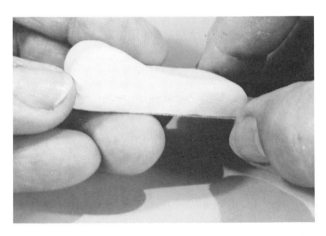

7-19. *A pillow for the back of the Morris chair is shaped of Polyform.*

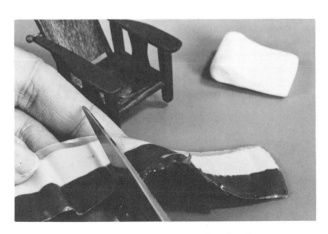

7-20. *Epoxy putty makes excellent "leather."*

7-23. *The pattern lines are pressed into the covered pillow.*

The next day, after the epoxy has set, more putty can be rolled between palm and finger into very tiny "buttons," or slightly flattened balls, which are gently pushed into the joint lines. It is a good idea to roll many more balls than are needed, and to use only those that match.

The edging for the pillows is made as described earlier by stretching the putty into threads of the desired thickness. If they are laid in place immediately, they will cling to the pillows and need not be glued. If they are allowed to set overnight, they can be glued in place the next day.

The footstool shown in figure 7–24 was made from two slightly irregular, thick discs of Polyform, pushed together. An indentation, left by the many tired feet that have rested on it for years, was pushed into the top. The stool was then baked and covered with epoxy putty, and the edgings were glued on later.

THROW PILLOWS

When making miniature throw pillows for beds, chairs, window seats, and so on, the same question arises: Which is more important to the craftsman, realism, or the appearance of it? If the former, miniature pillows should be made just as full-size pillows are made, with a soft filling and an outer casing. In addition, bed pillows should have an outside slip, open at one end. The only drawback to pillows made this way is that they remain puffed and perfect when in place on the furniture. It is not possible for very small pieces of cloth, no matter how fine, to bend, drape, or hang naturally, and when a filling is inside the cloth, the problem is compounded.

Again, Polyform or a clay material comes to the rescue. The pillows are shaped as the craftsman wants them to look when in place on the furniture. If a round pillow, for example, is to lean

7–24. *The completed "leather"-covered Morris chair.*

Clear "glass" drinking glasses can easily be
made by using a razor blade to cut clear plastic
straws into equal sections. If clear straws cannot
be found in a grocery store or drugstore, a small
paintbrush encased in a clear tube can sometimes
be found in an art supply store. One such tube
will make a whole set of glasses, and the brush
can always be used. The glasses can be fastened
with rubber cement to a tray, or directly to the
shelf.

For stacks of dinner plates and saucers,
Polyform again comes to the rescue. A thick
piece of the material is rolled into a cylinder until
its sides are straight and its diameter matches
that of the desired stack of dishes. Its two ends
are trimmed flat with a razor blade, and one end
gently indented to make a curved surface of
top plate. A thread, stretched tightly between the hands, is then used to mark lines on
surface, representing the edges of the individual plates. The thread must be held straight
the lines, which need not go around to the
be parallel. The stack is then baked in a
(250- to 300-degree) oven for about 25
until the material has set but has not
A stack of plates made in this way
and close inspection but is most
when used on a crowded shelf or
ed glass.

perfectly round cylinders to be used
for mugs, straight-sided jars, vases,
and so on, Polyform is rolled around
dowel. Since the ends of the roll will
should be made longer than needed
be cut off later and discarded.
and dowel are baked together in

a slow oven (about 300 degrees) for about 30
minutes. The tapered ends are then cut off with a
razor blade, the dowel slipped out of the tube,
and the tube cut to the length desired.

After the first baking, such things as handles,
slightly flattened flowers, or thin rolls of the clay
laid on in a design can be added. After a second
baking, the pieces can be painted as desired.

For a perfect little "china" plate that costs
nothing, the reader is advised to look into the
screw-on top (not cap) of a soda bottle. The thin,
white plastic lining can be removed by lifting an
edge with a screwdriver, then pulling it out with
the fingers. Although the piece is a little too wide
to be used as a dinner plate, it makes an ideal
serving plate, or it can be hand-decorated and displayed on a rack or hung on the wall.

PLASTIC PANES

In any phase of making miniatures, it is always
better, where possible, to use the real material instead of a substitute, but there are times when a
choice must be made between a lookalike and
nothing at all. Examples would be the glass in a
curved miniature door, and the glass covering a
small, framed picture. In both cases, clear plastic
would have to be substituted, because glass can
only be curved during its manufacture, and the
writer knows of no glass that is thin enough to be
used on a very small frame and still be in scale.

If a rule must be made, then, it is that glass
should be used where it looks just right, but the
craftsman should not hesitate to use plastic if it
looks better. Since some miniature makers, the
writer among them, have a strong and often blind
prejudice against anything plastic in miniature

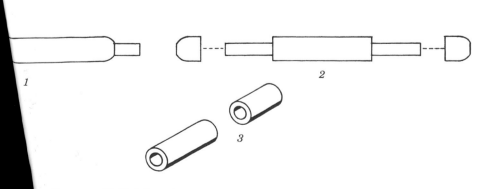

s, and so on. (1) Polyform is
baking, the ends are trimmed.
ths.

against the arm of a sofa, the pillow is first shaped of clay, then put in place on the furniture and pushed gently against the arm so that it bends, just slightly, in the right place. The custom-shaped pillow is then baked, and a fabric covering is glued to it with Duco Cement. An edging is added to cover the seams.

Though all pillows should not be dented, draped, or shaped, those that should can be made far more convincing with the use of clay rather than soft fillings.

Glass, like metal, is a material t' to work with at home. Unlike n glass cannot be filed, sawed, or s it be drilled and fastened with c but a professional. About all t do at home without special e flat panes of glass and grind accessories, such as dishe vases, chandelier parts, bought manufactured or buttons and beads, or su' for them.

Fortunately, however tured miniature glass in recent years, and t' china and glass p similar pieces that in even the most c Some of the piece isting painted fl proved upon.

However, th pieces is not afford to dis dishes in a glass and c an averag every dir while it front s shelve two sau the ar o

7-25. *A pillow shaped against a sofa arm —*

7-26. *— looks more inviting.*

7-27. *Making mugs, vase rolled on a dowel. (2) After (3) The tube is cut into leng*

against the arm of a sofa, the pillow is first shaped of clay, then put in place on the furniture and pushed gently against the arm so that it bends, just slightly, in the right place. The custom-shaped pillow is then baked, and a fabric covering is glued to it with Duco Cement. An edging is added to cover the seams.

Though all pillows should not be dented, draped, or shaped, those that should can be made far more convincing with the use of clay rather than soft fillings.

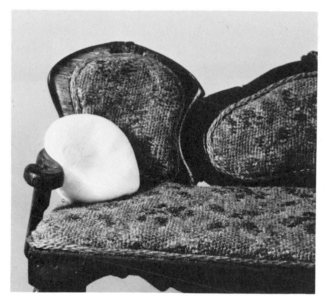

7-25. *A pillow shaped against a sofa arm —*

7-26. *— looks more inviting.*

GLASS AND CHINA SUBSTITUTES

Glass, like metal, is a material that is difficult to work with at home. Unlike metal, however, glass cannot be filed, sawed, or soldered, nor can it be drilled and fastened with dowels by anyone but a professional. About all the craftsman can do at home without special equipment is to cut flat panes of glass and grind their edges. Glass accessories, such as dishes, drinking glasses, vases, chandelier parts, and so on, must be bought manufactured or found in collections of buttons and beads, or substitutes must be found for them.

Fortunately, however, the quality of manufactured miniature glass pieces has been improving in recent years, and there is now a wide choice of china and glass plates, bottles, lamps, and similar pieces that are fine enough to be included in even the most carefully made miniature rooms. Some of the pieces can be hand decorated, or existing painted flowers or other trim can be improved upon.

However, the cost of the best miniature glass pieces is not low, and while most collectors can afford to display a special lamp, vase, or set of dishes in a miniature room, to purchase as many glass and china pieces as are usually contained in an average house would cost a great deal. Nearly every dining room contains a china cabinet, and while its doors may be of solid wood, the glass-front styles are usually more attractive. When shelves are visible, they should display not one or two pieces each, but a wealth of plates, cups, saucers, glasses, and similar pieces. In addition, the kitchen will need more china and glassware, and pantry shelves in most homes must be full to overcrowding.

A great many of these pieces will be seen on a shelf that can only be glimpsed through an open doorway or at the back of a crowded cabinet, and it therefore seems wasteful not to find substitutes for some of them. Finding substitutes for miniature dishes and glassware calls for a lively imagination combined with very little effort. Again, boxes of jewelry, buttons, and beads should be ransacked. Small glass or plastic buttons can make excellent bowls, and beads, both straight-sided and rounded, can substitute for drinking glasses, mugs, and vases.

Clear "glass" drinking glasses can easily be made by using a razor blade to cut clear plastic straws into equal sections. If clear straws cannot be found in a grocery store or drugstore, a small paintbrush encased in a clear tube can sometimes be found in an art supply store. One such tube will make a whole set of glasses, and the brush can always be used. The glasses can be fastened with rubber cement to a tray, or directly to the shelf.

For stacks of dinner plates and saucers, Polyform again comes to the rescue. A thick piece of the material is rolled into a cylinder until its sides are straight and its diameter matches that of the desired stack of dishes. Its two ends are trimmed flat with a razor blade, and one end is slightly indented to make a curved surface of the top plate. A thread, stretched tightly between the hands, is then used to mark lines on the surface, representing the edges of the individual plates. The thread must be held straight so that the lines, which need not go around to the back, will be parallel. The stack is then baked in a slow (275- to 300-degree) oven for about 25 minutes, until the material has set but has not discolored. A stack of plates made in this way cannot stand close inspection but is most convincing when used on a crowded shelf or behind frosted glass.

To make perfectly round cylinders to be used for drinking mugs, straight-sided jars, vases, lamp bases, and so on, Polyform is rolled around a wood dowel. Since the ends of the roll will taper, the roll should be made longer than needed so the ends can be cut off later and discarded.

The Polyform and dowel are baked together in a slow oven (about 300 degrees) for about 30 minutes. The tapered ends are then cut off with a razor blade, the dowel slipped out of the tube, and the tube cut to the length desired.

After the first baking, such things as handles, slightly flattened flowers, or thin rolls of the clay laid on in a design can be added. After a second baking, the pieces can be painted as desired.

For a perfect little "china" plate that costs nothing, the reader is advised to look into the screw-on top (not cap) of a soda bottle. The thin, white plastic lining can be removed by lifting an edge with a screwdriver, then pulling it out with the fingers. Although the piece is a little too wide to be used as a dinner plate, it makes an ideal serving plate, or it can be hand-decorated and displayed on a rack or hung on the wall.

PLASTIC PANES

In any phase of making miniatures, it is always better, where possible, to use the real material instead of a substitute, but there are times when a choice must be made between a lookalike and nothing at all. Examples would be the glass in a curved miniature door, and the glass covering a small, framed picture. In both cases, clear plastic would have to be substituted, because glass can only be curved during its manufacture, and the writer knows of no glass that is thin enough to be used on a very small frame and still be in scale.

If a rule must be made, then, it is that glass should be used where it looks just right, but the craftsman should not hesitate to use plastic if it looks better. Since some miniature makers, the writer among them, have a strong and often blind prejudice against anything plastic in miniature

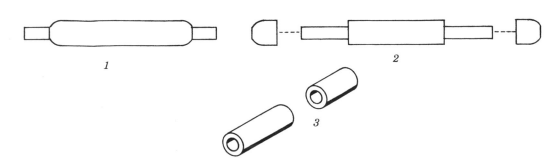

7-27. *Making mugs, vases, and so on.* (1) *Polyform is rolled on a dowel.* (2) *After baking, the ends are trimmed.* (3) *The tube is cut into lengths.*

rooms, its use is recommended only because there is no better substitute.

When using clear plastic for curved doors, the wood frame can first be wet and bent as described in Chapter 6 and the plastic glued to it. A second method is to use a section of a plastic bottle, whose curve approximates the needed curve, and to wet and bend the wood to fit it. If this second method is used, the wood frame and the curved bottle section should first be glued together before plans for the rest of the cabinet are drawn. The advantage of this method is that the pre-curved door "glass" will hold its shape better than will the flat plastic piece that has been glued to a curved frame.

When gluing the plastic to its wood frame, great care should be taken to avoid squeezeout. Certain adhesives, such as Duco Cement, contain acetone, which will permanently mar the plastic, and although white glue can be wiped off with a damp cloth, it will usually leave a smear that is very difficult to remove completely. Also, since the wiping must be done before the glue dries, the plastic is very apt to be pushed away from the frame if too much pressure is used, and the whole job will have to be done over.

Epoxy putty seems to be the best material for the delicate job of fastening the plastic to its frame. Very tiny balls of it can be spaced evenly along the gluing surface, or a thin thread can be pulled out and laid on it. The plastic is then pressed carefully into place. If care is taken not to use too much adhesive, there will be no squeezeout, and since the putty does not set quickly, as much time as necessary can be taken to do a neat and careful job.

The value of plastic as a substitute for glass is not necessarily limited to curved surfaces or framed pictures. In the writer's opinion, if there must be a choice, a pane of in-scale plastic is to be preferred to one of glass if the glass is even a little too thick to look just right.

7-28. *Plastic bottles and package covers can be used as glass in curved doors.*

WORKING WITH METALS

Metal, like glass, is a material for which substitutes must be found occasionally if miniature rooms are to be complete in all the important details. Fortunately, such substitutes are available. Materials such as wood or clay, for example, can be treated to be indistinguishable from metal if the finished miniatures are not handled. In the writer's opinion, it is preferable to use these substitutes than to display anything in the rooms that is even slightly out of scale or lacking in detail. However, there is still a great deal that can be done with metals at home, using material from one of the following four sources:

1. Sheet Metal

Thin sheets of brass and copper can be found in many hardware, craft, and hobby stores. Some of these sheets are as thin as foil; others are thicker but can be cut with scissors; and some are so

7-29. *Wood can be made to resemble metal.*

thick that they must be cut with a saw. These sheets have many uses, including the making of boxes, planters, clock faces, fireplace screens, and furniture trim, such as edgings, drawer pulls, and ornamental hinges.

2. Wires, Rods, and Tubes

Rolls of wire and a few lengths of rods and tubes of various metals are almost a must for the craftsman to keep among his supplies. Rolls of brass and copper wire can usually be found in any hardware store, and most hobby shops, particularly those specializing in model train supplies, carry brass rods and square and round tubes of various thicknesses. Much of the tubing will nest into the next larger size, a most useful feature when making an adjustable piece, such as a brass drapery rod.

Materials can be ornamentally shaped with the use of a pair of wire benders or needlenose pliers, and they can be soldered together or to other metals. Such curved pieces are almost a necessity when making most styles of chandeliers and when improving upon ready-made brass pieces, such as too-simple dollhouse beds, lamps, fire screens, and so on. Short pieces of the thinnest rods can also be used to suggest hinges on accessories that are too small to take workable hinges.

3. Old Jewelry

The most important source of small metal parts and pieces is a collection of discarded jewelry, as much of it as possible. With that collection, a good imagination, and a metal or wire-cutting tool, miracles can happen. In addition to the more obvious things, such as picture frames, which will probably emerge from the collection in greater numbers than the craftsman can use, small metal bowls, vases, trivets and the like, and harder-to-find things will also appear.

A section of a filigree bracelet can make a perfect fireplace fender or, painted and framed, a music rack for a grand piano. There will be parts for brass chandeliers, sconces, drawer pulls, and door handles. The list of usable pieces and parts that can be found will be limited only by the size of the jewelry collection and by the craftsman's imagination.

7-30. A variety of brass materials are available.

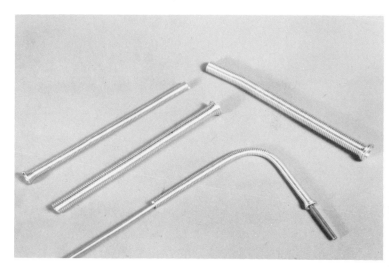

7-31. Tube-bending springs prevent tubes from collapsing while being shaped. The spring in the foreground holds brass tube.

7-32. Watch parts contain many useful metal pieces.

7-33. *Pot-metal pieces can be refined by filing and painting.*

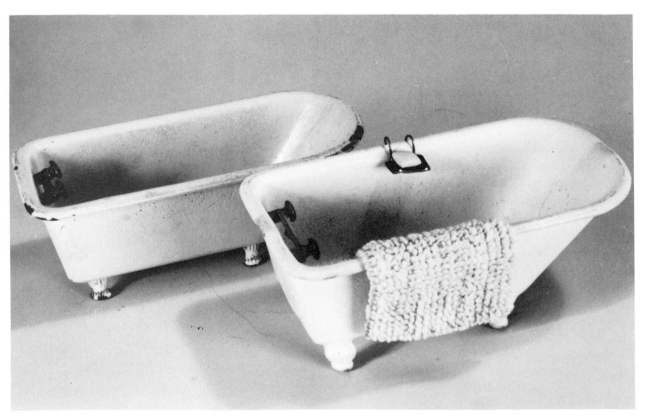

7-34. *The tub.*

4. Pot Metal and Lead

An excellent source of metal with which the craftsman can work is manufactured pieces of pot metal or lead. Pot metal is a material often used in miniature metal furniture today, particularly in the inexpensive pieces, and nearly every shop specializing in miniatures carries a variety of unpainted pot-metal accessories ranging from fairly elaborate chandeliers on down to such smaller items as shoes, skates, dolls, candlesticks, pots and pans, and so on. Much pot-metal furniture is painted, and feels so smooth and heavy that it seems almost to be made of steel, but the material is so soft it can easily be sawed or filed to any shape desired.

An example of such altering is illustrated in figure 7-34. An old Tootsietoy bathtub was long enough for the writer's 3/4-inch scale, but was too narrow. The tub was sawed in half lengthwise on the jigsaw, and narrow strips of plywood of the correct width were inserted to widen the tub. Polyform, molded and smoothed to match the rest of the piece, held the wood strips in place. New feet were shaped over the smaller, old ones to change the design to one more in keeping with the period of the bathroom and to heighten the tub a little. The tub was baked in a 275-degree oven for about 20 minutes, then painted a little unevenly to suggest an old, well-worn fixture. The faucets, which were now more widely separated, were connected with a pipe and a spout.

The washbowl and toilet that came with the bathtub was also modified. The base of the washbowl was sawed off, and the bowl was widened in the same way as was the tub. The toilet, which was large enough to be in scale for a small fixture, was given an oak seat and tank, and "porcelain" screw heads on the base. The result was a set of bathroom fixtures (shown in the color pages) that were correct in scale and detail, made quite easily from old toys.

Many pot metal accessories are roughly cast, with metal ridges left along the edges. Refining, reshaping, and painting them in any way desired is quite easy, however, and since some of the accessories, such as a typewriter, are not easy to find anywhere else, are well worth buying and improving.

Pot metal is quite brittle and any necessary bending should be done very slowly and carefully. If breakage does occur, the pieces can be treated as wood and rejoined with the use of drilled holes and a wood dowel, or with a tiny ball of epoxy putty, or both.

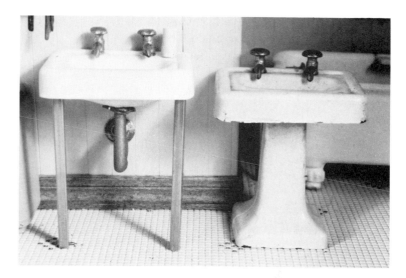

7-35. A washbowl (left) made from old Tootsietoy (right) was widened to suit scale.

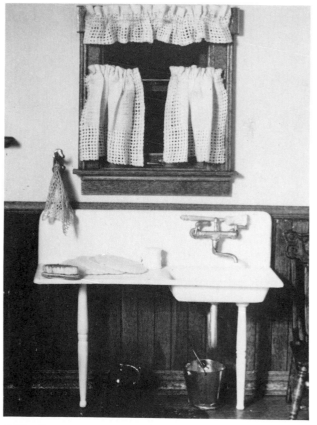

7-36. Legs were removed from the old Tootsietoy sink. New ones give added height.

Heating and Plumbing Pipes

When pipes for heating and plumbing fixtures are visible in a full-size room, it is important that they also be visible in the miniature copy and that they be given the correct curves and thicknesses for whatever they represent.

To make the pipes, a soft wire of the correct diameter can be bent to shape and its ends either glued to the wall or the floor with tiny balls of epoxy putty, or pushed through holes in the wall or floor that have been drilled to fit the ends as tightly as possible. To make the whole arrangement more convincing, small, flat, metal washers should be glued to the floor or wall around the pipe ends. If washers small enough cannot be found, small circles can be cut from thin wood and colored with a metallic paste.

7–38. Polyform "pipes" ready for baking, trimming, and painting.

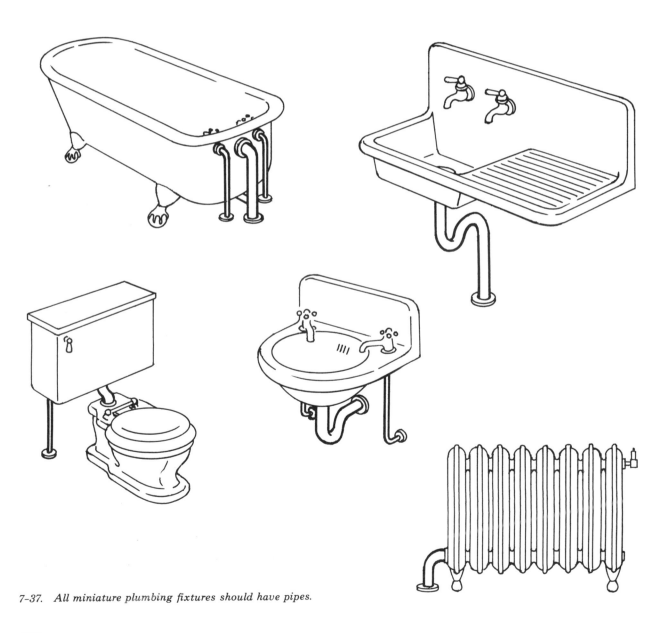

7–37. All miniature plumbing fixtures should have pipes.

An easier material with which to make pipes is the faithful standby, Polyform. The clay is rolled into a cylinder of the correct diameter. Since the ends will be narrower than the center section, and will be trimmed later, the cylinder should be made longer than needed. The rolled piece is laid on a metal plate or sheet, bent to shape, and baked in a slow oven (275 to 300 degrees) for about 20 minutes. Its ends are then trimmed with a razorblade or similar sharp edge. (Scissors will not give a squared-off, clean cut.) The pipe is finished with a coat of a metallic paint or paste, such as Rub 'N Buff.

Contact cement can be used to fasten the pipe ends to a wall or floor, although, again, epoxy putty does the work well. With a little extra preparatory work, the actual job of fastening the pipes in place can be made a great deal easier by using dowels. Small holes are drilled in the pipe ends and in the wall or floor, and small wood dowels are shaved from a toothpick. With this work done, it is a simple matter to fasten the pipe ends firmly in place, following the method for using dowels described in Chapter 6.

Faucets

The writer does not know of a feasible way to make metal faucets at home that will be fine enough, or detailed enough, to be worthy of a carefully made miniature kitchen or bathroom. However, all manufactured wash basins and bathtubs come equipped with them, and pot-metal faucets can sometimes be purchased separately. As with most other pot-metal accessories, manufactured faucets are very apt to be rough along the edges and too thick in places, but a small file can quickly reshape them into more refined pieces.

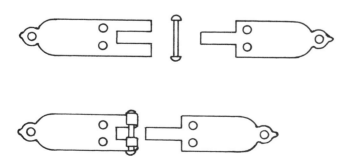

7-39. Ornamental hinges can be made by hand.

Hinges

Like faucets, manufactured hinges are better than those the craftsman could make at home. Most of them are made of brass, and since more styles and sizes are appearing on the market each year, it should rarely be necessary for the craftsman to make his own. The exception would be when a miniature replica of an old furniture piece is being made, and a certain style of ornamental hinge is important to its authenticity. Such a hinge can be made of sheet brass, with a small brass tack or pin substituting for the hinge pin. The second head can be added to the pin by putting a drop of solder on the tip, or the tip can be bent with a pair of pliers (figure 7-39).

Homemade hinges do not open and close as smoothly, and are usually not as strong, as manufactured ones, which are stamped from a heavier metal than the craftsman can handle. However, such hinges are strong enough to hold up if undue strain is not put on them.

Drawer Pulls and Knobs

Unlike hinges, drawer pulls are not required to do anything but cling very tightly to wood faces and look pretty. They are therefore easier to make. In addition, there are no set styles that must be followed, which greatly increases their sources. Gold-headed pins and tacks, beads, and the contents of indispensable boxes of old jewelry will probably yield all the drawer pulls the craftsman will need. The following are some suggestions for sources and for making pulls of various styles:

Round Brass Pulls

An art or craft supply store that sells materials for making jewelry usually offers brass pins with a selection of head sizes, some of them quite large. These pins can be used just as they are for plain brass pulls.

Wood Knobs

For cabinets and pantry drawers that require wood knobs, small balls of Polyform can be rolled, slightly flattened, baked, and painted to match the cabinet wood. It is a good idea to roll more balls than needed, and to select for use only those that match exactly. The knobs can be glued to the drawer faces.

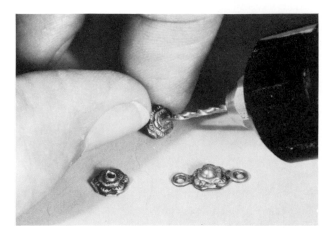

7-40. *Making drawer pulls. Holes are drilled in jewelry pieces.*

7-41. *The wire fastener is shaped and links separated are from a chain.*

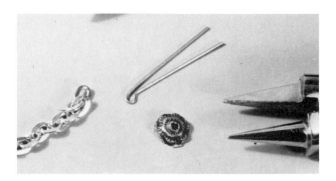

7-42. *Finished drawer pulls.*

7-43. *Simple drawer pulls made of shaped wires and chain links.*

Porcelain Knobs

Opaque white beads with the smallest possible brass pins slipped through their holes make convincing porcelain knobs. Very small white beads make excellent knobs for spice chests.

Miscellaneous Pulls

The jewelry collection, a pair of wire cutters, some old scissors, and a good imagination will yield a wide variety of pulls. Chain links, either plain or of unusual shapes and designs, can be fastened to the wood with brass pins, or can be combined with other jewelry pieces. Figures 7-40 through 7-43 illustrate pulls made of shaped wire, chain links, and small flowers cut from a jewelry piece.

Manufactured Pulls

There is a fair variety of manufactured knobs and drawer pulls on the market. However, unlike hinges, most of them are easily recognizable by anyone who wanders from shop to shop, as most miniaturists do, looking for the unusual. Therefore, where such pulls are exactly right on the furniture, it is recommended that they be used, but at other times and wherever possible the craftsman should create his own.

Fastening Pulls

Pulls and knobs can be fastened to drawer faces with pins, an adhesive, or a combination of the two. If the drawer is to be opened fairly often, pins should be used, since they hold more strongly than glue. If the drawer is false, fastening the pulls with an adhesive is usually sufficient.

To use a pin or tack, a hole slightly smaller than the pin is drilled into the wood. A little effort should be needed to push the pin through.

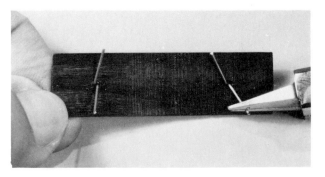

7-44. *The wires are bent at right angles on the back of the drawer face.*

The bead or other pull is then threaded on the pin, the pin pushed into the hole, and pliers used to bend the pin end at right angles along the back of the drawer face or door.

If there are two wire ends, they are pushed through the hole, then separated at the back and bent in opposite directions (figure 7-44). Both the single pin and the wire ends should be bent as close to the wood as possible, so there will be no play in the pulls when they are used.

To fasten the pulls even more firmly, a strong adhesive such as Scotch Super Strength Glue or epoxy putty can be used to cover the wires and holes on the backs of the wood faces.

Concealing the Shine of New Metals

There are times when the high shine of a new metal accessory adds a jarring note to an otherwise carefully furnished period room. To conceal it, the metal can be rubbed with a paste color such as Rub 'N Buff. A mixture of copper and onyx colors will reduce the shine of new brass, and a little onyx mixed with silver will tone down shiny steel, aluminum, or other silver-colored metals. Although the colors can be removed from slick surfaces as easily as they are applied, the metal will remain dull indefinitely as long as it is not handled.

METAL SUBSTITUTES

It was suggested earlier in this chapter that since much metal furniture cannot be made at home, substitutes for metal can be used. The making of plumbing pipes with the use of Polyform has already been discussed. The following are some suggestions for using wood as a substitute for porcelain and iron:

As long as any furniture piece is to be painted, treating its surface to make it resemble a particular metal presents no problem at all. The craftsman has only to observe the qualities of the metal he wishes to reproduce and to treat the wood surface accordingly. If, for example, a porcelain surface is needed, the craftsman needs only to fill and sand the wood surfaces as often as necessary to make them glassy smooth. The wood is then sprayed with a semi-gloss white or off-white paint.

If the resulting pieces are then used to make a stove, as in the figure 7-45, the association in the viewer's mind of a gas stove with porcelain immediately transforms the smooth, white wood

to the expected material. The same is true of any metal, such as iron, aluminum, tin, and so on. Combining a material that looks as much like the desired metal as possible with a furniture piece or accessory that is traditionally made of that material creates an illusion that is completely convincing—provided, of course, that the piece is not lifted and tested for weight.

A black "iron" stove can also be made of wood. Since iron does not have the glassy smooth surface of porcelain, filling the wood is not necessary. On the contrary, if the wood is close-grained, the surface will more closely resemble iron if it is lightly pitted here and there with a fine-pointed instrument to reproduce the mold marks in cast iron. A matte black finish can make the wood so closely resemble iron that the deception cannot be detected unless, again, the piece is lifted. The important point is that the stove must be shaped as perfectly as possible. If it is not fat, with the proper thick bulges, no amount of careful surface finishing can convince the viewer that the stove is iron, not wood.

7-45. *The gas stove resembles porcelain partly because it is expected to.*

BENDING WIRE

Very often, commercially made metal furniture and accessories can be greatly improved by the addition of short lengths of brass wire, decoratively curved and soldered on. Some of the very expensive dollhouse beds are beautifully made, but those more widely sold need embellishing to be made suitable for miniature rooms. Manufactured brass chandeliers and other accessories can also be greatly improved with the addition of shaped wires.

For bending wire, a pair of either needlenose or wire-bending pliers is needed. The latter is available in two styles, one of which will bend either angles or curves, and the other both angles and curves, since it is equipped with one squared, and one rounded, jaw.

To bend wire into curves, the pliers are moved along a fraction of an inch at a time, bending the wire just slightly at each new point. Bent in this way, the wire will hold its shape as the work progresses. If the curves are made too deep with each twist of the pliers, those already made will tend to be pulled out of shape.

More often than not, curved, decorative wire pieces are needed in pairs, or in matching sets of three or four pieces. To make them match, a pattern of the desired shape should first be drawn on graph paper, and the wire section laid on it from time to time as the bending is being done. Working in this way, it is not difficult to shape each piece so that it matches the pattern exactly.

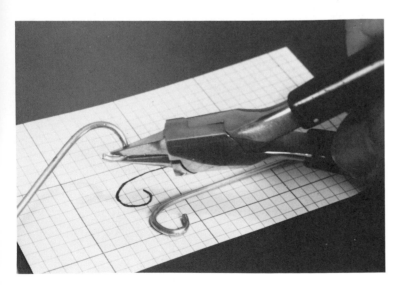

7-46. Bending wires by following a pattern.

DECORATIVE SOLDERING

The principles of soldering were covered in Chapter 3, where the making of electrical connections was discussed. For decorative soldering, the same principles apply: the hot soldering iron touches the metal to be soldered from below only; the iron *never* touches the solder itself. The solder is held above the metal, touching the joint to be made. The hot iron heats the metal, which, in turn, melts a bit of the solder, which falls onto the joint. When the solder has cooled, which it does very quickly, the joint has been completed.

There are three basic differences between soldered connections for electrical use and ornamental soldering:

1. Solder with a rosin core is not necessary for ornamental soldering; soldering wire with an acid core is preferred because it makes a stronger joint.

2. The appearance of ornamental joints is important; that of electrical joints usually is not. Fortunately for the beginner, however, soft solder is just that—very soft and easily filed to shape. Therefore, if a joint is thick and unsightly with solder, it can be filed down and painted to match the metal being soldered. Although such a joint is not ideal, it is reassuring to know that all is not lost when a soldering job has not been done just right.

3. Wires are first twisted together when an electrical connection is to be soldered. Metals to be soldered ornamentally are usually not fastened together before soldering. Like electrical wires, however, they must be touching or the joint cannot be made. It is therefore necessary to use two vises, clamps, or other holding devices to hold the metal pieces steady, in contact with each other, and in exact position for the soldering work.

The only metals the craftsman is likely to use that cannot be soldered with soft solder are pot metal, lead, and aluminum. Lead and pot metal will melt from the heat of the soldering iron, and aluminum must be soldered with a special aluminum solder.

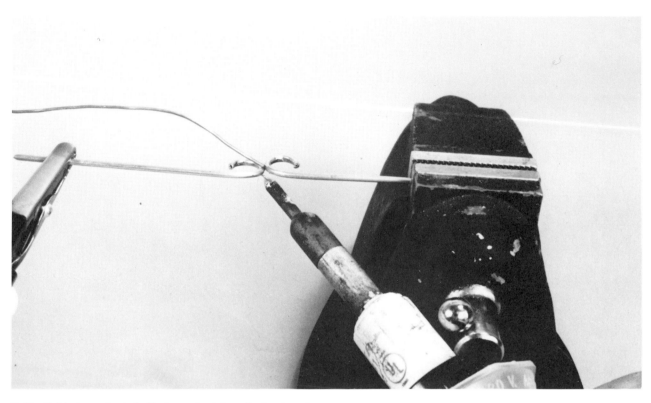

7-47. *Soldering wire is held above the joint, the hot iron is held below.*

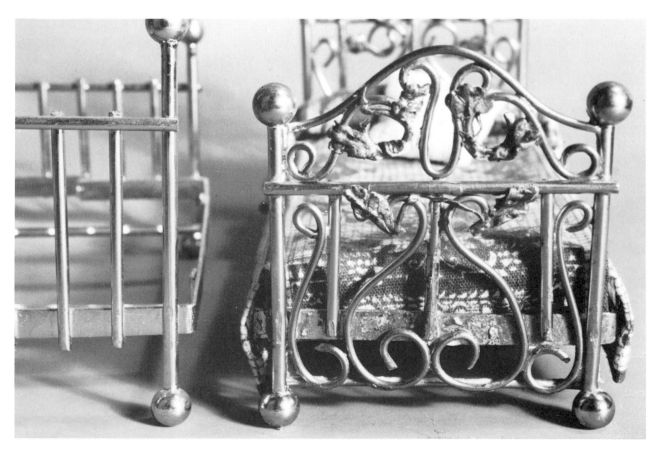

7-48. *A toy brass bed is altered and made elaborate with added, soldered wires.*

8.

The Finishing Touches

With at least one room built, painted, and papered, and with some of the furniture finished and ready to go into it, the home stretch has now been reached. The craftsman promises himself that just as soon as one pair of miniature curtains has been hung, he will put the work aside and do a few long-neglected, full-size chores. Several hours later, while hanging miniature pictures, he resolves to stop very soon now and call the fire department. His full-size house has been on fire for some time. Any craftsman who has reached the last stages of furnishing a miniature room will agree that the above picture is, or could be, factual.

The finishing work ahead consists not of simply filling an empty room with furniture and gluing a few pictures to the walls, but of painting a portrait of a new family that will move into it, and into the other rooms to follow. Although small, the family members are very real, and they must first introduce themselves to the craftsman so that the rooms he prepares for them will have personalities of their own.

Perhaps this new room is part of a large, old frame house on the outskirts of a middle-sized city. There are five in the family—the parents, a girl of twelve, a boy of seventeen, and a grandmother. The father owns a small retail store and is successful enough to support his family in comfort, if not in style. The mother does the cooking for the family and some of the housework, and a woman comes in twice a week to do the rest. The year is 1925.

The quality of some of the furniture, handed down in the family from past generations, is excellent. Other pieces, especially the utilitarian ones, were purchased from local stores as needs arose.

The new room that is about to be furnished is the parents' bedroom. A bed, dresser, chest, and rug have already been made for it. As those pieces are put into place, the craftsman realizes it is still a room that fits no one in particular. What is missing that will tailor it especially for the two people who will occupy it?

It is safe to assume that the mother and grandmother do the mending and darning for the family; in this year of 1925, a hole or tear in a piece of clothing does not mean the article is ready to be discarded. Even though there is a sewing room in the attic where dresses or whole pairs of draperies are made, many small jobs are done in the bedroom, often in the evening. The mother will need a chair, a low rocker without arms, and possibly a sewing stand or basket.

Often, while the wife sews, her husband likes to read in bed. There is a small table by the bed on which he lays his book and perhaps the evening paper. Behind him, hooked over the head of the bed, is a reading lamp, which was bought at Sears, Roebuck. It is a lacy, unmasculine affair, made of lavendar silk, not attractive but serving a very real purpose. On the table, on top of the paper, is a pair of eyeglasses, which will probably be forgotten in the morning and will be very much missed at the store.

In this house, there is never quite enough room for all the possessions the family has accumulated over the years. The mother has added as much storage space as possible to every room. In the bedroom being furnished now is a trunk, or carved chest, at the foot of the bed. It holds out-of-season bedspreads, a spare pillow, and a pair of sheets, embroidered by a grandaunt, that were much too fine ever to have been used.

The mother loves plants and can never find room for all she would like to have. In this bedroom, in front of a window, is a plant stand or a small, square table that holds a pot or two of geraniums or a single, large fern. Everywhere there is evidence, such as the lace dresser scarf and lace-edged scarf on the mantle, of her attempts to add elegance to her home, which, except momentarily, satisfies her quite well. All the members of the family love their home and their possessions, and have always found it difficult to throw anything away.

On the ceiling is an electric chandelier, and on the wall is a light switch for turning it on. If it is summer, there may be an electric fan near the bed or facing the sewing rocker, and no matter what the season, there is evidence of the house's heating system. There may be an open grill on the floor, or there may be a radiator against a wall.

There are five or six pictures on the walls, reproductions of oil paintings, a flower print, and some family photographs. The larger frames are hung from the picture molding, high on the walls. The smaller frames are fastened with cords to small hooks concealed behind the frames themselves.

One by one, the details are added. Each one, in its turn, should be given the same care and attention that went into the making of the finest furniture pieces, for it is the details that will be noticed first. A fly swatter, hooked over a door-knob for ready accessibility, will not be missed if omitted, but will be seen and appreciated if it is there. If there is a transom above a door, the rod on the wall by which the transom can be opened and closed will attract as much attention as a carefully made sofa or chair. The importance of these details cannot be overemphasized; they, far more than the furniture itself, lend the human factor to any living area, full-sized or miniature.

Following are some of the methods the writer has used for adding details to a series of rooms. These methods are by no means rules; they are suggestions that the craftsman may use, improve upon, or for which he may find substitutes.

HANGING PICTURES AND MIRRORS

If the craftsman will study pictures of rooms of the period in which he is working, he will probably not find a single framed picture or mirror fastened flat to a wall. The exception could be a very small print or photograph, but even this was usually hung by a cord or wire on the back of the frame hooked over a tack driven into the wall. Larger, heavier frames were suspended by wires that were sometimes concealed behind the

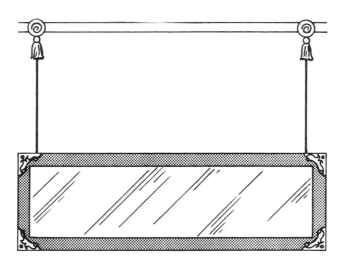

8-1. Long mirrors or pictures are usually hung from two cords.

frames, but very often they were carried all the way up to a picture molding at the ceiling level, or a foot or two below the ceiling. A very long, horizontal frame was sometimes suspended by two wires, one at each end. Another method of hanging pictures was to carry a wire a short distance above the top of the frame, where it was hooked over a nail or picture hook. Often picture hooks, whether at ceiling level or farther down on the wall, were concealed behind rosettes or tassels made of heavy, silk cord.

In today's homes, one does not see pictures slanting out from a wall at 30- to 40-degree angles, but this was seen in some homes in the nineteenth and early twentieth centuries. In those same years, however, other pictures were hung fairly close to the walls, as they are today. Apparently, then, how a miniature picture is hung is the craftsman's choice. The only rule is that it must not be glued flat to the wall.

How far the top of the frame hangs out from the wall is determined by where the wire ends are fastened. If they are fastened to the top corners of the frame, the picture will hang nearly flat against the wall. The lower they are fastened on the back of the frame, the further the picture will slant out at the top.

The weight of a full-size mirror or picture is enough to hold it in position, with the bottom edge touching the wall, and the top edge standing away from it. A miniature frame, however, does not have enough weight to draw the picture wire taut, so the natural look must be achieved by artificial means.

For all miniature frames that are to be hung, a narrow wedge should be sawed out of scrap wood. The wedge should be a right triangle, with the side that will be glued to the wall forming a right angle to the top (figure 8–2). The thickness of the wedge will determine how far the frame will lean from the wall.

The wedge is glued to the back of the frame, with its lower edge flush with the frame's bottom edge. If the picture is to be hung on a far wall, facing the viewer, the wedge can be glued in the center of the frame's back. If it is to go on a side wall, the wedge should be glued to the far edge of the frame, away from the viewer. The narrower the wedge, the less the chance that it will show. It need only be wide enough to hold the picture in position against the wall; 3/16-inch should be sufficient for any frame.

If the picture is to be hung with a short cord that would not show above the frame, and if the frame is to be hung fairly close to the wall, there is no need to add the cord, since it will not show. The wedge can simply be glued to the frame and the wall and the work is done.

However, for a heavier picture that will lean far out, or for any picture whose back can be seen, a cord should be used. A small tack or section of a pin, including the head, is pushed into a hole drilled with a pin vise behind the spot where the picture will be hung. The ends of a thread, cut to length, are then fastened to the back edges of the frame, and the thread is hooked over the tack as the wedge is glued to the wall. Small pieces of paper, glued over the thread ends, will hold the ends to the back of the frame. A gentle pull downward on the picture as the glue dries will then pull the thread tight and straight.

Heavy button thread is suitable for hanging most pictures. If the thread is sprayed thoroughly with Krylon or a similar material and stretched straight as it dries, it will become more manageable and will hold a sharp bend at the point where it is hooked over the tack or picture hook.

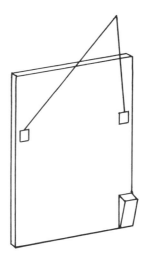

8-2. Pictures should not be fastened flat to wall.

USING A PICTURE MOLDING

If the room has a picture molding at or near the ceiling, hanging pictures from it by means of long "wires" is a most effective way to add an important detail.

Picture hooks are first made by cutting narrow strips, possibly 1/12-inch wide, from a thin sheet of brass with scissors. Brass sheets of various thicknesses can be found in many hobby shops, and the brass used for the picture hooks should be stiff enough to hold its shape when bent, but thin enough to be cut with scissors. If sheet brass cannot be found, wire can be used, although wire will not offer the same gluing surface and is more difficult to handle.

The strips are cut into short lengths, which are then bent into elongated S-shapes (figure 8-3). A wire-bending tool can be used for this, or the strip ends can be shaped over a round form, such as a nail or stiff wire of suitable thickness.

The picture hooks are then fastened to the molding directly over the place where the picture is to be hung. Although any adhesive may be used, the best for the purpose is a tiny ball of epoxy putty laid in place on top of the molding. The hook is then pressed down firmly on the putty, which, when set, will hold the hook strongly and permanently in place. The putty ball should be small enough so that it will not spread out beyond the edges of the hook when pressed flat.

One end of a Krylon-sprayed thread is then attached to a back edge of the frame. With the picture held against the wall where it is to hang, the thread is brought back down to the frame, where it is trimmed short. The end is then glued to the other back edge of the frame. Next, the wedge is glued to the wall, with the thread caught in the hook above, and pulled tight.

Picture wires were sometimes covered with silk or other materials. Two or three strands of embroidery thread, again Krylon-sprayed, can be substituted for button thread if desired. The concealing rosettes, mentioned above, can be made of the same thread glued in a coil. Such rosettes were usually edged with a fringe or decorated with a tassel.

WINDOW FIXTURES

If the craftsman did not drill holes for curtain rods before the room was assembled, now is the time for regrets. The holes that could have been drilled easily on separate walls with an electric drill must now be done in a more cramped position with a pin vise. Although the room can be turned on its back or side, making the windows more accessible, the work of installing the rods and arranging the folds in the curtains so that they hang naturally will be somewhat more difficult.

Whether on separate walls laid flat, or in completed rooms, all miniature windows should be treated in some way. The following are suggestions for hanging curtains and draperies, and for making and hanging the rods to support them. The making of the curtains was covered in Chapter 7.

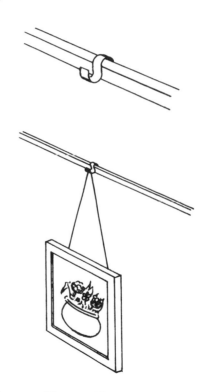

8-3. *Picture moldings and hooks add a touch of realism.*

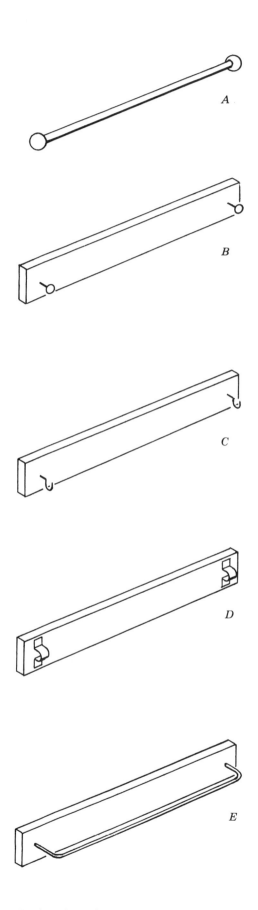

Rods and Brackets

The simplest curtain or drapery rod to duplicate in miniature is probably the straight bar supported on each end by a bracket (*A* in figure 8-4). A knob at each end of the rod prevents the rod from sliding off the brackets. The bar can be made of a brass rod that conforms in thickness to the craftsman's scale, or of a thin wood dowel. Each material has its advantages and disadvantages. The brass rod looks more real but is slippery, a quality that makes hanging curtains realistically a little more difficult. Attaching curtains to a wood dowel is easier, but if the dowel will show, it should be painted to resemble brass. Also, unless the dowel is to be used as a heavy rod for draperies over a doorway, it is apt to be a bit too thick for scale.

Small, gold-colored beads at the ends of the rod can serve as knobs. If the hole in a bead is too large for the rod end, it can be filled with a tiny ball of epoxy putty and the rod can be pushed in before the epoxy sets. If the curtain rod is made of a wood dowel, the chances are good that the dowel end will be too large to fit into the hole of any small bead. In such a case, the bead must be attached to the dowel end with a strong adhesive such as epoxy putty or super-strength glue. Although the bond will not be very strong, it should be sufficient to do the job, since, once the knobs have been attached, no further pressure will be put on them. If beads cannot be found that are small enough, they can be shaped from epoxy putty or Polyform and painted gold.

Supporting brackets for the rod can be made of tiny brass tacks or the heads of pins tapped into holes drilled into the wood with a pin vise. Such brackets are shown in *B* of figure 8-4. *C* of figure 8-4 shows brackets made of lengths of brass wire, bent to shape. The holes drilled for them should be so small that pressure is required to push the brackets in. The brackets shown in *D* of figure 8-4 are made of the same brass strips described previously for making picture hooks. The strips are shaped as shown, the cutrain rod is slipped into them, and the brackets' flat faces are then glued to the woodwork.

A Combined Rod and Bracket

An easy way to hang curtains is to make a combined rod and bracket by bending the ends of a brass rod at right angles as shown in *E* of figure 8-4. The ends of the rod should be made as long

8-4. A variety of curtain rods and supports.

as possible, and the holes should be drilled deeply enough to receive them. In this way, the rod will remain in position and steady, and can still be pulled out of the woodwork when a curtain needs cleaning, or needs to be changed in any way.

Another advantage of this type of rod is that the curtains can be brought around the corners all the way to the wall, thus giving a soft, three-dimensional effect. Curtains hung on bracketed rods must go straight across the window. However, since both styles are much used in trimming full-size windows, either can be used in miniature to good effect.

Between-the-Frames Curtains

When hanging a curtain between two opposing faces of a deep window frame, or the even deeper faces at the ends of a window seat, a thin wood dowel makes an excellent rod. Since, with the curtains in place, the ends of the rod will not show, the rod need only be cut a little longer than necessary and can be forced into the given space.

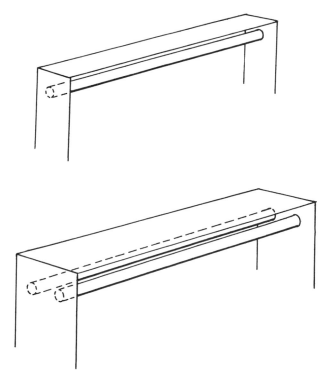

8-5. Wood dowels used as curtain rods between frames.

Alternate measuring and filing of one end will give the exact length needed, so the rod will stay in place without the use of an adhesive but will not be so long that it will bow out under pressure.

Two such rods, close together between the faces, can be used for double-hung, sheer curtains pulled back with ties. Both single and double wood rods are shown in figure 8–5.

Hanging Heavy Draperies

If draperies made of velvet or any heavy material are to be hung in a doorway or over a large window, it is very difficult to fold the material over the rod at the top without the appearance of bulkiness. This problem can be solved by sewing small chain links, just large enough to fit over the rod, to the top of the draperies, and by slipping the links over the rod.

Commercial Rods

A final suggestion for sources of curtain rods and other window fixtures is the manufactured pieces that can be found in shops and catalogs. Some of them are quite attractive, and while the wood rods do not always conform to scale, they can safely be used if they are not overly thick and if they will be covered by curtains.

WINDOW SHADES

Where appropriate, window shades, with or without curtains, can add a great deal of charm to miniature rooms. Unless the period being represented is a very early one, miniature shades on rollers can be used in nearly every room in a house. Shades belong in the category of details that will not be missed if omitted but, if included, will be much appreciated by viewers.

To make a window shade, a narrow wood dowel is cut long enough to fit tightly between the wood facings of the window. A strip of paper of appropriate color and weight is cut a little narrower than the dowel's length. The paper should be as long as wanted for the shade, plus about 3/4 inch to allow for a hem and for a section to be wrapped around and glued to the dowel.

The color of the paper used is optional, although most window shades range from a deep tan to off-white and occasionally white. All window shades turn yellow in the sun, however, so a white shade would indicate one that is almost brand new.

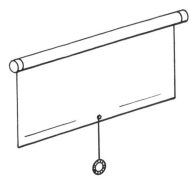

8-6. Where suitable, window shades are an important detail.

8-7. A window shade and no curtain suits an attic playroom.

One end of the paper is wound tightly around the dowel and glued to it. The other end is trimmed to a little more than the desired length, and a narrow end is folded and glued. The roll of the shade should be visible from the front, with the curtain hanging behind it (figure 8-6). The hem should be turned toward the window, with the smooth side facing the room.

A small hole is next punched in the center of the hem fold, and if a tiny grommet can be found, it is pushed into the hole. Such grommets are sometimes sold by hobby shops specializing in model train supplies; they come in handy for other phases of miniature work. If grommets cannot be found, however, the pull cord is simply threaded through the hole.

Any shade pull the craftsman wishes to make will do the job; all that is needed is a straight cord with a small, round loop at the end. One simple method of making such a pull is to braid three lengths of thin sewing thread together, glue the ends to prevent raveling, spray the braid well with Krylon, and glue one end into a loop. The other end is then pushed from the front through the grommet or hole in the shade's hem and held in place with a small dab of glue on the back.

Other pulls can be made of a single strand of heavy button thread, of a cluster of embroidery threads, of twisted silk thread, or of a length of thread stitched on a sewing machine in which there is no cloth. Whatever material is used should be made stiff and straight with a spraying of Krylon or similar material.

MAKING LIGHT FIXTURES

It has been said that in combining fresh flowers and in decorating Christmas trees, there is no such thing as bad taste. The writer is tempted to add the designing of light fixtures to the list in order to encourage the craftsman to enjoy himself to the fullest when constructing his own.

A study of chandeliers of the past will show a range of everything from simple, one- or two-shade fixtures joined to the ceiling by a thin brass tube, to monstrous, amazing arrangements of glass and metal that have an overpowering charm of their own. Almost any design within these two extremes, if suitable to the room, is acceptable. This means that the craftsman can spend an enjoyable hour or two selecting pieces from the boxes of old jewelry, beads, and odd metal pieces that he has by now accumulated.

After the above open invitation to let the imagination run free, a few words of caution: Although large crystal chandeliers and many-armed brass and glass fixtures were much used in certain types of homes, a study of a few books picturing interiors of the period being followed by the craftsman will probably show that the average home did not have such elaborate affairs hanging from its ceilings. Large homes of the rich and upper middle class did have them, but not in the quantity seen in dollhouses and otherwise carefully made miniature rooms.

It will be seen that even in some fairly large homes, lighting fixtures with two or more shades joined by a simple, curved brass tube were fairly common. Such fixtures are shown in the sewing and play rooms in the color section of this book. Other plain styles, such as a white glass bowl fastened to the ceiling, or a fairly flat, circular metal piece with a number of frosted bulbs attached to its underside, were very common dur-

ing the early years of the twentieth century.

If a very elaborate lighting fixture is suitable for a room, it will be fun to make. If a simpler fixture is called for, it will also be fun to make and will look right in the room because it will be appropriate.

If a room is to be lighted by gas or candlelight, the arms of a chandelier should point straight upward so the flames will not touch any part of the fixture. On the other hand, the arms of an electric chandelier point downward, and usually a little outward, so that the light will be spread over as wide an area as possible. A miniature candelabrum can therefore be used as the basis for making an electric chandelier by turning it upside down and bending the arms slightly outward. Similarly, a candlestick makes a good start as an electrical fixture by fastening its base to the ceiling and attaching a burst of bulbs and shades to its lower end.

8-8. *A collection of possible parts for light fixtures.*

Unlighted Fixtures

Fixtures that will not be electrically wired are comparatively easy to make because appearance is the only consideration. Many of the candlesticks, candelabra, and other odd metal pieces the craftsman is apt to use will be made of pot metal, which cannot be soldered. However, such pieces so often suit the purpose when nothing else will do that they should be used in spite of the handicap. Holes can very easily be drilled in pot metal, and the pieces fastened in place with a dowel or with wires threaded through the holes. Pot metal can also be glued with a strong, contact-type of cement, or with small balls of epoxy putty.

The obvious answer to finding light bulbs for unlighted fixtures is in a collection of beads. Clear glass or white beads will probably answer most of the craftsman's need for bulbs, but finding shades for them is a little more difficult. Some buttons or jewelry pieces can serve the purpose, and some shades can be made of frosted plastic, but the writer has found a gold mine in the inexpensive, white plastic wedding bells sold in shops specializing in greeting cards and party supplies. Suitable for either the 3/4- or 1-inch scale, they can be sawed, filed, glued together, and painted to make a variety of styles. How these bells can be used is shown in the bathroom, kitchen, and playroom in the color section of this book. The kitchen ceiling fixture is made of two bells, the lower one sawed short, inverted, and glued to the upper one. The wall light by the sink is the upper part of a bell, sawed short and its edges filed smooth.

An increasingly wide selection of ready-made light fixtures and parts can be found in shops. Some of the manufactured fixtures are detailed enough to be used as they are, while others can be improved upon with the addition of extra ornamentation, such as shaped brass wire pieces, more lights, and so on. Also available are such parts as brass ceiling and wall plates, chandelier arms, and hollow rods.

Although the room cannot be turned upside down to fasten a chandelier in place, it is usually better to install an unlighted ceiling fixture after the room has been completely furnished. More than any other accessory, the suspended fixture is at the mercy of every giant hand that comes near it, and a great deal of exasperation can therefore be avoided if it is the last thing to be fastened in place.

For fastening a light fixture to a ceiling or wall, nothing has been found to be more effective than a small ball of epoxy putty. Because of its heavy body, it will hold even a large fixture in place immediately, and after the adhesive has set overnight, the fixture cannot be pulled away.

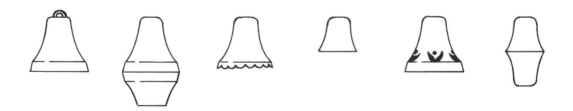

8-9. Plastic wedding bells can make a variety of shades.

8-10. *A kitchen ceiling fixture made of two bells, one sawed in half.*

8-11. *Two painted bells make an attic fixture.*

8-12. *A ceiling fan and light made of an inverted pot-metal candlestick, the top of a toy milk can, four wood blades, and a white bead.*

8-13. *The shade from a miniature oil lamp is fastened over a hole in the ceiling. The light source is an electric bulb above the ceiling.*

168

Lighted Fixtures

When planning a fixture that is to be lighted electrically, aesthetic design must take second place to wiring. In an unlighted chandelier, for example, curved arms with bulbs and shades at the ends can be made of heavy brass wire, but in a lighted fixture, the arms must be hollow so that wires can be threaded through them, as discussed in Chapter 3. Therefore, if a lighted fixture is to be an accurate copy of a full-size one, it should be of a fairly simple design. It would be very difficult, for example, to add as many lighted bulbs to the miniature copy as there would be in an elaborate, full-size crystal chandelier.

A small frosted- or cut-glass bowl, either fastened to the ceiling, or turned upside down and suspended from a wire or chain, makes an excellent lighted fixture. The "Tiffany" shade over the dining table in the color section was made from such a bowl, painted with glass paints. The "lead" strips between the colors are short lengths of heavy thread, glued into place. However, there are now on the market well-made plastic Tiffany-type shades, and they are suitable for either the 3/4- or 1-inch scale.

A lighted fixture may consist simply of an inverted, ornamental reflector that will bounce the light against the ceiling and light the room indirectly. In fact, any design at all can be used as long as the craftsman can see, as he makes his plans, how the necessary wires can be concealed and how the bulbs can be shaded.

Most manufactured lighted fixtures today, which come complete with battery cases, wires, and bulbs, are not of a quality suitable for a carefully furnished miniature room. This quality will probably improve as time goes along, but until it does, it is recommended that the craftsman be very selective when buying a ready-made chandelier, or that he use what parts are available, and design and make his own.

Unlike an unlighted fixture, which should be fastened to the ceiling after the room has been furnished, the electrical fixture should be installed in an empty room. Obviously, the work of wiring the room and installing the fixture will be made easier if the room can be turned to any desired position.

LEAVES, FERNS, PALMS

There are a number of materials, including paper, cloth, and plastic, which can be used to make the miniature green plants with which the mother of the house will fill every available space in her home. However, none has a better color for such plants, or a more convincing texture, than epoxy putty.

After the yellow and blue sides of the putty ribbon have been thoroughly kneaded together, the material is allowed to set for a few minutes until it is no longer sticky, but is still very pliable. It can then be shaped in any desired way.

For grass-thin shoots, the putty is pulled apart until it threads. Short pieces of the threads are cut off and laid on Saran Wrap, where they are allowed to set overnight.

Wider leaves can be made by stretching the epoxy into a thin sheet. Leaves can then be shaped and allowed to set, or the thin sheet can be left overnight to harden and leaf shapes can be cut out with scissors the next day. Palms and ferns can be made by laying pointed leaves of the correct sizes and shapes across a center stem. The pieces will stick together as they set.

Leaves made of epoxy putty will remain flexible permanently, but will always return to the shape in which they have set. Therefore, if curves are desired, the epoxy pieces should be laid across the side of a bottle, glass, or any object with the desired curve until they have hardened.

AVOIDING UPSETS

Every dollhouse owner at one time or another has accidentally knocked a miniature accessory off a table, upset a lamp, tipped over a chair or, even more painful, stood by helplessly while a visitor did these things. It is an unpleasant experience, particularly when the hand that reaches in to repair the damage is apt to upset something else at the same time.

A well-furnished miniature room is particularly vulnerable, because it will contain more pieces than do most dollhouse rooms. In some miniature rooms, tables, fireplace mantels, and shelves may be completely filled with pictures, statues, and family mementos that are at the mercy of every monstrous human hand that reaches, however carefully, into it.

The solution is quite simple. In most cases the craftsman does not wish to glue his accessories into place permanently, but if he will put a small dab of rubber cement on the bottom of everything he wishes to discourage from falling over, a gentle tug, as opposed to an accidental nudge, will be needed to pull it out of place. If similar dabs are put on chair and table legs, and on the bottom of all furniture that might tip easily, the whole room can be moved, or accidentally jostled, without a single piece falling over.

The cement can be rubbed from hard and semi-hard surfaces with the fingers, and can be cleaned from some fabrics with rubber cement thinner. (Thinner should not be used on delicate fabrics.) The amount of cement used on each piece, however, should be so small that even if a tiny dab should cling to a carpet after furniture has been moved, it would probably be invisible.

KEEPING RUGS FLAT

Loose rugs and corners of carpets, even if they lie flat when first laid, have a way of curling up with changes in temperature and humidity. This can be overcome by using rubber cement or small pieces of double-faced adhesive tape at trouble

spots. If the latter is used, the tape should be thin and semi-transparent. Double-faced white tape, if used close to the front edge of the carpet, is too apt to show, but may safely by used at the side and back edges.

THROUGH THE WINDOWS

"A window with a view" is a phrase that is synonymous with pleasant surroundings, even though "view" can mean anything from a blooming hillside to the solid brick wall of a next-door factory. What one sees through a window does tend to set the tone or feeling of a room and, to a great degree, the mood of its inhabitants.

The view through a miniature window is no less important. What the craftsman chooses to show there can deepen whatever mood he has tried to give a room. It is possible, with a judicious choice of a window view glued to the inner wall of the channel, to make a room seem larger and more elegant, smaller and more intimate, or to locate the neighborhood of the house, whether in the city, the suburbs, or the country. The feeling of

8–14. A collection of scenic pictures will be useful for through-the-window views.

height in an attic room can be increased by using a picture of clouds behind the window with, ideally, the tips of tree tops visible at sill level.

Needless to say, the view through a miniature window should be in harmony with any furnishings in the room that indicate the season of the year, such as an electric fan, a fire in the fireplace, or a supply of wood or coal in containers on the hearth.

It is a good idea to collect promising pictures from magazines, or any other source, as they are discovered. At best, it is difficult to find just the right view for a particular window, and finding it at just the time it is needed is often impossible. Not only must the chosen picture show the right season, it must also be in the right perspective. Only rarely would it be desirable for a tree to be pressed against a window, or for a fence, laden with snow, to be only a foot or two from the window. Nor would a second-floor bedroom window be on the same level as a ground-floor flower bed.

In addition to these considerations, the scale and size of the picture is important. If the window is of a normal size and has been constructed on the 1-inch scale, the picture must be in keeping with that scale and large enough so its edge will not show, no matter from which angle it is viewed. A side window, if located near the front of a room, will give quite a long view toward the back of the channel. All of the channel that can be seen must therefore be covered with the picture. It is easy to see, then, that a folder of pictures for possible future use can be a most valuable and useful collection.

The chosen picture should be held against the wall of the lighted channel and viewed through the window. When it has passed the test of size, perspective, and so on, it can be glued into place. Any adhesive may be used, but if rubber cement is applied at the corners, the picture can easily be removed later if a more suitable one is found.

Whatever feeling the craftsman is trying to give his miniature room can be enhanced by making three-dimensional outside additions to the window. If it is winter, snow made of white clay can be laid on the outside lower and middle frames of the window. A few evergreen branches, heavy with snow, can be glued in the channel with only their tips showing through the window. In the spring, a branch may hold a bird or a half-hidden bird's nest. If such details are added,

however, they must be in scale and should not be overdone.

THROUGH THE DOORS

Miniature doors that open into channels present another challenge. They must all lead to an adjoining room, a hallway, or the outdoors, and in every case, to achieve a feeling of realism, the view must be fairly well detailed. If the craftsman does not wish to make additional furniture to be glimpsed through an open door, he should plan the room so that this will not be necessary. The door can be omitted altogether, kept closed, or left only partly ajar so that nothing can be seen through the opening.

The main room will be that much more attractive, however, if another room beyond is shown in part, or at least suggested. A hallway adjoining a living room may show a glimpse of a front door, a table with a mirror above, a grandfather clock, or the last few steps of a staircase. Through the door of the dining room might be seen a butler's pantry or a less elegant pantry with oilcloth-covered shelves holding serving pieces, glasses, cups, and stacks of plates and saucers. A back door leading from a kitchen might give a view of a back porch with a railing, a broom or bucket, a milk bottle holding a note for the milkman, and so on. Easy access to a channel can be gained, of course, by removing the panel, which is held in place by four screws on the outside of the room box.

No matter what glimpses through half-opened doors are given the viewer, there should be no letting down on the quality of the pieces made. It would be a mistake to show a miniature room with furniture and accessories made as perfectly as possible, and to have an adjoining room giving glimpses of second-rate pieces, made carelessly simply because they will not be in full view.

The writer does not belong to the school of thought that believes everything made in miniature should be perfect, but to the group who believes everything *in sight* should be as perfect as possible. The craftsman who would glue a cabinet door shut with rubber cement rather than use out-of-scale hinges would receive the approval of many miniature enthusiasts, including the writer. Others, however, would have him sent out of town on a rail. Again, *de gustibus non est disputandum!*

Metric Conversion Table

In the following conversion table, full-size measurements are given in the left-hand column and, moving to the right, matching figures are given for the 1-inch and 3/4-inch scales. Needless to say, if a certain full-size number is not included in the left-hand column, it can be found by adding the proper figures. For example, 25 inches is not included in the left-hand column, but 24 inches and 1 inch are. If the 1-inch scale is being used, the two figures of 2 inches and 1/12 inch are added to make a total length of 2 1/12 inches.

For those who wish to use them, metric equivalents are also given. Although in the metric system, numbers smaller than 1 are often given in millimeters, for the sake of simplicity, all figures in the table are given in centimeters. For those who would prefer their smaller numbers in millimeters, it is only necessary to move the decimal point one place to the right. That is, .16 centimeters are equal to 1.6 millimeters.

Full-Size		1-Inch Scale		3/4-Inch Scale	
Inches	Cm.	Inches	Cm.	Inches	Cm.
1/4	.64	1/48	.05	1/64	.04
1/2	1.27	1/24	.11	1/32	.08
3/4	1.90	1/16	.16	3/64	.12
1	2.54	1/12	.21	1/16	.16
2	5.08	1/6	.42	1/8	.32
3	7.62	1/4	.64	3/16	.48
4	10.16	1/3	.85	1/4	.64
5	12.70	5/12	1.06	5/16	.79
6	15.24	1/2	1.27	3/8	.95
7	17.78	7/12	1.48	7/16	1.11
8	20.32	2/3	1.69	1/2	1.27
9	22.86	3/4	1.91	9/16	1.43
10	25.40	5/6	2.12	5/8	1.59
11	27.94	11/12	2.33	11/16	1.75
12 (1')	30.48	1	2.54	3/4	1.91
13	33.02	1 1/2	2.75	13/16	2.06
14	35.56	1 1/6	2.96	7/8	2.22
15	38.10	1 1/4	3.18	15/16	2.38
16	40.64	1 1/3	3.39	1	2.54
17	43.18	1 5/12	3.60	1 1/16	2.70
18	45.72	1 1/2	3.81	1 1/8	2.86
19	48.26	1 7/12	4.02	1 3/16	3.02
20	50.80	1 2/3	4.23	1 1/4	3.18
21	53.34	1 3/4	4.45	1 5/16	3.33
22	55.88	1 5/6	4.66	1 3/8	3.49
23	58.42	1 11/12	4.87	1 7/16	3.65
24 (2')	60.96	2	5.08	1 1/2	3.81
36 (3')	91.44	3	7.62	2 1/4	5.72
48 (4')	121.92	4	10.16	3	7.62
60 (5')	152.40	5	12.70	3 3/4	9.53
72 (6')	182.88	6	15.24	4 1/2	11.43
84 (7')	213.36	7	17.78	5 1/4	13.34
96 (8')	243.84	8	20.32	6	15.24
108 (9')	274.32	9	22.86	6 3/4	17.15
120 (10')	304.80	10	25.40	7 1/2	19.05

Index